NO REFUGE FOR WOMEN

THE TRAGIC FATE OF SYRIAN REFUGEES

MARIA von WELSER

TRANSLATED BY JAMIE MCINTOSH

GREYSTONE BOOKS
Vancouver/Berkeley

Originally published in Germany in 2016 as *Kein Schutz—nirgends: Frauen und Kinder auf der Flucht*

First published in English by Greystone Books in 2017

17 18 19 20 21   5 4 3 2 1

Greystone Books Ltd.
www.greystonebooks.com

Cataloguing data available from Library and Archives Canada
ISBN 978-1-77164-307-8 (pbk)
ISBN 978-1-77164-308-5 (epub)

Copy editing by Stephanie Fysh
Cover design by Will Brown
Cover photograph by Joseph Eid, Getty Images
Photographs by Peter Müller/BILD-Zeitung and Maria von Wesler
Printed and bound in Canada on ancient-forest-friendly paper by Friesens

We gratefully acknowledge the support of the Canada Council for the Arts, the British Columbia Arts Council, the Province of British Columbia through the Book Publishing Tax Credit, and the Government of Canada for our publishing activities.

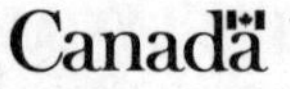

Canada Council for the Arts   Conseil des arts du Canada

CONTENTS

PREFACE TO THE ENGLISH EDITION

For most of you who will read this, Syria is far, far away. It is 6,681 miles from the center of North America to Aleppo, the second-largest city in Syria, and 7,447 miles to the middle of Australia. But in the fall of 2015, a photograph of a small boy lying on his stomach in the sand on the coast of Turkey was engraved in the minds of people around the world as if it was right in front of us. With the tragic death of 2-year-old Alan Kurdi in September 2015, the war in Syria became more of a reality even in distant countries, filling hearts with compassion. Since then, governments everywhere have discussed the flight of Syrians. Citizens split into camps: "do-gooders" wanting to offer help and protection, and skeptics and scaremongers warning of terrorists among the asylum-seekers.

What is happening to this world? The accommodation of refugees and migrants is woven into the historical DNA of so many countries. Over the centuries, people have fled from wars, from starvation and economic hardship. Today, 65.3 million people are displaced in the world, 60 percent of them women and children. But we who can comfortably remain in our homes? So many of us readily close our eyes to the dramatic scale of the situation.

With this book I not only tell the stories of people in flight but also provide facts that can take the wind out of critics' sails and equip people struggling for freedom and migration with good arguments. But above all, I want to show how refugees' lives differ from other migrants' lives: Migrants leave their homelands in the hope of a better life, because they feel that that homeland provides no future for them or their children. Refugees, in contrast, flee for their very lives—threatened by bombs, snipers, gas attacks, grenades, imprisonment. For migrants, governments everywhere have clear immigration laws and regulations; these vary from country to country, according to local needs. Refugees from war zones, however, need the protection of everyone in this world. After all, it was not for nothing that in 1951, after the Second World War, 147 nations signed the Refugee Convention in Geneva.

As I write this, the war in Syria has been raging for seven years. The United Nations High Commissioner on Refugees speaks of the greatest refugee crisis in a quarter-century. In February 2017, the international refugee organization stated that there were 4,898,353 registered Syrian refugees—including 2.3 million children under the age of 18. Above this, within Syria 13.5 million people are internally displaced, trying to flee from Assad's barrel bombs, Russian airstrikes, and the tanks of the ISIS terrorists. But to where? The asylum-seekers I met in camps in Lebanon, Turkey, and Jordan and on the island of Lesbos all wanted to return "home" when the war is over. For this reason, 87 percent of Syrian refugees remain in these neighboring countries.

But the living conditions I encountered there were anything but fit for human beings. So when, in the summer of 2015, the World Food Programme cut monthly payments to refugees there in half, many of the refugees registered for the UNHCR's resettlement program, in the hope of finding safety in places as faraway as the United States and New Zealand. And it was then that many of Europe's twenty-eight nations began to dig in their heels, while Germany opened its borders to 1.2 million asylum-seekers—a story that will be told in the pages that follow. Today, 890,000 asylum-seekers no longer live in reception camps but are on the more or less arduous path to integration.

Today, millions of women and children remain stranded in refugee camps, hoping that they will make it to Europe or be accepted for resettlement in the West. But the obstacles to resettlement are immense. The UNHCR reported that in 2015–16, Canada absorbed 39,671 Syrian refugees; the United States, ten times Canada's size, 18,007; Australia and New Zealand, 15,897 and 750 (!) respectively. I don't like looking at these figures in relation to the total number of inhabitants in the two largest countries of the North American continent—the United States has a population of 318.9 million, compared with Germany's 83 million. It's a disgrace! What has happened to people's humanity, morality, and empathy?

It is precisely these countries that became strong through migration, including that of refugees. Beginning in about 1830, it was mainly poverty and starvation that forced increasing numbers of people to leave Europe for America—18 million people over the course of a century. They came from Great Britain and Ireland, Italy, Spain, and Portugal; from Austria-Hungary, Germany, Sweden, and Norway. In the early twentieth century, 1 to 1.5 million people were leaving Europe annually. In later decades, while Turkish and then Italian *Gastarbeiter*—guest workers—were enticed to Germany by recruitment treaties, the Vietnamese "boat people" found refuge and new homes in North

America. Fifty thousand of those fleeing the Communist regime in Vietnam in the 1980s found refuge in Canada, and 200,000 were resettled in the United States.

Yet as the Syrian refugee crisis emerged four decades later, the response was not the same. David Miliband, former foreign secretary of the UK and now president and CEO of the International Rescue Committee, an organization supporting refugees wanting to resettle in the West, formulated the situation depressingly: "The United States has always been a leader in refugee resettlement but 1,500 [Syrian refugees] over four years is such a minuscule contribution to tackling the human side of this problem."[1]

He said this before Donald Trump became president, long before the first closure of U.S. borders to all Syrian refugees. Even before Trump, the resettlement of refugees from the camps in Jordan and Lebanon to the United States was a complicated process, with multiple rounds of background searches, medical tests, and interviews. During the Obama presidency, Department of Homeland Security staff visited the camps and interviewed applicants' families with the intention of hindering extremists from blending in with genuine refugees, and that was only one of many checks—more than are done by any other country. But even with this process in place, Republicans spoke out against increased quotas for Middle Eastern refugees. Meanwhile, there was (and still is, as I write this) no case of terrorism committed on American soil by a person admitted to the United States as a refugee.

The same applies to Canada. The man who killed six people and injured another nineteen at a mosque in Quebec in January 2017 was a 27-year-old non-Muslim white Canadian who appears to have become noticeably radicalized after a visit by the French right-wing extremist Marine Le Pen and by the election campaign of Donald Trump. In spite of this, the White House press secretary saw the atrocity as further evidence of the importance of an entry ban on Muslims. A hush shrouded the White House when it became apparent that the perpetrator was Canadian-born and white.

In Canada, this tragedy led to large demonstrations of solidarity and a closing of ranks across the political spectrum. In Parliament, Prime Minister Justin Trudeau emotionally addressed Canada's Muslim population: "We are with you; 36 million hearts are breaking with yours."[2] Canada's Liberal administration, under Trudeau, was already explicitly committed to a generous refugee policy in the North American spirit, accepting one of the highest proportions of its population in refugees in the world—higher than Germany, though Canada has not contended with anything close to the numbers of non-UNHCR-sponsored asylum-seekers that Germany has. Canada has long supported the integration of migrants with a range of programs. Trudeau himself was present as the first sponsored Syrian refugees arrived in Canada. He wants to continue Canada's long tradition of immigration.

The refugee system in Canada is humane and includes individual citizens. Since the 1980s, every Canadian has had the opportunity to personally support refugees: 40 percent of all refugees are privately sponsored. Groups of citizens submit an application to the government, pay a large fee to cover government expenses, and set aside a large sum of money in advance—enough to feed, house, and integrate the sponsored refugee or refugee family for a year. Canadians thronged to support Syrians in this program beginning in the fall of 2015, and the news media often reports that too few refugee households are being allocated to would-be sponsors and that the process takes too long—over a year now before privately sponsored refugees arrive, though for government-sponsored refugees, it is a matter of only a few weeks or months. In its Syrian resettlement program, Canada currently accepts only women, unaccompanied children, and families and individuals considered particularly vulnerable. Refugees registered by the UNHCR in the resettlement program are brought to Canada not only from Syria but from all parts of the world. And as in Germany, people in flight can find their way to Canada (though that requires airfare) and then apply for asylum. They are allowed to work, however, only once their refugee status has been accepted.

In the United States, on the other hand, it takes 18 to 24 months for the UNHCR to resettle a refugee. But even that is now history. When the first Trump executive order on immigration was signed in January 2017, refugees who had high hopes of asylum in the United States and were even on their way were refused entry. How heartless and bitter that must have been for people who had fled war, struggled to survive in refugee camps, been accepted to the UNHCR resettlement program, and gone through up to two years of interviews and checks to finally be turned back!

In the state of Connecticut, the staff of IRIS—Integrated Refugee & Immigrant Services, the country's largest refugee settlement assistance organization—were stunned. A week after the disruption of visas for citizens from seven predominantly Muslim countries and the indefinite entry ban on Syrian refugees, the men and women of IRIS sat at their desks, still appalled and furious. They agreed that the order was un-American, inhumane, and in violation of the Constitution. In February 2017, a panel of the Ninth Circuit Court of Appeals unanimously put the executive order on hold pending decisions in several lawsuits, but a new order was expected. Chris George, IRIS's executive director, however, didn't plan to give up: "The new order is an assault on our work, and the more refugees who live here the more likely it is to break down prejudices."[3]

Everyone at IRIS was convinced, said George: "People working with refugees don't believe the conservative scaremongers." So it still exists, the spirit of earlier immigrants—people with empathy, people who are willing to help, people who are involved. In Connecticut, doctors treat refugees without charge and student lawyers help new arrivals with paperwork. In 2015, when now vice president Mike Pence, as governor of Indiana, refused to allow a Syrian family to resettle in his state for "security reasons," Connecticut's Democratic governor, Dannel Malloy, was personally there to welcome them to *his* state. If fewer refugees can now come to the United States, organizations like IRIS will receive less funding from Washington. But George is not too worried: "Solidarity increases daily and can be felt everywhere. Last weekend 2,500 men and women ran five kilometers to fundraise for refugees. Over $200,000 was raised to help refugees." This is encouraging and a genuine signal that there is hope.

The Syrian men, women, and children in the refugee camps neighboring the war zone, however, are not banking solely on North America for UNHCR resettlement but also on Australia and New Zealand, countries with 23.13 and 4.47 million inhabitants, respectively. Australia has pledged to resettle 12,000 UNHCR refugees a year. But it, too, is sealing itself off—people trying to reach its shores by boat to claim asylum are returned to Indonesia or transported to Australia's offshore detention islands. The country's approach has three components: preclusion, insulation, and detention. The government in Canberra is a signatory to the Geneva Refugee Convention and has, as a result, been at the receiving end of some fierce criticism from aid organizations like Human Rights Watch and Amnesty International. Hardly any boats reach the continent, while in the detention centers, inhumane conditions prevail. In desperation, the boat people detained there try to take their lives; people have set themselves on fire, and there have been reports of sexual abuse of women and children and refusal to provide any form of aid. The Australian government has come to an agreement with Cambodia, a corrupt state, and paid $23 million to resettle refugees there. But hardly a single refugee has accepted the offer. It all sounds very similar to the March 2016 EU treaty with Turkey, discussed in this book. People who have managed to reach Greece and thus Europe do not willingly return to Turkey.

And New Zealand? It accepts few refugees, mostly women and children, people with disabilities, and the badly wounded. Here, too, the government refuses entry to people arriving in boats. All refugees entering the country have to be registered already with the UNHCR.

The United Kingdom is a particularly sad case. The European discussion about refugees was one reason that the majority of Britons voted to leave the European Union. What is for me the most colorful country in Europe no longer wants to absorb foreigners, let alone Muslim refugees. The United Kingdom is colorful because all hues of skin are represented there and lived in peaceful coexistence until the Brexit referendum. I worked there for three years as a correspondent, and I still can't grasp why the Britons suddenly want to seal themselves off. In 2015–16, the country, with a population of some 65 million, accepted 8,118 Syrian refugees. According to the government, it wants to offer protection to unaccompanied children in particular. But up until September 2016, not one child from the Syrian war zones was recorded in the UNHCR resettlement program there. Hundreds of thousands of unaccompanied children have fled Syria, many taking months to cross Europe and gathering at Calais, France, managing to reach England only by hiding in trucks about to enter the Channel tunnel. The French government cleared the chaotic camp and dashed hopes of a life in the UK. The refugees there were moved to better-organized facilities in the center of the country. But they don't want to be there—they would rather risk sneaking into the UK through the tunnel, landing in a country without compulsory registration, where they could somehow bluff their way into small jobs and live with the steady hope of a better future. But the UK too is now blocked off, no longer a welcoming culture.

This is also becoming open for discussion in Europe, in Germany. "From receiving country to rejecting country" many people muse when considering the developments since this book was first published. Chancellor Merkel, however, is convinced that only through rigorous deportation of rejected asylum-seekers can help be given to those really in need of assistance. Meanwhile, it is becoming increasingly difficult for people in genuine need of protection to reach Europe. The Balkan route has been hermetically sealed since March 2016. Fleets of inflatable dinghies with 2,000 to 3,000 refugees no longer complete the hazardous crossing from Turkey to Greece night after night. Boats from Libya are intercepted in the Mediterranean. The laws have become tighter.

The war in Syria, however, continues. Aleppo has, since this book was first published, fallen to Assad's troops. As I write this, the 1.5 million people still living in the city need relief supplies—blankets, sleeping bags, and winter clothing to survive the cold months. In some regions of the country people are fighting for mere survival. Time and again there is talk of a ceasefire, but one never materializes. Russia, Iran, and Turkey meet to negotiate the future of the country, but war still rages. Those who can—those with some savings—try to flee. But Turkey long ago sealed its borders; Lebanon too. Jordan allows entry to women and children only after assessment. Neighboring Iraq has to contend with 1.5 million displaced persons. Under these circumstances, those who do manage to cross the borders to the neighboring countries have taken an enormous step forward—but not toward humane conditions.

Meanwhile, the world looks on. In this book I turn that gaze to the plight, fears, and worries of women and children in the refugee camps and on the road to asylum. We who can have to take a close look, listen, and negotiate. It cannot be possible that the rich nations of Europe, North America, and the Pacific cannot manage to help some 5 million Syrian refugees.

Maria von Welser, March 2017

A NOTE ON TERMINOLOGY

The word *refugee* has a specific legal meaning: a person who has been registered as such by the UNHCR or accepted as such under a particular country's immigration laws. It is, however, sometimes used here to mean an "asylum-seeker" or "person in flight."

ISIS (Islamic State of Iraq and Syria) is chosen here for the name of the Salafi terrorist group also known in English as IS (Islamic State), ISIL (Islamic State of Iraq and the Levant), and Daesh (its Arabic-language acronym).

INTRODUCTION

WHERE ARE THE WOMEN AND CHILDREN?

As I visit refugee camps around the world, I ask myself, "Why are these women and children fleeing without protection? Where are their men, their fathers and brothers?" All the while I know the answer, and it makes for a long, bitter story. With this book I want to tell this story so that it won't be forgotten.

IT STARTS LIKE this: As the first images of Syrian refugees flickered on our TV screens in the spring of 2015, we rubbed our eyes in incredulity. We sat warm and safe in our living rooms, watching as thousands of people disembarked from tiny boats or wobbled, scared and hesitating, down the gangways of larger ships onto Italian soil. Some, at least, were wrapped in blankets and had warm hats. Later, the European Union's border control agency, Frontex, reported that in Italy almost seven times as many men as women had arrived. Seven times!

But it was still far away. We had managed to grasp that refugees leave destitute countries or dictatorships in Africa, flee from war in Syria, seek safety from insecure Afghanistan, but who exactly was arriving we weren't so sure about. We in Germany had been quite happy for years to leave Greece and Italy alone with the floods of refugees. Anyway, Germany seemed to have been paralyzed for months by other topics: the Greek financial crisis and its consequences, the right-wing mob attacks at Heidenau, and the question of where to spend our summer vacations. Everything was completely normal... well, almost.

Only with the photos of the endless lines of people in the summer heat on the Balkan route to Passau, of people huddling in the Budapest and Vienna train stations, of desperate faces at the barbed wire fences in Macedonia did we suddenly become startled. At the time I studied the scenes closely and discovered, almost exclusively, men—fathers, brothers, sons. Very seldom did I manage to find a woman in those photos of cramped boats, of lines at fences, administrative offices, or toilets. Where on earth were the women in this refugee summer of 2015? It almost seemed as if there *were* no destitute women and children, as if the communities caught up in civil war in Syria, or communities in Afghanistan, Eritrea, and Iraq, were simply a man's world.

And that is just how the refugee summer of 2015 will be written in the history books: as a mass exodus of young men. Two-thirds of applications for asylum in Germany that summer were made by men. Germany's Federal Office for Migration and Refugees (BAMF) later noted that over 70 percent of applicants were under 30. Among the refugees aged 14 to 34, the proportion of men was even higher, reaching three-quarters.

THE QUESTION OF the women and children plagued me. I read about the thousands of women and children from northern Syria and northern Iraq who were forced to flee the terrorist militia Islamic State (ISIS). UNICEF Germany sent out newsletters to committee members reporting the dreadful living conditions of women and children in the refugee camps of Jordan and Lebanon. I knew from many years of research into wars in the Balkan states, Chechnya, and Rwanda that it is women and children who are primarily at risk. Systematic rape has long been used as a strategic weapon of war, and the kidnapping and sale of girls to soldiers or Internet bidders is one of the barbarous techniques used by the ISIS terrorists.

But I also know *these* figures: globally, 60 million people are in flight, and according to the United Nations, every other refugee is female. They flee their homes because of war, either staying within their country or looking for rescue beyond their borders. Never in the twenty-first century have so many people been forced to leave their homes as now. So, where, in the summer of 2015, were the women?

I BEGAN TO research the countries that have sheltered the most Syrian refugees: Turkey, Lebanon, and Jordan. It is there that most of the women—mothers and grandmothers, with their children—are stranded. It soon became clear to me that the great trek of Syrian men began the moment that the UN's World Food Programme (WFP) halved its prior monthly payments from U.S. $26 per refugee to $13, simply because many countries had failed to make their financial contributions to it. The program is funded entirely by voluntary payments, and receives no core funding from the UN. Thus, money for millions of Syrian refugees was lacking—a disaster for those affected. Already in 2014, the program's executive director, Ertharin Cousin, had warned that "a suspension of WFP food assistance will endanger the health and safety of these refugees and will potentially cause further tensions, instability and insecurity in the neighboring host countries,"[1] Turkey, Lebanon, and Jordan.

At that moment many refugee families must have said, "We have no future here in the camps near our former homes—it would be better to climb on board an inflatable boat on the Mediterranean than to starve here." Their meager reserves of available money were then scraped together and invested in the flight of the "strong" men—in the fathers and sons—so that they could make the dangerous journey to a secure European country then arrange for their families to join them. It was an understandable decision, as one man is more likely to make it alone than with his whole family in tow.

The first stop in my search for the women and children was Turkey. Without complaining, the country, with a population of 76 million, had, up to 2016, afforded shelter to 2.8 million refugees—mostly Syrian families, and mainly women and children. I traveled to Diyarbakir, the Kurdish capital in the southeast of the country. Altogether, twenty-five tent settlements have been erected by the Turkish army along the Turkish–Syrian border.

Yazidis from the Iraqi Sinjar Mountains have sought refuge here. Their men are either dead or still fighting; some are on their way to Europe. In the huge but, in summer, incredibly hot military tents, the women told me their sad stories—of their tears for their war dead, of their grief for daughters kidnapped by ISIS, of their fears of being stranded here in the Kurdish part of Turkey. Time and again I heard that one hundred years ago, the Yazidis, a non-Muslim community, were victims of a horrific genocide implemented by Muslims in precisely this region of Turkey. They kept asking me, "Why doesn't Germany take *us*? Why only the Syrians?" At that time, selfies of Angela Merkel with Syrian refugees were circulating on the Internet.

I also met brave Syrian Kurdish women who were billeted in camps near their destroyed hometown, Kobanî, and wanted to go back across the border as soon as possible, even though war still raged there. Many were even prepared to leave the children with their grandmothers and to fight against ISIS, like many Iraqi women, some of whom have joined the Kurdish *peshmerga*—the military forces of the autonomous region of Iraqi Kurdistan—to confront the ISIS forces. These women are courageous; they don't give up but take up arms themselves. They have exciting stories to exchange with one another.

The situation of the women and children stranded in Lebanon, on the other hand, is much more hopeless. The country, with a population of 5.8 million, kept its border with neighboring Syria open until January 2015. Since then, however, the border posts have been closed, and the roughly 1.2 million refugees remaining in Lebanon have to provide for themselves. This small country doesn't have the financial resources to offer them things like organized camps and secure shelters. The refugee families have to organize these things for themselves; they live in improvised accommodation made from cardboard, paper, bits of wood, and plastic sheeting, or in narrow, dark rooms with mold on the walls and threadbare mats on the cold floor. It's pitiful. I see the aid organizations doing what they can, but the stories the women and children tell give me sleepless nights. Above all, the hopelessness of their situation is harrowing.

Rape, forced marriages, and forced prostitution are everyday occurrences in the camps in Lebanon and Jordan, especially if male members of the families are absent. Families offer women and children protection; without men, they lose this security. The only thing that can help is the combined force of strong-minded women who can defend themselves and who are there for each other. I have seen it happen in Lebanon, and the same applies to Jordan.

In these countries, trafficking in women has become a flourishing business. Arabs are fond of buying Syrian women as second or third wives (as permitted by the Qur'an), and are prepared to pay up to $10,000. Syrian women are not only beautiful but apparently much more obedient than Arab women—the Lebanese women told me this.

However, the refugee families' dire financial situation often forces women into prostitution. This happens in refugee camps as well as outside, in cities. The fact is, however, that it doesn't concern the governments of the host countries or society generally. Although the women's and children's living conditions are degrading, nobody lifts a finger. In this wealthy world it is a mystery to me that the UN cannot manage to provide for the refugees, to ensure that no women have to be sold and that no father has to hand his daughter over to a stranger for money.

WHILE IN 2015 it was mainly men arriving in Germany as refugees, in the first months of 2016 the tide turned. There they were: the women and children. But against a backdrop of amendments to German asylum laws at the beginning of the year, refugees feared that men would no longer be allowed to have their families join them. In Greece alone now, 55 percent of the registered migrants were women and minors, according to the United Nations High Commissioner for Refugees (UNHCR). Even more dramatic: according to UNICEF, the UN child welfare organization, 36 percent of the refugees making the hazardous journey from Turkey to Greece in inflatable boats were children.

I wanted to witness this with my own eyes, so I traveled to the small island of Lesbos, where the first of the "hotspots" (EUsupervised registration centers) was supposed to be in operation and where most of the mainly Syrian and Afghani refugees had arrived. Tears came to my eyes on seeing people with babies in their arms arriving on the beach in winter, soaking wet and freezing. Thousands of young volunteers waited for them, providing warm clothes, hot tea, and some comfort. Registration actually seemed to be working, and twenty-four hours later, 1,000 or 2,000 people were standing in the line for the ferry to the mainland. I stood by the gangway and could only wish them luck on their travels. They were all so happy, hoping that at last, after a long journey, they could look forward to a secure life. But I read on my iPhone at that very moment that Macedonia was closing down the Balkan route, that more and more refugees were arriving at the border camp at Idomeni, on the Greek side of the border, flocking there through dirt and mud in icy-cold temperatures. Again a drama loomed. On top of this, Europe had agreed to a settlement with Turkey about the security of Turkey's borders. After March 20, refugees without an asylum application in EU member nation Greece could be sent back to Turkey.

All this has to be given a chance to work. But one thing is certain: refugees will continue to arrive—the war in Syria is not over; the situations in Afghanistan, Iraq, and Pakistan are uncertain. Life in Eritrea remains dangerous for its people. Never in the history of humankind have there not been refugees. Flight is a part of our world, and always will be. After the Second World War, 12 million displaced people from East Germany arrived in West Germany, were accommodated, and were integrated. My husband was a refugee child. His mother fled to Dresden with her 6-year-old son and a newborn in a pram, later landing in Garmisch-Partenkirchen, in Upper Bavaria. Her husband was a prisoner of war in Russia for many years. Integration of this mother and her children was a success, as was the integration of millions of other refugees and displaced people. When we consider the sheer numbers, the material hardships, and the political uncertainties of that time, we can see that it was a much more difficult task to overcome than what we face today, even if the refugees come here now from a very different part of the world. The historian Andreas Kossert, in his important book on displaced people after 1945, wrote of the "cold homeland" when describing the reception of refugees at that time, but eventually integration did prevail. So why shouldn't it be possible today, in 2015, to integrate just 1.3 million refugees?

In the meantime, of course, women and children require special protection. As early as July 2015, I read the first reports that female refugees were more often victims of attacks in communal living quarters. There were cases of physical violence, sexual harassment, even rape that were often not reported by the women for fear of the authorities. Unaccompanied women, for example, were driven out of the facilities' laundry rooms and kitchens. This is disgraceful, and in no way should it be allowed to continue. But society in Germany has become sensitized, especially after the attacks by thousands of North African asylum-seekers outside train stations at Cologne, Hamburg, and other German cities—targeting young women, sexually harassing them, and stealing cellphones. This, too, is disgraceful and should never be allowed to happen again. But to blame all male refugees would be wrong, and unhelpful in the debate on refugees. According to a 2015 review by the Federal Criminal Police Office and the various states that make up Germany, refugees committed no more offenses than did the native population,[2] though PEGIDA and the AfD—both right-wing populist organizations—claim the opposite.

FOR THIS BOOK I have highlighted the story of Miryam, as it is always the fates of individuals that particularly touch us. Miryam is Syrian, and she fled with her five children. Today she lives in a container settlement for families in Hamburg, in a unit with three rooms plus a small bathroom and a kitchen. Hers is an impressive story, about how she managed to reach Hamburg through the rebel lines in Syria, then across to Sudan, through the Libyan Desert to Tripoli, and from there across the Mediterranean—impressive and, I believe, a positive indication of the strength of Syrian women.

Miryam, together with her four daughters and young son, made it, but hundreds of other families mourn the loss of their children during their flight. Every day from September 2015 through spring 2016, on average two refugee children drowned in the eastern Mediterranean, right in front of their parents' eyes. To date this had meant more than 420 dead children. UNICEF assumes that the actual figure is much higher, as many bodies are not found. By the end of 2015, about 300,000 children had arrived in Germany with their mothers. In the first three months of 2016, more than a third of the 80,000 refugees who landed in inflatables on the Greek islands were minors—28,000. National governments and local authorities are faced with a Herculean task.

First and foremost, refugee children always have to be treated as *children,* with their own rights as laid down by the UN Convention on the Rights of the Child. This means that they require special protection. I am alarmed by reports that thousands of children who arrived in Europe have apparently vanished—simply gone. Europol, the European Police Office, talked in March 2016 of at least 10,000 untraceable children.[3] In Germany, in April 2016, the figure was 5,835.[4] They could have landed in the hands of criminal gangs exploiting them for child labor or prostitution—for every child a nightmare, for Europe a scandal. Here, children are not being protected, particularly those traveling alone—children who have been dispatched by their families to the reputed safety of Europe.

According to the aid organization Save the Children, these children are mainly between 15 and 17 years old and come mostly from Eritrea, Somalia, and Syria. They are sent off alone in part because their parents hope that the unaccompanied children will be able to fetch them after their asylum procedures have been completed. This is, at the moment, hotly debated by politicians, but it would be disastrous to make examples of the few young refugees just to stem the overall flow of refugees. In 2015, only 105 unaccompanied minors received subsidiary protection (protection for people who don't qualify as refugees but who would be placed in harm's way if returned to their country of origin) in Germany, and they are covered by the amendments to the asylum laws.

The destinies of the refugees who arrive in Germany are linked to political decisions. Chapter Eight, "Germany 2015–16," outlines this context. The German chancellor plays a central role there, and a section in that chapter describes Angela Merkel's stance, in statements and interviews, because it is she above all who granted protection in Germany to the refugee women and children.

Before you turn to the personal stories in this book, I would like to quote the political theorist Hannah Arendt. She wrote in 1951 about her flight from Germany from Hitler's henchmen, "What is unprecedented is not the loss of a home but the impossibility of finding a new one." And a little later the Jewish emigrant full of vision and wisdom added: "This, moreover, had next to nothing to do with any material overpopulation; it was a problem not of space but of political organization."[5] I hope today that we in Germany will give these refugees a new home, that our politics can get organized, and that the stories in this book soon become history.

ONE

SYRIA

MIRYAM'S STORY

PART 1

EVERYDAY LIFE IS HELL

She holds her bleeding child in her arms. Akilah, 17, has been badly hurt. It's the fall of 2014, and Assad's henchmen have once again dropped barrel bombs on Kafr Sousa, a suburb of Damascus. Here, in the eastern quarter of the capital, resistance to the government is strongest. Miryam knew that, but up until now it hasn't meant anything. The 35-year-old wasn't interested in politics, only in her family: her son, Amir, recently turned 4, and her four daughters, Olcay, 6, Kalila, 12, Djamila, 16, and Akilah. But now she is certain—she has to go, to get away from the chaos, to rescue her five children, to leave everything behind. Right now. Otherwise, her daughter will bleed to death.

With a neighbor's help, she pushes Akilah in a wheelbarrow through the dust and dirt. Three streets away is a hospital. Quickly, quickly! Miryam begins to panic—so many people are thronging at the huge gates ... so many people with injuries. She looks up at the sky, hoping that no more helicopters are dropping their evil barrels of high explosives and shrapnel.

In the hospital, Miryam manages to find a doctor she knows. He takes care of Akilah, and the relieved mother can take a breather. The doctor sends her home to the other children. In the streets, the dust has settled somewhat.

When Akilah is released from hospital, Miryam packs their belongings. Now she is sure: the president of Syria, Bashar al-Assad, is fighting his own people in his own country. Unconcerned by international bans on barrel bombs, he continues to allow them to be deployed. They fall uncontrolled from great heights onto civilian populations; on impact they explode, killing and injuring people; metal splinters cover their bodies. At times dozens of these projectiles are dropped every day around Aleppo, in Daraa, and, above all, in certain suburbs of Damascus. Whole districts have been razed to the ground, including now Miryam's own suburb of Kafr Sousa. Later, refugees in Germany, including Miryam, will insist that they fled Assad's barrel bombs, not the terrors of the ISIS militia.

I'M SITTING WITH Miryam in her home in Hamburg. A white headscarf covers her tidy hair, and a loose cardigan engulfs her diminutive body. She's a beautiful woman. With an open face she looks at me, the unfamiliar German, warmly. She is ready to tell me the story of her flight, is willing to answer all my questions so that I can understand her actions. Her voice quivers when she talks about her parents, about her friends, because where, in her Damascene suburb, once stood markets, schools, clinics, and houses now are only trails of death and destruction. Her parents still live there, but under the worst conditions imaginable. Miryam's cellphone is her last link to her home—to her family and friends. She tells me that you can recognize a falling barrel bomb by its faint hum but you can only tell exactly where the harrowing deaths will occur just before impact. Akilah, who was at the market to buy fruits and vegetables, was unlucky. She later explained that she had heard the humming but unfortunately sought shelter on the wrong side of the road.

Hesitantly, Miryam continues. She is half Syrian, half Palestinian. Her husband had a good job as a barber and was able to feed the family of seven—until 2011, when civil war broke out in Syria after the Arab Spring, when uprisings spread through much of the Middle East and North Africa. Their house was bombed and severely damaged. They remained, however, in the ruins, with filled-in holes and makeshift structural repairs to the walls. It seemed to them, at the time, to be safe. Yet both parents agreed, especially after Akilah's injuries: mother and children must flee. But how? Where would they find the money? "By then," Miryam tells me, "Assad's troops had sealed off the suburb, arrested my husband, and imprisoned him in a military camp, and I couldn't get Akilah out of the hospital because of the constant bombing in the area."

Miryam was prompted into action. She had to sell the wrecked house and the land—at a giveaway price, but never mind that. She sold all the gold jewelry that her parents had given her at her wedding as a traditional dowry and that was to be used in hard times. She sold her kitchen utensils, the children's beds, the living room sofa and chairs—all at bargain prices and all because she was sure of one thing: they would need plenty of cash reserves if the flight with the children was to succeed.

But while all this was happening, Miryam and her children had to suffer every day. Even while she stood in line for bread, Assad's bombs fell; Syrian rebels bombarded them from positions in the neighboring mountains. It was hell. The schools in Miryam's district had all closed. Nationally, at least 2 million children were going without lessons. Miryam asked around, among friends and reliable neighbors, about how to get in touch with a trafficker, how to get out of there.

In earlier times, everything had been fine in her country. Having a large number of children meant much social esteem, and is considered the duty of all good Muslims. Before the war the birth rate was 3.5 children per woman. Miryam, with her five children, was well above the average. And they meant she had enough to do. Her marriage had clearly defined rules about who was in charge of the household. Miryam cooked, did the washing and shopping, and changed the baby's diapers. Today she says, "My husband never ordered me around. If, in his opinion, I hadn't carried out my duties—say, the meal wasn't cooked when he got home—he would never complain." Who knows, I wonder, if that really was the case?

She continues, "It was perfectly normal for mothers to have jobs, in our area and in the country as a whole. Especially with the increasing pressure of *having* to earn money—many families couldn't survive without a second income." For Miryam everything was fine, though: she was responsible for looking after the five children, and she didn't need to seek additional employment. Her husband's earnings were enough.

She remembers that there had never been much support from the state for mothers or their families. Working women were entitled to maternity leave only under exceptional circumstances. Civil servants, like her sisters-in-law, were allowed to remain at home for three months on full pay, but in the private sector few women were entitled to leave. There were also hardly any government-run childcare facilities. Kindergarten? Daycare centers? Not a chance. Not in those days, and certainly not since the war put a stranglehold on the country and its people. In Syria, the streets have always been the traditional playground, including for Miryam's children. But this is no longer thinkable; even the daily trip to the shops for necessities is a perilous undertaking.

MIRYAM'S HOUSE IN Damascus is in a once pretty, quiet new housing development far away from the dusty, lively hurly-burly that prevails in the center of the city even in wartime. Every day the police come by, gruffly asking to check the whole family's passports. They want to know whether the family still have them or whether they are preparing to flee. The Syrian traffickers take passports with the first down payment, supposedly for safekeeping and as proof that the family are serious about wanting to flee.

On the street in front of Miryam's house now, Assad's troops and the rebels are constantly engaged in heavy gunfights. For days on end she cannot leave the house with her children. At least Akilah is getting better, and Miryam can bring her home from the hospital. The teenager is weak; the wounds haven't yet healed, are just covered by bandages. Every night Miryam nestles on the floor with her five children. Next to Akilah lies Djamila, then Kalila and Olcay. Little Amir cuddles in his mother's arms as she hopes against hope that stray bullets won't hit them. Miryam takes a deep breath when she thinks about those days. But she also says, "To this day I'm thankful for my neighbor Mohammed. He put me in touch with a man who got us out of there, and who took us to the rebel forces so we no longer had to live with the acute danger of bombs."

Miryam had to pay the man 50,000 Syrian pounds (about U.S. $200 at the time) for her and the family. She realized that this was just the beginning: first of all they must get away from the fierce fighting on her doorstep—at night, in the dark. She hopes that this will just be a brief phase, the first steps before the flight proper, just a short while. But it will be one year and three months before Miryam and the children can go. By then the children will be a year older: Akilah, 18, Djamila, 17, Kalila, 13, Olcay, 7, and little Amir, 5.

"I only left for the sake of my children," Miryam tells me now. "I no longer care about my life. But my children should have a future." Miryam knows that she will never go to Happy Land, a Damascus amusement park, with them again. Never ride the roller coaster, slide into the swimming pool, or eat candy floss until they're almost sick—all that is in the past. The colorful lights of the merry-go-round are a distant memory. The meeting places of her youth are also long gone. Pizza Hut, Kentucky Fried Chicken—all have vanished. Zara, her favorite boutique, is barricaded. Many neighbors have moved out. Best friends disappeared over night; she sometimes find out where they are via WhatsApp. At night her husband whispered that the only way to save the family was to flee, but they waited too long. After one such night, Assad's soldiers came for him at dawn and forcibly recruited him to fight, like thousands of other Syrians.

THE SYRIAN CIVIL WAR

Miryam's story is only one of hundreds of thousands. It is easy to forget for those of us far away how the war in Syria started—why, by spring 2016, 4 million Syrians had left their homeland, why over 500,000 had requested asylum in Europe alone. Inside the country itself, 8 million people had had to leave their homes to seek accommodation elsewhere in Syria. The worst thing about it is that half of them were children. By the beginning of 2016, 470,000 people had been killed in this civil war—shot, tortured, killed, blown to pieces by barrel bombs; many who survived have been marked for life by chemical weapons.

At the beginning of this civil war, peaceful demonstrations by Syrians received no notice in the world media—not a line in a newspaper or a one-minute broadcast—although it had been clear for some time that Syria had become a brutal police state in which secret services and various mafia-like organizations had taken control of government finances, the economy, and business. All was approved of and fostered by the president, Bashar al-Assad, an Alevite (follower of a mystical Islam) who chose cronyism as his form of government. *Wasta*—"connections"—was the magic word leading to success and fortune. But the majority of the population had nothing to gain: they did not have the right *wasta*. So the division between the rich and influential elite on one side and the extremely poor on the other became increasingly apparent.

After some boys were arrested for spraying graffiti, just for fun and because it was "in," thousands of infuriated and courageous Syrians took to the streets in 2011 against their president and his system. First they spray-painted hearts, then words critical of the government, on a couple of walls in the southern city of Daraa. They had seen reports on TV from Tunisia, Egypt, and Libya during the Arab Spring. Assad's much-feared military secret services reacted brutally: they arrested twenty schoolchildren and tortured them savagely over the weekend, killing a number of them. The regime, not for the first time, felt surrounded by conspirators who wanted to topple the government. Its reactions to criticism of the government or even to the slightest hint of conspiracy were merciless. The war began with the deaths of the tortured children. The cynical message from the secret services addressed to the mourning, broken-hearted parents was "Just make some more."

That was too much. Enraged citizens took to the streets throughout the country, no longer peacefully—no, this time with arms. Now it was a civil war. "Assad out!" chanted the demonstrators. The response was raw violence that hasn't stopped to this day.

THIS CIVIL WAR divided the country. As of April 2016, over half of its territory was controlled by the terrorist militia ISIS, though they had had to evacuate the embattled city of Palmyra, driven away by Assad's forces and Russian bombs. Government troops continued to hold the capital, Damascus, and eleven of the thirteen provincial capitals. Rebel groups like the Free Syrian Army, the Islamic Front, the Kurdish militia, and an al-Qaeda offshoot, the al-Nusra Front, controlled the remainder of the country. From a one-time population of 22 million, only 16 million remained in the country. Those that could had fled to wherever they could.

Of those left, 12.2 million people as of that spring—half of them children—desperately need humanitarian aid. There is no longer enough to eat, no treatment for diseases, hardly any sanitary facilities; 25 percent of the schools have been destroyed. Rani Rahmo, of SOS Children's Villages, has reported that children are forced to eat grass just to have something in their stomachs. Half of the hospitals have been destroyed. Westerners who claim that there isn't war everywhere in Syria, so we could simply deport the refugees to safe areas of the country, are being cynical. The director of SOS Children's Village in Syria is enraged by such suggestions: "The situation outside Damascus is particularly dramatic. The children there live under the constant fear of bombardment. They are traumatized. If the situation continues, up to 2 million Syrians will make the trek to Europe. The passport authorities in Damascus are already overwhelmed. Five thousand people wait in the line every day."[1]

But back in 2011, this was just beginning. In the first years of the war, the world simply looked on, apparently indifferent. An Arabic speaker on Twitter bitterly summarized the situation: "2011—We're worried, but it's probably not that bad. 2012—It's got worse, but not so bad that we have to worry about it. 2013—Now it's really bad, but won't we only make it worse if we interfere? 2014—It's got much worse. We should intervene but we have no idea how. 2015—It's so bad that any action now would be too late. We should have done something in 2011."[2]

THE FACT IS that Syrians are fleeing primarily from the troops, from the bombs, from attacks and rockets sent by their president, Assad—not from the terrorist militia ISIS. Nicolas Hénin, a French journalist, was held hostage by ISIS for ten months. The author of *Jihad Academy*, recounting his experiences in captivity, stressed, "The West thinks that in Syria there is the choice, Islamic State or Assad. But ISIS is only the symptom—the reason for the horrific conditions is the regime."[3]

And British chemical weapons expert Hamish de Bretton-Gordon, who has worked for decades in the Middle East, states, "Europe and the Middle East region are looking at a million refugees needing help today, which could easily escalate to five million by the end of the year unless there is a significant policy shift by the international community towards Syria ... The refugee problem in Europe is of our own making, a result of inactivity towards Syria hitherto. In particular, we, globally, ignored the stated red line on use of chemical weapons after the Ghouta chemical attack in August 2013, which killed up to 1,500 people."[4]

What is stopping the governments of the United States or Europe from intervening? From creating peace and enabling the people to have a future? Certainly, Syria was always a contested country, a bone of contention for the superpowers. Yet it was rich in culture long ago: when the Greeks and Romans, Arabs, Turks, or Crusaders were smashing skulls there, they still managed to build temples, palaces, fortresses, and even whole cities.

Today, too, the military rivals outside Syria are all but united in their aims. The only common denominator is the will and need to fight ISIS. The Russians and Iranians want to rescue Bashar al-Assad's regime, thereby strengthening their own standing in Syria and the region. Turkey and the Sunni Gulf states want to topple Assad because he is allied to Iran, a rival regional Shi'ite power hostile to Sunni Muslims. The United States while under Barack Obama, France under François Hollande, and the other Western countries have above all been interested in fighting ISIS. Russian involvement in the war in support of its old friend Assad began in 2015, mostly with bombardment of the rebel forces, after which the United States and Europe closed ranks against Vladimir Putin, who cunningly claimed to be targeting ISIS forces, which was later proven to be untrue.

The involvement of Russia led to a fateful imbalance in the war. This can be seen in, among other things, the drama in and around the city of Aleppo. Over 100,000 Syrians fled toward the Turkish border in early 2016. Turkey had by then closed its borders and set up a refugee camp inside the Syrian border. On March 16, a little while after a ceasefire, albeit a fragile one, had come into effect at the end of February, Putin suddenly announced that Russia was withdrawing from Syria. His objectives had been accomplished.

The rest of the world was left to ponder which objectives the Russians had actually achieved with their offensive. ISIS troops still occupied a third of the country and were behind suicide bombings in Turkey and North Africa. There was no end in sight to the refugee drama for millions of people, despite the agreement between Europe and Turkey on March 18. The average length for the trek was two and a half months, so the time when fewer Syrians would be underway was still a long time off. Refugees were still managing to flee the war-torn country using hazardous routes. On top of all this, 500,000 people were still trapped in Aleppo and Homs. Aid transport in the whole country was having difficulty getting through, let alone reaching the besieged areas.

DATA AND FACTS: SYRIA, SPRING 2016

- Syria's population at the outbreak of the civil war was 22 million.
- 4 million refugees have been registered by the UN in neighboring countries since 2011.
- 470,000 have been killed in the war up to now.
- 8.2 million Syrians, half of them children, have fled to other parts of the country. They all require humanitarian aid, including food and medical support.

- Since the beginning of the war, Syria has probably had a population of only 16 million.
- Syrians living in regions not controlled by the warring parties are totally reliant on aid from nongovernmental organizations.
- Assad's regime has huge financial problems, due among other things to reduced revenues from taxes and duties.
- Oil export has stopped. Before the civil war, it amounted to one-fifth of the national budget.
- The country is printing money to survive and receiving credit from Iran to keep the oil refineries running.
- The average income of a Syrian citizen is only U.S. $100 a month.

STRANDED AT THE TURKISH BORDER

The plight of the 100,000 Syrian refugees stranded on the Turkish border since the beginning of 2016 remains grim. They were fleeing from the three-year struggle for the trading center of Aleppo, from Russian air attacks, and from Assad's barrel bombs. Safiye Mahmut, a 26-year-old mother of three children, is totally desperate. She no longer believes that she can return. "My city has been reduced to rubble," she explains, adding pragmatically, "I say, we stay here." By "we" she means she and her three children. Her husband is fighting with moderate Syrian rebels. The children still wear their summer clothes; their shoes are sodden from the journey to the border in the rain. They are freezing, hungry, and scared stiff. It's an appalling image.

Safiye was, with thousands of other Syrians, part of a refugee trail to the Turkish border. They tramped as quickly as possible with their children, along the road connecting Aleppo to the border, some 42 miles. She made it across the border to Turkey and ended up in Demirciler, a suburb of Kilis. Kilis is a small city, but since early 2016 it has become a great symbol of hope. Kilis accommodates as many refugees as it has inhabitants: 130,000. The mayor, Hasan Kara, is convinced that Europe can learn the real meaning of solidarity from his city. "We share willingly," he says, adding, "but now, after three years, we've reached our limits. We can do no more."[5] His city now uses three times as much water as before the war; five times as much garbage is produced; and in many apartments there are three, sometimes four, families. "I need 10,000 new apartments, new garbage trucks, new sewage treatment facilities" from the EU, pleads the 47-year-old mayor. Now it's the EU's turn. It has already helped with a payment of €100 million. One hundred million euros—that's less than 3 percent of the promised €3 billion ... peanuts.

SOME 70,000 REFUGEES are marooned a short distance to the south on the other side of the border, in Syria, at the Öncüpinar crossing. These Syrians didn't make it across the border. It is to them that the Turkish president, Recep Tayyip Erdoğan, said, "The limits of capacity have been reached. Newcomers will be absorbed in camps on the Syrian side of the border." There has long been no more space available for additional tents to supplement those the Turkish and international aid organizations have already erected. People are forced to sleep in the open, in the rain and cold, on pieces of cardboard. They all want to leave Syria as soon as possible. But in Turkey there is no more mention of an "open door" policy. Those times have gone. So the refugees now have to endure the makeshift camp, some of them sleeping on the streets in temperatures just above freezing. Only when aid transports make it across the border do they receive supplies of blankets, food, and milk. It is a human catastrophe, and hardly anyone is offering help. Only the injured and sick are allowed across the border by the Turkish authorities. At least after medical treatment they are not sent back across the border but are accommodated in the Turkish container settlements that have sprung up along the border since 2016 and that house 20,000 Syrians. The Turks are preparing for a long war with many injured and countless refugees.

THE RUSSIAN AIR offensive continued nonstop until the middle of March. The Russians were not, as they had assured, targeting ISIS, whose troops were positioned east of Aleppo. Instead they bombarded villages along the only remaining supply route between Aleppo and the Turkish border, the lifeline of the once largest city in Syria, its commercial hub, a World Heritage Site.

In spring 2016, Aleppo is divided between the regime and the rebels. The Russian bombers support Assad's government troops, who, together with the Lebanese Shi'ite militia, Hezbollah, officers of Iran's Revolutionary Guard, and Shi'ite mercenaries from Iraq and Afghanistan, fight against the once rebellious citizens of Aleppo. The circle is closing; Aleppo is almost completely surrounded. A population of 350,000 still lives in the part of the city controlled by the moderate rebels. Roughly another million live in other parts of the city, where Assad's forces are entrenched. "There are no Syrian Free Army posts in the city center, only civilians," claims a young doctor in a hospital in Aleppo. Thirty doctors remain in the beleaguered city. Time and again one of them gives up and tries to flee. Initially, they were treating light wounds, the effects of tear gas and baton charges. Since Assad's regime started deploying the dreaded barrel bombs, however, the injuries have become more severe. Now it is pure horror. Every two or three hours, waves of fighter bombers fly above the city, aiming at anything that has not yet been destroyed—houses, schools, hospitals... The doctor continues, "Previously, we had ten seriously injured patients a day. Today the number is fifty." And, tragically, the Russians always attack "when the children are on their way to school."[6] How inhuman!

Syrian observers fear that Aleppo and its inhabitants will soon be totally cut off from humanitarian aid, as happened previously in the towns of Madaya, Darayya, and Talbiseh. This would lead to an even greater humanitarian catastrophe. For reference, in 1992, during the Bosnian War, Sarajevo, with its population of 300,000, survived only three years with the help of NATO airlifts. In 1994, the peace treaty was signed in Dayton, Ohio, and at last that war ended... at least for now.

In Syria, in contrast, no airlift to Aleppo, to the almost completely encircled population, is possible—not as long as the airspace belongs to the Russian bombers and American fighters. Despite the much-heralded withdrawal of Russia's forces, Russian bombers, pilots, and weapons still remain on the west coast of Syria. The first peace talks in Geneva are history. They didn't work out—the opposing sides couldn't even agree on an air corridor at the start of the talks, let alone on an evacuation strategy to allow the civilians to flee. We can only hope that the next round of talks will be more productive. The UN certainly doesn't want to give up, and shouldn't.

The ceasefire agreed upon at the end of February 2016 was a small ray of sunshine on the horizon. Even if it appeared fragile, for the first time the majority of aid convoys were getting through to the long-suffering people in the country, and there were new dates for a continuation of the Geneva talks.

Above all, there has to be agreement on the internationally outlawed cluster bombs. They are not only extremely dangerous to people because of their localized and instantaneous explosive forces, but many of the submunitions they contain don't explode on impact: they explode when moved or touched, which can be much later, even years after a war has ended. Human Rights Watch has been tireless in condemning the use of cluster bombs as a form of warfare. Images from bloggers in Syria vividly demonstrate the power that their blast has on victims—images mostly of children who have picked them up, believing that they've found something valuable.

ALSO IN THE spring of 2016, Turkey introduced other measures to seal off the borders to Syrian refugees. While the civilians who fled from Aleppo endured the bad conditions, in dire need on the Syrian side of the border, the Turkish government was replacing the barbed wire with huge concrete walls. The wall is the final phase of what the Turks refer to as the "safety zone," intended to prevent Syrian Kurds from controlling the border region. Turkey is more afraid of the Kurds than of either the thousands of refugees from Syria or the terrorists of the so-called Islamic State. But if Turkey no longer allows refugees to cross the border, it creates, in effect, a zone on the Syrian side of the border that comes under the auspices of the international community—an ingenious policy, considering that the Turkish government fears the foundation of a Kurdish state far more than a devastated Syria with its millions of refugees.

At the same time, large-scale kitchens and bakeries were appearing on the Turkish side of the border and small businesses were relocating to supply the needs of the refugees "over there," on the Syrian side. But by this time, Miryam had long since arrived in Europe.

FROM SYRIA TO SUDAN

Miryam and the children had to remain with the Syrian rebels in the mountains for one year and three months, often without electricity and with hardly anything to eat, sometimes going for days without water. She lived with constant fear of exploding shells and bombs, and with endless worry about her children. It is obvious to me that Miryam struggles to continue to relate her experiences of the flight—how she was eventually picked up by her friend and taken to the rebels, her children in tow, still without contact from her husband, still with no news of him. As someone who had been forced into military service, was he still at the Yousef Deip military camp, or had he already been transferred elsewhere? Had he been tortured? Was he even still alive? Could she pay to have him discharged? One of her husband's friends who was fighting for the anti-Assad rebels had claimed that to do this, she would need to raise 500,000 Syrian pounds—about $2,300.

She is unwilling to part with that much at the moment; the whole affair is too risky. She has often heard that money is paid to the Assad regime but the men are not released. And Assad is running low on soldiers: many have deserted, refusing to fight for him against their own people. Nobody gets away from the clutches of the armed forces that easily.

At long last it's time for Miryam and the children to move on, first to a former military airbase near Damascus. The passage for all six costs 125,000 SYP ($580). The next destination is Khartoum, the capital of Sudan, where, Miryam has been assured, everyone speaks Arabic.

Each child and their mother is allowed to take just one backpack. Miryam hides what's left of the cash from the sale of her household in Damascus in her underwear. One warm jacket per person, one change of underwear, one pair of sneakers—that's it.

Besides this, passports, a little loose change—you never know when you might need it—banking documents, the house deeds, and a couple of photos of the good old days (Miryam will show me these later in Hamburg). With a heavy heart, she has left behind blankets and warm clothing in Syria, although her neighbor advised her, "Put them on, no matter how hot it is—you never know what's coming." An older and more experienced friend added, "You might not be able to return home as quickly as you think." *Especially,* Miryam thinks to herself, *as home doesn't exist anymore.* She's loaded other family photos onto her cellphone: pictures of the house, the children's birthdays, their first days at school, and her wedding photos—although, and this will come to light much later, it hasn't been a particularly happy marriage.

What would await them in Sudan? They had no idea, says Miryam, shaking her head and laughing at the memories. *Destination: Khartoum.* These were the last words her Syrian helper said as she and the children boarded the small turboprop plane.

Sudan is a strict Islamic country with a population of some 40 million people, 8 million of whom live in the capital. It's also one of the poorest countries in Africa. Perhaps this is the very reason why Sudan has become a destination for Syrian civil war refugees who can afford it. But for Miryam, it is anything but a safe place. Khartoum is dominated by men and is a hub for global traffickers. And it is a brutal society. Women's rights? Nobody talks about them in Khartoum—just the opposite: *Shari'a,* the Islamic laws, prevail here. Even in the plane Miryam worries about what will happen if one of the children becomes ill in Sudan. She hopes they'll remain healthy. She inhales deeply and calms herself down with the thought that Akilah is again in stable condition. And at least Miryam's not pregnant again, as she has already heard that women in Sudan die by the dozen during childbirth. The mortality rate at birth is 1:31 in Sudan, making it the highest in the world.

She and her four daughters were advised to wear long, enveloping robes, and it was impressed on them how important this was. Women in Sudan are goods. They are worth nothing in themselves, but they do have a monetary value. They are kidnapped and sold, and also whipped if they dare to wear European clothes, especially pants.

She should also be very careful about her beautiful daughters. Rape is not a criminal offense in Sudan. When women are raped in Sudan, they don't report it to the police, and certainly not to the courts, as judges consider women who have been raped to be partly to blame. In the worst cases, women are imprisoned as punishment for having enticed the men to rape them. Countless other laws discriminate against and marginalize women. But it is to this country that Miryam is flying with her four daughters and her small son.

She knows that she must be properly veiled; the importance of this has been impressed on her. Straight after landing, she pays her first bribes to the airport staff: this one to the border officials; she knew this too in advance. In a rickety cab, she and the children are driven through the city and out to a rural area called El Grief. This is the first port of call for all newcomers from neighboring areas, like Darfur, South Sudan, Eritrea, Somalia, Ethiopia, and Chad. The list of places people are fleeing is long.

The small Syrian family moves into a stall next to a farmhouse, their new "home." With its crumbling walls, it is a mixture of refugee camp and old ruin. It lacks electricity and clean water. Miryam grits her teeth and sets about calming the children down. She tells me now that they lived like animals. And her children? They quickly learned to imitate the other animals, befriended them, and were soon so dirty that it was almost impossible to tell them apart. So, everything was perfectly normal. Above all, they were able to sleep well there, despite the hard concrete floor—no bombs, no shelling. Today Miryam can laugh about her experiences, but she tells me, "At that time, at night, I often wished that we had all died in Syria." She shudders: she would prefer to forget the memories of life in the stall in Khartoum. If only it were possible. One thing that she kept repeating deep inside was: "I must save the children." It was the only thing that helped her at that time. Thank God—or in Arabic, *Alhamdulillah*—Miryam didn't know that the worst was yet to come.

In Khartoum, another Syrian family with children is housed next door, in a similar stall-like hut. They come from Aleppo, from the Salah al-Din district, right on the front between the government troops and the rebels. The children play "snipers" together. It seems to help them cope with their experiences. The snipers in Aleppo got their kicks from having women, children, and the elderly in their sights and shooting at the ground between their legs. The official casualty figures for 2015 list 389 children shot over two years.

In the game in Khartoum, the children duck behind the stalls; one aims, and the others have to run away as quickly as possible. They are not allowed to look up while escaping because, as the children from Aleppo explain, you should never look a sniper directly in the eyes. At night, when quiet shrouds the two stalls in Khartoum, Miryam often hears screams and crying from next door. She is then glad that she managed to get the children out of her besieged Damascus suburb just in time and that they are now, hopefully, on the way to a safer future. She knows that children react particularly strongly to disturbing events. She knows this from the experiences of families in her own neighborhood after the bombs and shells fell. There is still no news of her husband, and she suppressed all thoughts of him. The most important thing is the children—and the next stage. Which will be when? Miryam is totally dependent on the trafficker, who mumbled something like "next week." It didn't sound convincing. The other family is also waiting and hoping. It is 100 degrees Fahrenheit (38 degrees Celsius) in Sudan.

THE PERILOUS LIBYAN DESERT

Miryam knows that the next stop is Libya. In the preliminary talks in Kafr Sousa, a possible flight via the Balkan route was rejected. The costs would have been considerably higher, and anyway, everyone had dissuaded her, as a woman alone with five children, from taking that route. Right—so the plan is to continue on to the North African coast. From Khartoum, as the crow flies, it is a distance of 1,500 miles. Driving on something resembling a road, there are two possible routes. One, through Chad, Niger, and Mali, is some 4,000 miles; the other goes along the Nile, through Egypt, then west along the Mediterranean coast, a distance of 2,600 miles. The Google route planner reckons it would take about 125 hours, more than five days of nonstop driving.

The traffickers, however, drive through the desert, to the northwest of Sudan, between Chad and Egypt, where there is a small stretch of shared border with Libya. This route is the safest for them, with few towns or oases and hardly any control posts. Miryam's contact, called Mohammed like her neighbor, dropped by to say, "Tomorrow morning, very early. There will be twenty refugees on the back of the pickup. Everyone can only take one backpack and enough money."

Sleeping that night is unthinkable; only the small ones, Olcay and Amir, dream blissfully, sleeping soundly next to their mother.

The traffickers arrive at four in the morning with dimmed headlights. The back of the truck is packed with people. *Where,* Miryam asks herself, *is there space for the children and me?* It isn't the turn of the neighboring family from Aleppo yet—they're still fast asleep, and she hasn't told them that she is about to leave. *Okay,* she thinks, *so let's go.* First, up go the children, then she follows onto the dirty truck bed. The others mutter, making space only when pushed aside by the driver. The best places, behind the driver, where you can lean against the cabin wall, have long since been taken. At the back is some sort of grip, as long as you can keep your hands on the hinged guardrail. In her backpack, Miryam has packed two 5-liter canisters of water and sweaters for the desert nights. She hopes that the sweaters will be warm enough and that this is enough water to keep them all alive. She then prays, the first time for a while. Miryam is not particularly devout, but she is scared about this trip and hopes that Allah will protect them. Before she got onto the pickup, one of the two traffickers took $10,000 from her. For the rest of the trip was the agreement. Now she has very little money left, but on the positive side, she doesn't have to hide so much money.

How long will they be traveling? She can no longer remember the map she used to look at in geography lessons at school. "Seven days and seven nights" someone in the pickup, better informed, tells her. Some of the others sit on thick wooden sticks that they have jammed between their luggage and their water canisters. On the long journey, this proves useful only so long as they keep a firm grip on something; otherwise, they end up on the floor, together with their sticks. Failure to hang on can mean falling off the pickup and landing in the desert. Hardly any drivers will stop—not for a single refugee.

Miryam and the five children stand for seven days on the back of the truck and sleep seven nights on the sand next to it. Then they are passed on to the next trafficker. Will they make it?

MIRYAM DOESN'T KNOW it, but women in particular are in great danger on this route. The UN reports that almost all women on this refugee route experience some form of sexual assault, including rape, and that thousands of children are sold as child soldiers or sex slaves, bringing the smuggling gangs a lot of money. People become commodities and are put up for sale. Even worse, women can't fail to be noticed on this route, and are in short supply elsewhere. It seems to help Miryam and her daughters that, apart from a slit for the eyes, they are fully veiled, as if they're wearing niqabs. They huddle together in the hope that no one will notice them.

At every arbitrary checkpoint, the police, border officials, military personnel, and militiamen cash in on the refugees. At these checkpoints all the refugees have to get down from the back of the pickup, and each time are forced to pay $40 per person, Miryam included. Six times $40 equals $240. Luckily, she has enough funds to cover this. Those who refused to pay or who have no money risk being beaten with sticks, belts, or tubing. Miryam tries to cover the small children's eyes so that they don't have to witness the horrific scenes. The officials also force the refugees to part with their jewelry and watches. Those who fail to voluntarily hand over their possessions are prevented from continuing on. That's worse than all the beatings: the trucks just hurtle away through the dusty sand; where they are heading, no one knows. Would the next truck pick up the castoffs? Extremely unlikely, especially as the refugees have nothing to offer.

The women were mostly worse off than the men, remembers Miryam later. They were dragged off to the back rooms of the stations, beaten, and raped. The route through the desert is extremely dangerous, and for many fatal. Especially for women traveling alone, many refugee organizations consider the route through the Sahara to be as hazardous as the trip across the Mediterranean. The numbers of people actually left behind are known only to the people-smugglers, says Maliki Hamidine of the International Organization for Migration in Agadez, Niger.

But Miryam will make it. She and her four daughters somehow manage to grip onto something, clutching little Amir, brace themselves when the truck jolts or swerves or when the driver speeds over a hump and all four wheels hang momentarily in the air. At anxious moments like this, everyone in the back of the truck holds their breath, hoping that they will land safely in the sand.

The traffickers take turns driving, and started from Khartoum on a Monday evening, as they know that on that evening, convoys of police and military vehicles also head north on the same route. Then they know that they're traveling safely in the slipstream—safe from the many gangs of bandits, whose numbers have swelled since the waves of refugees began to cross the Sahara. One result, however, of this "security" is an increase in costs at the new checkpoints that have sprung up along the route. Ultimately, everyone wants to cash in on people who have already been prepared to dispense with several thousand U.S. dollars for the journey to Europe. After all, later, when their flight is over, *they* are the ones who are all going to be rich. That, at least, is the conviction of those who remain behind in the desert. They take the money; the refugees, as they see it, get a new life.

LATER, MUCH LATER, in Germany, Miryam talks, above all, of her fears for the safety of the children during the journey through the desert. The traffickers had already threatened to carry on should anyone fall off. In the meantime, the twenty people in the back of the pickup got to know each other a bit better. The adults were willing to let the children remain in the middle of the truck bed, looking after them when they cried or when they were hungry or thirsty.

Miryam's fears began to recede a little, but never at night, when the huge star-studded sky sparkled and blinked above her, when they huddled together in the sand next to a wheel and froze.

The contrast was almost unbearable—during the day, temperatures reached 110 degrees Fahrenheit (43 degrees Celsius), and at night dropped to near freezing. Only people who have spent a night in the desert know this dramatic temperature drop. Every part of Miryam's body ached—her hands cramped up from constantly gripping the guardrails or a neighbor's wooden stick; her back ached from the jolts from deep potholes in the road, her throat from inhaling the sand and dust, her knees and legs from standing for hours on end in the same position while trying, as often as possible, to hold the small ones in her arms. The older children were a great help. Akilah, her eldest, who had been so badly injured in the bombing in Damascus, had been suffering from bad pains since the second day, but all the painkillers had been used up. Miryam was very upset about that.

The journey from Sudan to the Libyan capital really did take seven days and seven nights. On arrival, the refugees were so weak that they hardly managed to get off the pickup. Everything ached and their eyes were encrusted with sand, but they knew they wouldn't be able to take a shower yet. This was just a short break. At least they had arrived; it felt as though they had passed through a hundred checkpoints. They were able to refill their water canisters, and there was rice and pita bread to eat. The driver dropped them at the gates to Tripoli, and there they boarded an old bus. They saw nothing of the once beautiful city; the windows were filthy, and their eyes were still coated with dust and dirt from the trip.

Tripoli, with 1.8 million inhabitants, is the largest city in Libya but it is not the only capital. Two governments are fighting for ascendency, one based in Tobruk, with the parliament, the other in Bayda, with the government. This doesn't interest Miryam or her children in the slightest. They just want to move on—on to a boat, on to the sea toward Europe. She ends up with her five children and fifteen other women in a single room, and they are warned not to go out. Once a day, a young man on a motorbike brings them water and something to eat, usually rice and pita bread. The showers and faucets don't work, the beds are unmade and filthy, and Miryam can't bear to think about how many people have already slept there. But first things first: just stretch out, try to find a bit of peace and quiet. She wraps a piece of cloth around her nose to try to avoid the stench. The children cuddle up to their mother.

LIBYA TODAY IS considered a failed state. It was ruled until 2011 by the dictator Muammar Gaddafi, but since the end of his regime, brought about by a civil war and international military intervention, the country has been shaken by battles between rival militias. There has been civil war again there since 2014. The terrorist group ISIS is also involved in the struggle for power. In addition, refugees keep arriving there by the thousands; the exact numbers are unknown as nobody keeps track. The domestic oil industry could be a new source of revenue for the ISIS troops, who have come under pressure in Syria and Iraq. In times gone by, the brutal dictator did ensure order. The EU paid him millions of dollars to keep refugees who had reached his country away from the coast, using questionable methods. Some refugees found work as gardeners or domestic helpers: many Libyans could afford the cost thanks to the prosperity that the oil reserves had brought the country. But now Gaddafi is dead and the borders are open—for all.

In these chaotic conditions it is easy for the people-smuggling cartels to transport hundreds of thousands of migrants for thousands of dollars through the desert and onto boats. The network is incredibly successful, tendril-like, and, according to the experts, more profitable than the arms trade or drug business—in particular because the migrants regard the smugglers as friends and helpers, as indispensable facilitators in order to survive the flight. No matter how inhumanely the smugglers behave during the flight, no matter how violently they force the refugees into overladen boats, leaving them to their own destinies, no migrant will betray a smuggler. The trafficking mafia is the real winner in this flood of migrants.

NIGHT AFTER NIGHT, while Miryam tries to keep up the spirits of her children and to remain calm about the catastrophic hygienic conditions, small fishing boats put out to sea from the Libyan coast. With twenty to thirty refugees on board, they head out to sea for a rendezvous with larger cutters. One hundred, two hundred uncomplaining people are then squashed together in a confined space with the promise of a safe passage to Italy. The government in Tobruk has apparently come to an agreement with the EU, and after "positive dialogue" now wants to stop the flow of refugees. But these men in the so-called government are, in reality, powerless to act. If the EU really wanted to achieve something, they should have negotiated with the warlords in Tripoli, which will not have been made easier by an increase in hostilities in the port of Benghazi and in Tripoli. The EU mission to strengthen border protection in Libya was forced to withdraw to neighboring Tunisia for security reasons.

The operation against the traffickers had, for the time being, failed. There is no more talk of Libyan support... a green light for smugglers and refugees. This suits Miryam fine.

DATA AND FACTS: LIBYA, SPRING 2016

- Libya lies on the Mediterranean and borders Egypt and Sudan to the east, Niger and Chad to the south, and the Maghreb countries of Tunisia and Algeria to the west.
- Since the fall of the Gaddafi regime, brought on by civil war and international intervention, the country has been shaken by rival militias.
- Two separate alliances struggle for power in the country: the official government groups and the terrorist group ISIS.
- The official capital is Tripoli, parliamentary sessions are held in Tobruk, and the seat of government is in Bayda.
- The country has 6 million inhabitants.
- The Sahara covers 85 percent of the country.
- 30 percent of the population is under 15 years old.
- The country, until recently, was relatively supportive of women, but over the last few years, veiling of women had been on the increase.
- Libya has the highest per capita earnings in Africa.
- Libya has Africa's largest oil reserves.
- There is compulsory education, with free schooling for all 6- to 15-year-olds.
- Illiteracy rates are 29 percent for women and 8 percent for men.

- There are universities in Tripoli and Benghazi.
- Since 2015, the United Nations has considered Libya to be close to economic collapse.

NON-SWIMMERS

Following the advice of a friend in Syria, Miryam had planned her flight for this time of the year, the end of September—before the heavy storms on the Mediterranean in the fall and when the desert is no longer so hot. This turned out to be poor advice. But the sea route between North Africa and Italy at this time of year is smooth compared to the crossing to the Greek islands from the west coast of Turkey. There, the waves are much higher and the dangers of capsizing much more serious.

Miryam knew all this in Damascus when she was planning her escape. Now she learns that she is again to be collected at night, that she has to hide in thick woods near the beach so that the Libyan police patrols don't find her. She has to be totally silent, and this information she repeatedly passes on to the small children. "The smugglers," she tells me later in Germany, "said that the crossing would take only one night and two days." This was untrue. It is, after all, 200 miles to Lampedusa—across open sea. On the beach of Garabulli, in Libya, the sand dunes and thick undergrowth hide the refugees from the sight of the patrols out in the bay. The Italian navy patrols this stretch of the coast and impounds boats. Out of fear of arrest by the Italians, many traffickers now leave the refugees to navigate their boats alone.

This isn't the case for Miryam and the children. Yet once again nothing goes according to plan. First, she has to pay more—$2,500 for the crossing. "This is now totally safe. Don't worry," the man collecting her money promises her. Will her remaining money last until Europe? She has to give him another $100 for provisions on board—they are supposed to provide bread, canned tuna, and milk for the children. She is told that the bus will collect them at two in the morning, and the man disappears. *In this business, people don't say goodbye,* she thinks to herself; anyway, she won't see him again. Once again, another man... The whole business is a man's world; women are nowhere to be seen.

A NUMBER OF buses stop in front of the dilapidated buildings and the passengers quickly board. Most of them are women from Miryam's house. The men have already been gathered from other houses. It's cold on the beach as they duck behind prickly shrubbery. Miryam clasps Amir tightly; he is shaking with fear. Dark figures emerge and herd the migrants onto a small fishing boat. They stumble and fall in the sand—at least it's soft—then wade through the shallow water to the boat and clamber aboard. The Libyan fisherman fires up the outboard motor and chugs out onto the dark black sea.

Miryam and the children feel sick. They are very scared, so scared that they can hardly breathe. They've never been out on a lake, let alone the sea. None of them can swim. The traffickers never mentioned anything about lifejackets, for the obvious reason that there are none. They just claimed, again and again, "Everything will be okay. It's totally safe."

After only ten minutes, they reach a bigger ship, which they have to board by climbing a rope ladder. Amir is crying now. Up to this moment, he has been incredibly brave for his five years. A tall man gathers him in his arms and climbs up the rope ladder.

Miryam, still below, takes a deep breath. She is the last one to board; the children were first, followed by the men.

On the bigger ship now, she scans the deck. There are, she is certain, 300 people there, huddling together in the darkness—crouching, frightened, freezing. Some of them try to keep each other warm. Miryam searches for a space sheltered from the wind near a guardrail, and clasps the children close to her, which seems to calm them down a bit. The tall, dark-haired man in the steering cabin starts up the engines, and they head farther out to sea.

"The crossing took two nights and three days," she tells me. Even this long after the event, Miryam is reluctant to go into details about the journey across the Mediterranean. She can no longer talk of her panic and fear as the so-called captain appeared to no longer know the route, of how the engines spluttered and died, of how more and more water gushed on board until it was up to their shoulders. Most of the refugees had had to hand in their cellphones before the boat trip. Now none of them was able to contact the rescue services or send out an SOS. Miryam was sure that she and the children would die. She held Amir in her arms, later heaving him up onto her shoulders so that he wouldn't be the first to die. At the last—the very last—minute, as she says today, rescue arrived in the form of an oil tanker. Its crew rescued all 300 people. The Italians—"They were Italians, and we were all given pasta to eat"—gave them as many blankets as they could find. They fed them and made their own cabins available to the women and children. Miryam could hardly believe it. Saved, survived—all of them.

On the Italian island of Lampedusa, her family of six disembarked, full of gratitude to their rescuers. The reception from the Italians was not particularly warm, but never mind: the most important thing was that they were all alive.

In 2015 alone, over 3,000 people died on this crossing. The Italian coast guard recovered the bodies; there is no count of those who washed up on the Libyan coast. Hundreds of battered remains of black inflatable dinghies languish in harbors large and small along Libya's 1,100-mile coastline, reminders of failed crossings. An engine missing here, an occasional lifejacket there, but no trace of people from Syria, Eritrea, Somalia, or Nigeria, the countries where most of the refugees originated. A few personal belongings sometimes remain in the boats: passports and ID cards, cellphones, cash, faded family photos—all testimony to the people who didn't survive. What survivor would leave behind any of these vital possessions?

THIS IS AS far as we'll go for now with Miryam and her children's adventurous and dangerous escape. The family's flight from Kafr Sousa at the gates of Damascus to Lampedusa cost a total of around $13,600. You'll learn how she and her children got from there to the German border and then to Hamburg in the second part of their story.

THE WOMEN OF SYRIA

Until the beginning of the war, women in Syria had rights. They were better off than many women in neighboring Arab countries. Nevertheless, even before the conflict the proportion of women in professional and business life was very low. In 2010, just under 20 percent of Syrian women worked; most women abandoned their careers after marriage. As in other countries of the Middle East and North Africa, the number of girls going to school has increased in recent decades but did so without affecting the numbers of women taking part in working life. The reason for this, above all, lies in the patriarchal structures still embedded in family and social life. According to the Syrian constitution, women still have the same rights as men, but with the Ba'ath coup and subsequent Emergency Law in 1963, limits were set. Not until 2011, after weeks of protests, did President Assad formally suspend the Emergency Law, altering women's legal situation. However, it remained difficult for Syrian women to appeal suppressive and discriminating legislation through legal channels. It's true that women were allowed to open up businesses, earn their own money, and own property, but in practice, social pressures, lack of self-confidence, and lack of education often forced women to hand over social and economic control to male family members.

Additionally, even before the war, women's rights varied from region to region. In the cities, women could study and subsequently work without problems, despite male-dominated family structures. Their fathers—and later their husbands—still called the shots on many issues, but women had some freedom in some areas, even if it didn't extend to real self-determination over their own lives. In Syria's villages, on the other hand, the majority of women had only a minimum level of self-determination.

Still, girls went to school, and as a result, 81 percent of all Syrian women over the age of 15 can read and write. Illiteracy rates for young people aged 15 to 24 are relatively low, at 5.5 percent. This is because these young men and women grew up only just after the introduction of compulsory education. Until the beginning of the war, English was taught to 10- to 11-year-olds in state schools, which has proved especially helpful during this crisis to women who, as a result of the war in Syria, have become the main breadwinners of their families after so many husbands, fathers, and brothers lost their lives in the conflict.

But the constant, ongoing violence of this war is having a dramatic impact, particularly on women. Human Rights Watch reported in 2014 that rape, as a weapon of war, was common. Pressure on women to conform to the norms of strict *Shari'a* laws is also growing, particularly in areas run by rebel groups like Hezbollah and the al-Nusra Front, who act almost like jihadists. Family honor must never be defiled, and thus in this war the rights of women dwindle.

If courageous women nonetheless continue to live visibly in public, they experience pressure and condemnation. There is very little left of Syria's once liberal constitution, which guarantees equal rights to both sexes. A forty-seven-page Human Rights Watch report on seventeen women refugees and their experiences of human rights violations is a bitter testimony to these developments. It shows that women in Syria are threatened, arbitrarily imprisoned, detained, and tortured, both by government and by opposition forces. The women interviewed were physically abused and tortured, and dramatically restricted in their choice of clothing and freedom of movement. "Women have not been spared any aspect of the brutality of the Syrian conflict, but they are not merely passive victims," said Liesl Gerntholtz, Women's Rights director at Human Rights Watch. "Women are taking on increasing responsibilities—whether by choice or due to circumstances—and they should not have to pay with intimidation, arrest, abuse, or even torture."[7]

A HORRIFIC BALANCE

The war in Syria is the greatest refugee crisis in the last quarter century, according to the UNHCR. The number of refugees who have fled the Syrian conflict to neighboring countries now exceeds 4 million. Furthermore, by the end of 2015, the number of displaced people within Syria amounted to around 8 million. Many of them are in inaccessible areas.

DATA: SYRIAN REFUGEES, SUMMER 2015[8]

- 1,805,255 in Turkey
- 249,726 in Iraq
- 629,128 in Jordan
- 1,172,753 in Lebanon
- 132,375 in Egypt
- 24,055 at various other locations in North Africa

In the EU, 1,294,000 asylum applications were registered in 2015, over 476,000 in Germany alone. Although the last weeks of 2015 may have left the impression that the majority of refugees were using Austria and Hungary as transit routes to Germany, this is not entirely true. Many remained in those countries. In absolute figures, Germany does indeed absorb the most refugees in Europe, but in proportion to their populations, Austria and Hungary are both ahead of Germany. Sweden, up to the end of 2015, remained unchanged at the top of the table.

THE LOST GENERATION

"We should stop and ask ourselves how, in all conscience, can we continue to fail the children of Syria?" remarked Anthony Lake, the executive director of UNICEF, in 2013.[9] He was not the only one who believed that the international community had failed to do anything about this war. The survival and welfare of a whole generation of innocent people is at stake—people who have lost their homes, their families, and their future. Even after a successful flight to another country, they remain traumatized, most of them utterly in despair. This applies to at least 2 million children and young people who have fled to foreign countries to escape the horrors of this conflict.

The number of affected children inside Syria is much higher. Hardly anything is reported about them because journalists, bloggers, and photographers increasingly risk losing their lives for such research. Due to the ongoing hostilities, the civilian population is increasingly dependent on humanitarian aid. Many live in unreachable terrain. There, only 40 percent still have access to semi-drinkable water; many are able to obtain food only once a day, if at all. The UNHCR estimated in January 2016 that 8 million people—half of them children—will never be able to seek refuge in other countries.

TWO

TURKEY

THE FORGOTTEN

The next act in the refugee drama takes place in Syria's neighbor, Turkey. An estimated 2.8 million refugees have found refuge here, 64 percent of them from Syria. Some of them have been registered, but many are here illegally in the country that straddles Europe and Asia. In Germany and in EU headquarters in Brussels, people have been saying, "The key to the solution of the refugee crisis lies in Turkey." Just like that—as if we can do something, as if there is a solution outside of Europe's borders, as if Turkey is a buffer zone between us and the fleeing people.

Two-thirds of Turkey's refugees come from Syria, the rest from Afghanistan and Iraq; those from Iraq are mostly Yazidis and Kurds. But the male refugees—fathers, sons, and brothers—try to leave Turkey as quickly as possible. In 2015, this meant across the Mediterranean to Greece then on to the Balkan route. Destination: Europe, and above all, Germany. In the winter of 2015–16, up to 2,000 refugees set off each night, often in stormy conditions, from the western Turkish coast and landed on one of the Greek islands. Turkey, Europe, the rest of the world—everyone else just looked on.

WHAT HAPPENS TO the women and children they have left behind? Before January 2016, nobody spoke about them, nobody told their stories. Only in the early months of 2016, as more women and children began arriving in the inflatable boats, as more women and children were registered in Passau, Germany, than ever before, did a few Germans begin to sit up and take notice. I had been asking myself for a long time: Where are they, where are the women of the fleeing men? The mothers and grandmothers of these unaccompanied young people?

So, my first destination was eastern Turkey, along the Turkish–Syrian border where the camps had been set up as early as 2014, when Turkey hoped that the war in Syria would be swiftly resolved and the refugees would be able to return to their villages and cities. It was for this reason that the camps were sited on the border, near to the refugees' homes. But it didn't work out as hoped. In 2016, the war was in its sixth year. Six years of living in camps. Six years of being a begging refugee, dependent on the generosity of others. How were people coping there? And were they really mostly women and children?

I set off for Diyarbakir, a city of 1.6 million in eastern Turkey, right in the center of what used to be the "wild Kurdistan" known to German readers of Karl May's American-style western novels. From Istanbul the cross-country plane trip is almost two hours, first along the incredibly long Black Sea coast, then over barren steppes, where very little grows—hardly any green but plenty of gray—and through meandering dry river valleys and treeless mountain ranges. My iPad weather app told me back in Germany that the average temperature in September in

Diyarbakir is 100 degrees Fahrenheit (38 degrees Celsius). I will soon discover that this was far from accurate.

As for my research in Afghanistan for a previous book, I am accompanied by Peter Müller as photographer. We are already a well-oiled team. In the evening sun we have a gentle landing at a small, nondescript airport. Everything runs smoothly, even the trip to the hotel. A Kurdish man, Mansur, collects us; he will be our driver for the next several days. The hotel is within the city's famous picturesque Roman basalt walls, which stretch unbroken for almost four miles; here it sits between mosques and churches, surrounded by businesses small and large. Soon we see the famous gigantic watermelons, the largest of which is supposed to have weighed 110 pounds. The Tigris River, which winds through the eastern part of the city, irrigates the large valley where the refreshing fruit grows.

With WhatsApp, you really can make phone calls to any country in the world for free, and everyone has WhatsApp—at least, that's what Peter Müller has claimed. And, as if by magic, I manage to reach Feray, our interpreter, whom we will meet at ten the next morning, for our journey to the first refugee camp. We are satisfied with the ease of our travel arrangements and drop, exhausted, into bed. Thankfully, the rooms are air conditioned, for although it is late evening, the temperature is above 100. *How high will the mercury climb at midday tomorrow in the camp?* I wonder.

DATA AND FACTS: TURKEY, SPRING 2016

- Turkey has a population of 74.9 million.
- Its system of government is parliamentary democracy.

- 2.8 million refugees and asylum-seekers are sheltered there.
- The country consists of two regions: Anatolia, to the west, consists of 97 percent of the country's area and straddles two continents, while Thrace, on the European mainland, accounts for the remaining 3 percent.
- 99.8 percent of the population are Muslim, mostly Sunnis; 15 to 20 percent of Turkish Muslims are Alevis, a Shi'ite branch.
- The national GDP is around U.S. $851.4 billion
- Youth unemployment is about 20 percent.
- 42 percent of Turkish women are victims of domestic violence, although men and women are equal before the law.
- Since the mid-1980s, the Kurdish conflict has determined domestic politics.
- Some 18 percent of the population are Kurds, the largest ethnic group in the world without an autonomous country.
- The Turkish and Kurdish governments had moved closer together, but in the course of the war the relationship between the two governments has deteriorated.
- Turkey has repeatedly demanded the resignation of President Assad.
- Since May 2012, Syrian opposition combatants have been trained and armed by the Turkish secret services.

- Freedom of the press is severely restricted; in the World Press Freedom Index, Turkey ranks 149, behind Iraq and Burma (Myanmar).[1]

WOMEN HELPING WOMEN

In the morning we pay our first courtesy call to Kardelen, a center for women and children. Kardelen helped me organize my trip, found my interpreter, and recommended the hotel. Its director, Mukaddes, has already notified the refugee camp of our impending visit. As I discovered during research in Afghanistan and East Congo for a previous book, it is women who take care of people in need; in this case it is Kurdish women and the organizations they run.

Before our visit to the camp, Mukaddes explains that we shouldn't be surprised at the reticence of the women there. The Yazidis from the community around Mosul in northern Iraq now live in Turkey, but they are still terrified of Muslims. In desperation, they fled to a Muslim country, but, according to Mukaddes, their fear is still ever present. The story of a horrifying genocide of Yazidis one hundred years ago is passed on from generation to generation. On top of this, their once friendly Kurdish neighbors in northern Iraq and northern Syria did nothing to help them against attacks by ISIS terrorists. None of the Kurds there stood by them, defended them, or even hid them as the terrorists occupied their villages. I am to hear this again later from many mothers and daughters. In front of their eyes, the fanatical jihadists murdered their husbands and sons. Even worse was having to leave the bodies behind, being unable to give them a proper burial, unable to pay their final respects. We begin to understand how past and present merge in the minds of Yazidi women.

Feray translates sensitively and amiably, and, on parting, the dedicated director of the Kurdish women's center wishes us plenty of luck with our interviews. Once again she repeats, with deadly earnestness, that not one woman or girl will give an account of their personal experiences—the abuse and rape that they may have suffered—mainly because of their religion. I shouldn't even bother asking; it's futile.

WE DRIVE SOUTH out of Diyarbakir, initially along the Tigris. After thirty minutes a huge sea of gray tents surrounded by coiled barbed wire appears. Two men open a wobbly gate; we are already registered as visitors, so can proceed without delay. One year ago, straight after the first offensives against northern Iraqi towns and villages, 7,000 people found refuge here at the Fidanlik refugee camp. Today "only" 4,500 remain, housed in huge army tents and in wooden huts without walls, allowing a slight breeze to pass through in the scorching hot summers, making them much more pleasant for sleeping. Everything seems stable and orderly. But a refugee camp is a refugee camp.

Turkey has earned worldwide respect for its immensely generous intake of Syrian refugees. The refugee camps set up by the Turkish government inside its borders are considered exemplary compared to those in other countries. The *New York Times* actually went as far as describing the container camp at Kilis as "perfect."[2] But far from all refugees have found shelter in this camp, and after five years of war in Syria, the mood is changing. The Turkish government feels that it has been abandoned, that the burden of caring for the refugees is not being fairly shared. Ahmet Davutoğlu, then prime minister of the transitional government, even believed that Turkey has been let down by the international community and that Turkey has "effectively become a buffer between chaos and Europe,"[3] and the point cannot be entirely dismissed. Ankara stressed that they had spent U.S. $7.3 billion on refugees.[4] There is no reason to doubt these figures. Beyond them, the social costs are significant. So the Turks are seething while the refugees, some of them living in pitiful conditions, eke out a miserable existence. The refugees have no long-term status in Turkey, although the country was one of the original signatories to the Geneva Refugee Convention in 1951. According to an ancillary agreement concluded by Turkey, the refugee status foreseen in the Convention and the ensuing international protections applies only to Europeans, not Syrians, Afghanis, or Iraqis. These refugees can't apply for asylum or, as a general rule, for work permits. It's the same in Lebanon and Jordan.

This is bitter, especially as, according to UNICEF, only about 17 percent of the refugees in Turkey live in camps. The rest seek shelter in derelict buildings, ruins, run-down houses, or overpriced rooms and apartments. Large families live in small rooms in the most cramped conditions, or even on the streets. Women are forced into prostitution. Others scrape a meager living as day laborers or agricultural harvesters for starvation wages. They are considerably cheaper than Turkish workers, making them more enemies among the local population,[5] so much so that after five years, very little remains of the welcome in Turkish culture. The Turkish people would like to get rid of their refugees, but how? Already at the end of 2015 the twenty-five camps were full.

THE CAMP IN front of the Diyarbakir gates is one of those camps. I learn that only 1,600 Yazidi women remain here with their children. Here too, the men—the fathers and brothers—are en route away from Turkey.

My first impression of the camp is that it is very tidy, clean. Between the rows of tents, stone slabs have been laid close together to make walking easier. Occupants' shoes are placed in front of the tents, as is customary in this part of the world. Inside the tents are neatly piled stacks of blankets, contented children, and lots of babies in small wooden cradles, but no screaming or complaints. The women sit cross-legged, pretty headscarves covering their hair. Children are everywhere, holding their mother's hand or in her arms or leaning against her shoulder. So many women and girls—and so few men. And so many surprisingly blond children. They study me with interest: a foreigner, certainly not Turkish, also blond. *What on earth is she doing here?*

Together with our Kurdish interpreter, I am kindly invited into a tent. The photographer has to wait outside—men are a hindrance when women want to talk to women. We sit down on thin foam mats that serve as mattresses for the women and children at night. Seve, the Yazidi woman who courteously invited us in, is 42 years old. She proudly introduces me to her eight children. Her eldest daughter is just over 18; the youngest girl, 11 months, was born a refugee while they fled from the ISIS terrorists who entered Iraq from Syria in August 2014 and attacked Seve's hometown near the Sinjar Mountains. Over 20,000 northern Iraqi Yazidis tried to flee to the mountains to escape the atrocities of the ISIS militiamen, often enduring days without water or provisions in extreme heat. At that time only Kurdish

Iraqi *peshmerga* units, supported by air cover from the U.S. Air Force, were fighting the militiamen. The Yazidis were pursued for weeks by Sunni extremists while under continuous fire from ISIS terrorists who had tried to surround them and take prisoners. Only after a safety corridor was set up by *peshmerga* soldiers with U.S. air support were the desperate Yazidis rescued. Soldiers provided food and water, thus saving their lives.

Now Seve and her children, sister-in-law, and mother-in-law all live in this 160-square-foot tent provided by the Turkish army. They have been here for over a year. It is hot—over 100 degrees Fahrenheit (38 degrees Celsius) outside. A fan is on in the tent, but it just circulates the air and doesn't provide any effective cooling.

Politely we remove our shoes outside the tent. Inside, we start by asking about everyday life here but soon move on to the story of Seve's flight. An animated account of the events of a year ago gushes out—how twenty people, including Seve in advanced pregnancy, fled on foot for twenty-five hours, aiming just to get away, first east and then north. Their intention was to cross into Turkey at the northern Iraqi border. The gruesome images of the beheaded neighbor, the murdered children, were fresh in her memory. "They cooked them," she tells me, looking at me intensely, as if she wants to burn her words into my memory. "And then they forced us to eat the soup." I don't want to believe it. I feel sick. Feray is hardly able to translate the words.

THE BORDER IS OPENED

Seve skips over what happened to the daughters of her Yazidi friends next door. Mukaddes has warned me that these stories were taboo, that the Yazidis will not talk about topics like violence or rape. Seve goes on to talk about more harmless things: "Our Kurdish neighbors provided us with two cars for our flight." It was this act of kindness that enabled the refugees to reach the Turkish border. And there they came to a halt—the Turkish officials wouldn't let them cross. "Only after ten hours of waiting were we finally allowed to cross to safety. The whole time we were quivering with fear." As if by a miracle, the borders suddenly opened, Seve explains. There was no sign of the Turkish border officials. Seve and her family landed in the Fidanlik camp, a thirty-minute drive south of Diyarbakir, where they remain today and where we are sitting together... in safety, at least, but nothing more.

The camp administrator, Muzeyyen Anik Aydin, tells me later that a year before, 7,000 Yazidi refugees found shelter here after the first offensive by the ISIS terrorists. Many of them had to endure a wait of up to fifteen days at the Turkish border, without food and without water, above and around them the constant boom of mortar fire. Some were severely injured and, after the border opened, had great difficulty hauling themselves here to the refugee camp.

All this proved to be a huge challenge for the volunteers. The camp is run by the municipal authorities of Diyarbakir. They provide the tents and organize the catering, school classes, and medical treatment—an immense task. The Yazidis sought refuge here because, among other things, their language is related to Kurdish languages. Feray, our interpreter, speaks five Kurdish dialects and can communicate well with the Yazidis. A second, and even more important, reason often named for fleeing to the Kurdish region of the neighboring country and not to central

Turkey is fear of the Turkish state. In the Kurdish area, the Yazidis feel safer. But it often becomes clear that they don't feel really *safe*—just safer.

AT SOME STAGE in my conversation with Seve I raise the subject of men. Where is her husband? What has happened to all the other men? What if there are no funds available to pay the traffickers? "Some of them," says Seve, and this astonishes me, "have returned to Iraq."

Her husband is still there, she tells me. But she doesn't know any more than that, or she doesn't want to tell me. "Maybe they are fighting for the north Iraqis, the Kurdish *peshmerga*," she says, almost whispering, as if it is forbidden. But if he was with the *peshmerga*, it would be more than understandable—after all, their homes are at stake.

On top of all the harrowing personal stories, the mothers in the tents always asked me one question: "Why doesn't Europe let us in? Why only the Syrians?" Even here in eastern Turkey, news spreads like wildfire on the Internet. Every woman here has a cellphone—a phone is essential for contact with the outside world, with friends and relatives still persevering at home, and especially with their fleeing husbands and sons. So it is true: some of the men are on their way to Europe, have left their women and children behind in the hope of one day being able to reunite. But when? And what can be done until then?

Additionally, the Yazidi women deeply mistrust the Muslim patriarchal surroundings here. Mukaddes had already mentioned it to me. Seve becomes angry: "The Muslim Kurds in northern Iraq betrayed us all, knowingly sending us in the wrong direction, straight into the arms of the ISIS terrorists." Religion is a deeply dividing element between Yazidis and Kurds. Here a non-Muslim religious community, there the Muslim faithful. Everyone in the camp knows about the dreadful genocide of the Yazidi community a century ago in this very region, eastern Turkey—another reason the women and children want to get away from here as soon as possible . . . preferably back home, when peace returns to Syria. That is what they all say, but it seems a more distant prospect than ever.

One of Seve's daughters disappeared; two other girls are missing from the neighboring tents, on Seve's left and right. "They are back in Iraq" is the explanation given to me. I don't want to believe it, so I press her, asking why the daughters, of all people, would return to a region where they will be threatened by ISIS terrorists. They are mentally ill, I learn later: ISIS fighters gave them drugs that rendered them deranged. The women don't want to expand on this. Seve tightens her pretty dark red headscarf and looks into the distance. There is, indeed, a great reluctance to speak.

YAZIDISM

Some 35,000 to 40,000 Yazidis live in Germany; worldwide the number is 200,000 to 800,000. Yazidism is a monotheistic religion that is not based on a holy scripture. The Yazidis worship Nature as the ultimate good, and have been targeted by fundamentalist Muslims since the end of the Iraqi invasion of 2003. In Mosul, al-Qaeda issued a *fatwa* forbidding the provision of Yazidis with food, causing hundreds to die by starvation. The terrorist group ISIS considers the Yazidis to be unbelievers, and pursues and murders them. For ISIS, Yazidism is a "heathen religion from pre-Islamic times,"[6] which enables ISIS to "legally" sell captured Yazidi women and children into slavery.

About 7,000 Yazidis managed to flee to eastern Turkey after the ISIS offensive from Syria and the northern Iraqi Sinjar Mountains. Today, 4,500 Yazidis remain marooned there in various refugee camps.

TWENTY-FIRST-CENTURY SLAVERY

Thirty-year-old Sari lives in the tent opposite Seve. Her 11-year-old daughter, Eydan, has been listening to us, leaning, a bit lost, against a post at the entrance to the tent. Now she pulls me and the interpreter to her tent to introduce us to her family.

Two women sit on a bed made out of wooden planks, the others on the floor. A baby lies in a wooden cradle. I ask the age of the baby, about what life is like here, what they do the whole day. But after a while, as I inquire whether Sari's husband is back in Iraq, I seem to have touched upon a sore point. Suddenly the distraught mother and daughters begin to cry, and the tears are unceasing. I rummage around in my backpack for some tissues; Peter, who is waiting outside, passes in a whole pack. I feel ashamed that I initiated this outburst of heartache and sorrow with what was intended as an innocent, objective question. Later I learn that Sari's husband was a soldier killed by ISIS terrorists during their flight. But he wasn't the only one—the youngest son too, and, as if there hadn't been enough deaths in this family, the twin brother of 16-year-old Viyan. How was it possible that Sari's and the other families were able to escape at all? Up to today, they still don't know the answer. Shaken by memories, Eydan clasps her frantic mother. It is hardly bearable. And between the sobs, there is always the same sentence: "We don't know what to do when winter comes—how are we supposed to manage?"

Much later, after the tears have dried a bit, Sari talks about kidnapped girls—girls in general, but in such detail that I suspect she is talking about her own daughter. She speaks haltingly about how girls are sold on the Internet. The younger the girl, the higher the price. Twenty dollars is the current price for a 16-year-old. One girl, she tells me, was forced by ISIS terrorists to phone her parents and give exact details of what the "barbarians," as Sari calls them, did to her. She was imprisoned for days without water or food and brutally, repeatedly raped. Now, according to Sari, the girl is about to be married to an ISIS terrorist. If she shows any signs of hesitation, she will be either sold or killed. During the narration, Sari frequently breaks into sobs. How can people endure so much suffering? Fairly soon I am absolutely certain that she is telling us the story of her own daughter.

In northern Iraq, a full-scale slave market has been established by ISIS fighters. Arab and Kurdish dealers buy kidnapped girls and boys. They refer to the transaction as "liberation." And then they sell them on, this time back to their families. The ISIS terrorists also deal in Christian slaves, often for just under $125. Boys who are captured during ISIS raids are trained as soldiers and forced to convert to Islam. The dealers who buy and then sell these children on usually charge between $1,000 and $3,000. That is the price paid by friends or relatives of Yazidi families for the release of their children. It's a particularly dark chapter in this already horrific war in Syria—a twenty-first-century slave trade.

Canon Andrew White, former vicar of St. George's Church in Baghdad and now head of a foundation helping Yazidis and Christians, sees only one way out of the sex slave drama: "You have to pay the ransom for the girls, it's the only way to free them." At the end of 2015 there were thought to be 2,700 girls still in the hands of ISIS as sex slaves.

All this goes through my mind when, after many hours, we leave the tents at Fidanlik. Here, in this settlement, at least they are safe. But the question keeps returning: What future awaits them? What opportunities do the Yazidis and their children have here? Our comforting words seem very superficial, a further example of our helplessness. I promise them that on my return to Germany I will report about the fate of the Yazidis in eastern Turkey but tell them that we cannot help at the moment. I promise myself that when I have finished my research, I will visit these women again.

BENEATH THE SHADE of some trees we meet Sukran Nizrak, who sews, knits, and paints with the women in an attempt to distract them from their misfortunes and to make the long days in the camp seem a little shorter. She explains how difficult it was at the beginning to get through to the Yazidi women. The men were always hanging around, sitting under trees and at the side of the paths in the camp. Only when the idea of a women's center was realized did the situation improve. Sukran hopes that with time many families will change their minds and choose not to go to Europe but to see their future here in eastern Turkey. The Kurds here do a lot for them, she says—the local administrations in Mardin and Diyarbakir regularly send volunteers to the camp. Here, too, they rely on the help of volunteers—more evidence of the qualities of a civilized society.

A year has passed since ISIS attacked this religious minority. According to Kurdish reports, 3,000 people are still missing in northern Iraq. At least 2,500 kidnapped Yazidis are alive but in the hands of the jihadists in Syria. According to figures released by agencies in the Iraqi autonomous region of Kurdistan, 1,850 Yazidis have been released after payment of ransoms. The agencies also estimate that at least 1,000 Yazidi men have lost their lives in this terrible war.

I often ask, what exactly does the Turkish government actually do for those who are here? Bearing in mind the readiness of the European Union to pay €3 billion for assistance for the refugees in Turkey once the Turkish government organizes stricter border controls, what does the Turkish government provide to help the Yazidi women and children here? The answer I get from Harun Ercan, the liaison officer of the city of Diyarbakir, is bitter: "The Turkish state pays nothing here. Provision for the people in the five camps in east Turkey is greatly at risk. Money is running out—we can only provide the absolute necessities." This was in the fall of 2015. Since then, Turkey has broken off peace talks with the Kurdish minority and war is raging in the former Kurdistan. Little hope remains for the refugee women and children in the camps.

Feray, our interpreter, has promised to bring milk to two elderly women in the camp. It is our last stop for the day. Thank goodness, they have a fridge—at least the milk won't go off. At the moment they aren't living in their allotted tent; instead they have constructed an airy shelter across from it, made out of wooden planks. It has raised beds so that there is more of a draft, more fresh air; outside, the temperature is 107 degrees Fahrenheit (almost 42 degrees Celsius).

Sixty-year-old Rezan sits on the floor knitting bed socks and crocheting facecloths. Completely shrouded in white, she tells me an extraordinary tale. Her two sons have been in Germany for a long time, but they have never taken care of her and will not help her here. Her friend and former neighbor, Xoxe, has a son in the United States. He also has not contacted his mother or sent her money, let alone helped her to get away from here. This is almost unbelievable, as the devout Yazidis are considered to be always willing to help. Their religion obliges them to support each other. The two women seem to have already accepted their destiny. "We expect nothing more," they say sadly but calmly.

ONE SUICIDE BOMB

Depressed by the visit with the two old Yazidi women at the camp in Fidanlik, we return to our car. Mansur is waiting there for us, and we drive back to Diyarbakir along the Tigris, where children are swimming or playing knights with wooden sticks for swords. It seems for a moment that all is well in the world.

Tomorrow we plan to get up at six and drive to the Turkish–Syrian border, to Suruç, to the place where a suicide bomber has just killed thirty-four Kurds. We suspect that with this act, a new, brutal spiral of violence has begun—Turks against Kurds. Tough times lie ahead.

During the night I can't get the two hopeless women out of my head. Rezan, dressed completely in white, showed me her upper arm with her name tattooed on it. Feray was reluctant to translate the reason for the tattoo: "So that other people know my name when one day the ISIS terrorists chop off my head." What kind of prospect is that? What levels of fear do these people have to bear?

All this is still going through my head during the trip to Suruç, some 200 miles from Diyarbakir, directly on the Syrian border in deepest southern Turkey.

A few days ago, Suruç was the scene of a fateful suicide bombing by a young man. It was later reported that he had been sent by ISIS. He killed thirty-four Kurds—refugees and their Kurdish helpers who had gathered at a social center. In response, PKK (Kurdistan Workers' Party) militants attacked and killed two Turkish soldiers in another Turkish city—violence breeding violence, and all this in a region that has been contested for centuries. The Turkish president, Erdoğan, will seize the opportunity created by his soldiers' deaths at the hands of PKK militants to punish the Kurdish party HDP (Peoples' Democratic Party), who were successful in the previous elections. He is determined to force them out of parliament. With 13 percent of the votes in the election, they were the reason that Erdoğan couldn't form a coalition government and that, in late 2015, he no longer has unlimited powers. East Turkey is now finally simmering, and the heat is palpable everywhere, triggered by a suicide bomber and thirty-four dead Kurds.

TO RETURN TO KOBANÎ

But for the moment we drive peacefully and relaxed through the country, on perfect, well-laid roads similar to the German *autobahns*, and through modern cities with plenty of building activity and elegant skyscrapers. Just before Suruç we see a typical Turkish refugee camp, slightly more run-down than those around Diyarbakir. However, we want to first go to the border, 6 miles south of Suruç. The mercury again rises to around 100. We drive past police control points, metal fencing, and finally a long line of small trucks laden with beds, closets, mattresses, boxes, and suitcases. Do the refugees all want to go back to the war zone?

We are able to drive right up to the border. It is very dusty here, and very close to the destroyed city of Kobanî. We see hundreds of shell-damaged roofs, ruins, and houses without windows or doors. Here, at the border, only three large trees offer a bit of shade to people, most of them women with children who have been waiting here since five o'clock in the morning. Several explain that they waited here for twelve hours yesterday too.

Sara sits with her baby, breastfeeding him from time to time. She has been living in Turkey for a year since fleeing here from ISIS attacks. She left everything behind, and things haven't been easy here. This is confirmed by an 18-year-old, Meyisa. Sure, people gave them provisions—blankets, tents—and apartments, but they couldn't work and they earned no money, and they couldn't send their children to school. It was simply no way to lead a life even if they were safe. Now she wants to return home with the whole family, even though her father died in the fight against ISIS. Together with her 55-year-old mother, Rachmed, she is hoping for a better future. She speaks fluent English and thinks that she'll be able to work as an English teacher in Kobanî and thus be able to provide for her mother. Her house was destroyed, the apartment plundered, and they will have to start again from nothing, but that doesn't bother her—it's certainly better than remaining here in Turkey. "At home we can hope," she says confidently, smiling at me. I can only wish her luck.

All the women we talk to here at the border have the same thing to report: they want to go back to their city, to Kobanî, whether it has been destroyed or not. They have lived for over a year in the Kurdish region of Turkey but haven't been accepted, not by anybody, although they too are Kurds. The mood here, despite the incredible dry heat, is positive and motivating. The people seem to be looking forward to moving home and starting from scratch.

International aid organizations are highly alarmed that so many Syrians are considering returning. One reason the Syrians want to return is that they are unable to raise the thousands of dollars necessary to pay the people-smugglers to get them to Europe. According to UN reports, in 2015 alone, 94,000 Syrian refugees left Turkey to return to their homes. About half of them chose the route via Suruç on the way to Kobanî, to a town that was besieged by ISIS forces until the beginning of 2015, when the Kurdish *peshmerga*, with support from U.S. airstrikes, recaptured it.

The UNHCR is among those very worried about the rising numbers of refugees returning to Syria. "It is a dangerous choice," says Andrew Harper, head of the UN refugee agency's mission in Jordan[7]—relatives remaining in Turkey, Jordan, or Lebanon often receive sad news when the villages that the refugees return to are again bombed and there are civilian casualties.

PROBLEMS WITH SECURITY

We hope, however, that the Syrian Kurds here on this hot day who wish to return to Kobanî will be safe there. But suddenly, first two and then four security personnel appear in front of us—strong young men with stubbly hair and decided self-confidence. "What are you doing here? Do you have a permit to film?" The officials, dressed in civilian clothing, crowd round us extremely aggressively. We should get lost, we're told—and the cameraman, Peter Müller, should delete all photos and film footage. We produce our international press cards, but neither they nor

Peter's card from the newspaper *Bild* help. "Delete!" two of the men scream at him. But Peter refuses, and makes a stand, asking them repeatedly, "Why?"

Our Kurdish interpreter tries to defuse the situation but is visibly frightened. I slowly withdraw from the front line with my camera, replace the lens cap, and hope that they don't want me to delete my photos too. But the four men are concentrating on Peter, circling him with their broad shoulders. Peter has anything but a slight figure, but four against one . . . After a fierce battle of words, he concedes, showing them one of the films that he suggests deleting. With much toing and froing, the civilian officials are satisfied. Astonishingly, they haven't demanded to see everything that we shot—what luck! One of the officials then focuses his pent-up rage on a young man on his way to the line outside passport control. He approaches him aggressively, shoving him backward with both hands while screaming at him—not a good impression of Turkish police behavior toward others. Aggression is now to be felt everywhere. But this is just the beginning.

Slowly we withdraw but remain outside the fenced-off area. Any piece of shade, no matter how small, suits us fine—it is now 113 degrees Fahrenheit (45 degrees Celsius). While we wait at the border, not one single small truck passes us. The line hasn't moved. What are the Turkish officials actually doing inside? Why is everything taking so long? A couple of men say *inshallah* and plan to try again tomorrow morning at five. No one will stop them once they have crossed the border and are on their way back to their bombed houses in northern Syria, back to the war. Is it not, perhaps, better to remain in Turkey, where, admittedly, they are only reluctantly accepted but where they still have a measure of safety?

We drive back to Suruç and find a small restaurant full of men, where huge plates of meats and vegetables are served. Suruç is in the province of Şanlıurfa, where most of the "imam marriages" take place—marriages in which men can take a second or third wife in a ceremony solemnized by an imam, without any problems. In Turkey polygamy is actually no longer allowed, but with the large supply of pretty Syrians, this form of marriage is on the increase, according to both Feray and our driver. The second and third wives have no legal protection but, at least for the time being, they are supported within the family. For the husbands it is, regardless, a win-win situation. "More wives, more variety," says Mansur, grinning, and continues, "In the olden days only rich Turks could afford a second wife." But that has all changed now. And that's about as far as our small digression on the family situation goes. The others go to the small restaurant for lunch, but I choose to buy one of the famous Kurdish watermelons from a fruit stall. In these temperatures, I can eat no more.

Afterward I drink a Turkish coffee, which is not easy to find here because the Kurds, I learn, prefer tea to coffee. The rest of the team drink glasses of the famous *chai*.

ON THE WAY back to Diyarbakir we stop at a roadside refugee camp that we spotted on the outward journey. A couple of Kurds greet us cordially, and we are allowed to visit and talk to the refugees without any problems.

Resmis resolutely invites us into her tent. Both sides of the tent have been rolled up, and an electric fan hums. As always, we take off our shoes and sit cross-legged with Resmis and her children—Jala, 11, Hilava, 15, and Servan, who is just 9 and has a disability. They live here in a typical 190-square-foot tent together with their neighbor Dicle. But, as both Resmis and Dicle stress, not for long—they too want to return to their hometown, Kobanî, as soon as possible. The women are utterly convinced that they can rebuild their houses. Their husbands have found work in Suruç, so there will be a little money when they head for the border. A road now runs through the site of her old house, but Resmis is optimistic: "We will certainly get some sort of financial compensation," says the 42-year-old. She seems anything but depressed, far from hopeless, full of confidence—nothing like the mood of the Yazidi women in the other camp.

Resmis's husband used to be a mechanic at a car repair shop, and there will always be cars and there are always things that can go wrong with them, she says. Apart from that, she is convinced that after the battles in and around Kobanî, women should take the reins. She wants a women's revolution, and if need be she will join a women's army unit to fight against ISIS. There are still thousands of young women in the hands of the terrorists, she adds. Resmis and other female combatants want to liberate them, and she is sure they can do it. "If necessary I will leave the children with my mother-in-law," she says, unflinching.

So we don't have to worry too much about these refugee women. They are looking to the future and not backward; they speak about everything that they have experienced in this war, about all the horrors and violence, about what has happened to their daughters and to themselves—the rapes, the forced viewings of murdered compatriots. Despite all this, they have hope for the future. They are going home to their destroyed city.

Deep in thought, we drive back, smiling at the police officers in the white Golf who "hid" behind a tree to spy on us at the border and then followed us part of the way home. Feray is relieved when they turn back. The young Kurd has lived here long enough to recognize brewing conflict. Tomorrow, I will learn more about the political side of the refugee tragedy from the municipal authorities in Diyarbakir and in Mardin. I am certainly looking forward to it.

A YAZIDI WOMAN IN MARDIN

The next day produces some incredible encounters. First we meet a young woman who was born in Celle, Germany, studied politics at the University of Hanover, and today works as an adviser to the mayor of Mardin in eastern Turkey. Dr. Leyla Ferman is a Yazidi, like most of these women is very pretty, and is also extremely assertive. This assertiveness she probably brought with her from Germany.

We meet in the municipal building in her super-chic white office, with white cantilever chairs and an elegant desk. "We had to really struggle to get this office," she says, laughing. By "we" she means she and the two women with whom she shares the office.

Her concern: the plight of Yazidi women, and what should and could happen to them. Most of the remaining 3,800 refugee women come from the city of Shingar, Iraq, in the region to which some 500,000 Yadizis have escaped. The Sinjar Mountains, known now around the world, have been partially reclaimed by Kurdish forces, but the western flanks remain under the control of the ISIS terrorists and their jihadist state system.

I now learn from Leyla Ferman everything that the Yazidi women in the refugee camp didn't want to impart to a non-Yazidi. She tells me of severely traumatized women and children, of the high standing of men in Yazidi society. Of the kidnapping of girls, the murder of babies in front of their mothers, the execution of men in the presence of their families. She understands that these fleeing mothers and their children definitely have no wish to return to their former homes and that they are frightened of the Muslims who betrayed them to ISIS. Leyla Ferman also knows that the families want to leave eastern Turkey, preferably for the safety of Europe. Later, the women in the camps will often tell me that they feel surrounded by Muslims here, and anything but safe. And time and again I will hear the reminder that it was precisely in this area of Turkey one hundred years ago that the last genocide of the Yazidis took place.

Leyla Ferman is now pursuing another project. Together with another fifty international organizations in the Federation of Yazidi Societies, she wants to build a village for the refugees—now, before winter, and quickly, using prefabs. She claims that with the aid of Kurdish cities, she will somehow scrape the necessary funds together.

She is also at pains to point out why she is concerned about a project launched in the German state of Baden-Württemberg, a project that was much lauded in the media. The government offers traumatized Yazidi women the opportunity to stay there for a year and undergo therapy. Leyla Ferman's objections are understandable. After three months, the women and girls in the program can decide whether their families can join them in Germany. This causes tremendous pressure within families even before departure: the women are virtually forced to open up in therapy so that the family has the opportunity of coming to Germany. Revealing their personal tragedies, however, contradicts Yazidi religion.

Baden-Württemberg wanted to document and offer psychological treatment to 1,000 ISIS victims by the end of 2015. The program began with 250 women. Before the girls' departures, their mothers insisted that they be blessed by a high priest: technically, if a Yazidi has sexual intercourse with a non-Yazidi then they are excluded from the religious community, but the chief religious guardians have made it clear that due to the horrific experiences with ISIS, raped Yazidis are exempt from this rule. According to the mothers, the blessing will help them during therapy if they actually decide to go through with it.

Leyla Ferman, the official from Mardin, is writing a report about the plight of Yazidi women that she promises will be finished by the evening, and true to her word, at 11 p.m. an email arrives with an attachment—very German, very reliable.

It is not only in Germany that people are willing to help. In Iraq, an organization called Yazda, based in the city of Dohuk, is documenting what happened to the Yazidi women, looking after the returnees, and planning psychological assistance. A questionnaire is intended to clarify the most important questions: "Were you raped? Sold? Forced to convert? Beaten? Drugged? Forced to witness an execution? Did you have to pay for the flight? Have you received psychological support?" By the fall of 2015, 800 cases had been recorded and the data passed on to the Ministry of Labor and Social Affairs in Baghdad. The interviewees receive $100 and medical assistance—a first step. What happens to the pregnant women remains undocumented, though: everyone—counselors, psychologists, and certainly the women and girls involved—remains silent on that issue. In Iraq, abortion is illegal.

IN THE AFTERNOON, after an extensive walk through the pretty city of Mardin, we meet up with Harun Ercan, the adviser on international relations for the city of Diyarbakir. He too is involved in ensuring that the refugees can remain in Turkey, that villages will be constructed for them, that they will be allocated land even without support from the Turkish government, so that refugees can become more self-sufficient and more independent than they are in the camps.

Loaded with new information, I plan to return to the refugee women in the camp near Diyarbakir. We will see what they have to say.

Peter Müller and I quickly go to a small restaurant near the hotel in the old part of town, as we did on the first night. People here spray the sidewalks with water, which doesn't really help—it doesn't make it any cooler. We are slowly becoming accustomed to the heat. And in any case, the food is simple and good: chicken kebabs with rice, but no beer and no wine—after all, we are in a Muslim country. It is okay, though. We can do without.

NOT TURKISH VILLAGES—EUROPE

The next day, we drive back to the refugee camp, back to the women. This time I have a bag of small presents from Germany—candy, cookies, tissues, and chocolate. The last hasn't melted yet, as it is still early in the day.

Seve is visiting the doctor, but the other women invite us into the tent. Everything is like the first visit: spotlessly clean and tidy. The blankets are neatly folded and piled behind a curtain. They also have a fridge, and the fan is going, although it doesn't help much in these temperatures. Seve returns wearing a distinctive red ankle-length dress with long sleeves—actually too hot for these temperatures. I ask myself how she can bear it, and how she manages to breastfeed her baby in it.

I tell Seve all that I have heard in Mardin and Diyarbakir about the mayor's Yazidi employee's plans for the refugees. Her reaction astonishes me: she's furious. There is no way that they want to remain in Kurdistan—they would rather die. They want to go to Europe. I hear a lot about how Syrians are allowed in but not Yazidis. The other women all agree. After an hour and many arguments on my side, four men enter the tent. One can speak a little English, and he too says, "We want to go to Europe. We don't want a village in Turkey." They don't feel safe among the Muslims; they're frightened, *very* frightened. I think of Leyla Ferman's words: "The people are severely traumatized."

Sari, too, in the adjacent tent, shakes her head. "We would all rather die here than move to a house. We will not go to a village in Turkey."

It is exasperating, and even my argument about the children not being able to attend schools here hasn't convinced them. I try once more: "In a village at least there's a chance to educate the children." But I can't get through to the women. I'm banging my head against a brick wall. Admittedly, several families send their children to makeshift classes in the camp, with instructors from Diyarbakir, Mardin, and Batman, so that the children can receive at least some education—some reading and writing skills, a bit of math. But most of the Yazidi children stay near the tents, playing in the fields between them. These are lost years.

Two hours later, not only my legs ache; my head too is throbbing. The fact that Leyla Ferman, a Yazidi, is trying to do her best for them doesn't convince the women. They definitely don't want a village in Turkey—they want to go to Europe. "And when winter comes?" I ask Seve. "Then we will just die," they answer unanimously. And I shouldn't go on about them moving to a solid house in a village here in Turkey. "If need be," continues a daughter-in-law in Seve's tent, "we will take an illegal path, even if we die on the way." Gradually I run out of arguments; gradually I'm at a loss and in despair.

We leave the camp depressed and muted. We don't understand any of it. These people have long since run out of savings to enable them to reach the Bulgarian border and the gates to Europe, so nothing will come of that. Mahmood, one of the last remaining men, told me that Turkish soldiers would prevent it anyway. All that is left now is the hope that the Yazidi community in Germany will help, not abandon their fellow believers in their moment of need. Hundreds of thousands have made it to Europe, but they too are marooned in refugee camps.

DEFIANT WOMEN

But there are other, very different, Yazidi women. Not in Turkey but in northern Iraq, on the other side of the border. They are pugnacious, fierce, and furious. They are tired of being considered victims. They call themselves Sun Girls, and together they want to take the fight to ISIS. In fall 2015 they attended a training camp near Dohuk and learned how to load and unload, shoot, and clean a Kalashnikov and, above all, how to aim the weapon correctly. While researching in Mardin, I had heard that 120 Yazidi women aged 17 to 30 were already in training. They are affiliated with the *peshmerga,* the army of the autonomous region of Kurdistan in northern Iraq. This is very unusual for Yazidi women, as the religious group has clear rules and adheres strictly to its traditions. But times change, even for these young women.

Not only the Sun Girls are registering an influx of Yazidi women. The PKK, engaged in a bitter struggle with Erdoğan, is also training women in the Sinjar Resistance Units. The Yazidis are holding out in the Sinjar Mountains after fleeing there from the ISIS militia in 2014.

THE DAYS IN Diyarbakir, Mardin, and Suruç have passed quickly. We have a farewell meal with our assistants, Mansur and Feray. Peter loads his photos onto his computer, and I manage to find a *kilim*, a traditional rug, as a present for my husband—our wedding anniversary is the day of my return.

Later I can no longer recall why, but instinctively I pack my suitcase the evening before we are to leave and quickly fall into a deep sleep. Around midnight I am woken up by Peter hammering on the door: "Get up! The hotel's on fire!" I quickly pull on a pair of jeans, grab my cellphone and handbag with my money and passport, and head for the exit. Thick smoke is everywhere, but at the hotel entrance we realize that the smoke is from PKK weapons, and that they have attacked a police post some 1,500 feet away. Yesterday's sheer numbers of police control points signaled that war was about to begin between the PKK and the Turks, with the Kurdish civilian population shouldering the burden. The previous day the PKK had attacked a police station on the eastern border and killed a policeman. Now revenge is to follow; now things are really going to heat up.

BACK IN THE hotel after the exchange of fire, it is impossible to think of sleep. In the morning peace prevails, but tension remains. Peter goes for another "look," as he puts it, and I bring my luggage down to the lobby so that we can leave quickly. Then I get a text message: "I'm at the police station—they're checking my papers."

Suddenly I don't need coffee anymore—my adrenalin levels rise. I quickly pay for our rooms and head out to go to the police station, but there is no way through. A hundred-strong squad in body armor with weapons at the ready has sealed off the compound. Another text message: "Everything OK, depart, no worries." Nonsense! There's no way I would leave him behind. I call him and, to my surprise, he answers. "I'll send a policeman out to fetch you," he says.

A few minutes later someone appears, asks me for my name and nationality, searches my backpack, and escorts me to Peter. Four officials are scrutinizing the contents of his backpack and scrolling through his photos; discussions go back and forth. Then, finally, one of them passes me his passport and press card. Things are looking better; maybe we will even be able to catch our 11:50 flight. It seems to go on forever, and then—*merhaba* and *spas,* "goodbye" and "so long." We're out. Phew! That was a close call. But one of the officials had explained why three policemen with arms at the ready had arrested and forcibly taken someone into police custody for "looking": they were worried about foreign ISIS suicide bombers, and Peter had been shouldering an enormous backpack, for all his camera gear.

Now, we get out of there—off to the airport, check in, and off we go, out of this region.

Now, much later, we know that at that time other journalists were imprisoned for days and weeks, so we can consider ourselves lucky. Everywhere, it was obvious that the Turkish police were highly sensitive and anything but moderate in their handling of supposed enemies. Even then, on our way to Istanbul, seldom have I been so relieved to sit in an airplane. Suruç, Diyarbakir, Mardin—these cities became in the ensuing weeks and months scenes of bitter fighting between the Turkish soldiers and PKK combatants. The Kurds living in eastern Turkey, as always, bore most of the suffering, but this time so did the thousands of refugees living in the camps.

A FEW MONTHS LATER

"Eastern Turkey sinking into chaos" is how Feray, our interpreter, described the situation in an email a few months later. Turkey is engaged in a war against the Kurds; the population is under a strict curfew; every day brings more shelling and bombs. "I feel so bad because every day it gets worse," says Feray.

The number of refugees in the camps has diminished drastically; those who could have fled illegally, with traffickers, to the west coast of Turkey to try to reach Europe in inflatable dinghies—including many of the Yazidis we met. Only 1,300 remain in Fidanlik, mostly women and children without funds for the trek and elderly men no longer confident that they could survive the arduous journey. They all just want to get away, which is understandable, as they have stumbled from one war into another. Two women with their six children want to risk leaving Fidanlik by any means necessary, even with the last of the small savings that they have. "We have nothing to lose," they say, adding, "even if we drown, we will try to flee."

The municipal authorities in Diyarbakir and Mardin continue to try to supply the remaining refugees with necessities. The new villages are still to be built. In the winter, the local authorities delivered provisions and organized warm clothing. But it is still icy cold in the tents—they're not easy to heat, writes Feray. She is angry at the few old men still in the camp, who have first pick of the aid goods, with the women and children farther down the line. She writes in closing, "The women in particular are suffering because they are women and women are not equal to men in the Yazidi community."

TURKISH POLITICS

It could all have been so good: the Turkish government and President Recep Tayyip Erdoğan were on the path to a political solution to the Turkish–Kurdish conflict. Since 2012 the country had been able to offer shelter to over 2.8 million refugees. They were cared for in twenty-five relatively well-organized camps along the Syrian border or in empty apartments. But it all turned out differently—worse, more bitter, more threatening, as much for the Syrian refugees as for the Kurdish population of eastern Turkey, precisely the region where after their horrific summer of 2014 most of the Yazidi refugees had found shelter in five camps.

The Turkish president was furious when, in the June 2015 parliamentary elections, the governing party—the Justice and Development Party—got only 40 percent of the vote, failing to reach an absolute majority. Worse still, the pro-Kurd Peoples' Democratic Party had managed to break the 10 percent barrier, with 13 percent. No agreement had been reached on a coalition government, because, for one thing, Erdoğan didn't want one. He demanded new elections, aiming at an absolute majority this time, and won.

Since then there has been a pogrom-like atmosphere in Turkey. It all began with that suicide bombing in Suruç, in the province of Şanlıurfa, near the Syrian border. A 20-year-old shoe shiner from the Turkish city of Adiyaman, under ISIS orders, blew himself up, together with thirty-four other people—Kurdish refugees and volunteers in a cultural center. Seventy-four more people were seriously injured. The volunteers had been collecting donated medication, toys, and food for the Syrian city of Kobanî, on the other side of the border. In September 2014 the cultural center had been used as an initial reception point for the large number of Syrian refugees fleeing from the violence of ISIS and their Kobanî offensive.

On the day of the attack in Suruç, an appeal by a socialist youth organization had managed to gather some 300 left-wing and pro-Kurd activists to support the reconstruction of Kobanî. But again, nothing went as planned. The PKK accused the Turkish government of complicity in the attack in Suruç, as the government, not only in the opinion of the PKK, had allowed ISIS to gain strength and continued to support the terrorist militia. The government had indeed not made any serious moves at interrupting ISIS supply lines through Turkey. The oil business continued to flourish, and money flowed. And even today, extremists from all over the world can travel through Turkey, without hindrance, to join ISIS. Political observers point out that the Turkish government's favorable attitude toward ISIS is based on the fact that ISIS fights against both the Shi'ite-Alevi regime of the Syrian dictator, Bashar al-Assad—much hated by Erdoğan—and the Kurds in Syria.

Two days after the terrible bombing in Suruç, the PKK attacked a police station in Ceylanpinar, in the eastern part of the country, killing two Turkish policemen. That was the end of the ceasefire between the PKK and the Turkish government. The spiral of violence gained momentum. On October 10, 2015, there were two explosions in Ankara. The 102 dead and 500 injured had been taking part in a peaceful demonstration organized by left-wing and Kurdish activists against the continuing violence between the Turkish government and the PKK. The conflict escalated, although ISIS later claimed responsibility for the attack. Civilians fled from Kurdish cities; the Kurdish stronghold Diyarbakir was completely severed from the outside world. Road blocks and curfews impeded normal life.

In Cizre, the center of the banned Kurdish Workers' Party, where the HDP achieved an incredible 94 percent of the vote in the June 2015 elections, a strict curfew was declared. The city became a military no-go area: no one allowed in, no one allowed out. What happened there was concealed from the public. In spring 2016, not even regional politicians were afforded entrance, let alone human rights organizations.

At the end of 2015, Turkish newspapers reported that 200,000 people had left their homes in Kurdistan because of the hostilities and attacks, 10,000 from the Sur neighborhood of Diyarbakir alone. Journalists spoke of a civil war. Now it was no longer a battle between the Turkish government and the PKK but between Turks and Kurds. Against this background, the refugee problem slipped into the shadows. The fact that Turkey has taken on more refugees than all the European countries together—2.8 million people from Syria, Afghanistan, Iraq, and Iran—is no longer relevant. The refugees have been all but forgotten.

But at least after the attack in Suruç, the Turkish government came to support a U.S.-led alliance to combat ISIS. It had become increasingly apparent, even to politicians in Ankara, that ISIS and not the PKK was behind the attacks. Turkey established a 55-mile-long, 25-mile-wide security zone along the Turkish–Syrian border. In this area, there was to be no fighting, no shooting. International observers suspected that the government in Ankara was following a different agenda. Above all, Turkey does not relish the thought that the establishment of the security corridor has enabled the Kurds in northern Iraq and northern Syria to control a continuous strip of land from Iraq to Syria. A de facto Kurdish state, already a reality in the north of a disintegrating Iraq, is a frightening prospect for Erdoğan and his government. The government fears that it would drive a wedge between Turkey and the rest of the Arab world, and further encourage the separatist aspirations of the Turkish Kurds.

SO EVERYTHING IS interlinked: the war in Syria, the fleeing of the civilian Kurds from ISIS, the stance of the Turkish government, and finally the clear position of the international alliance against ISIS. On top of this diversity of interests came the refugee drama being acted out in Europe. By spring 2016, Turkey had become the focus of the crisis not only as a host country but increasingly as a transit country. EU diplomats in Brussels increased pressure on Ankara to take a firmer stance against traffickers. The Syrian Civil War was entering its sixth year, even though there was a fragile ceasefire in the winter of 2015–16 and even though the Russians unexpectedly withdrew most of their planes and pilots from Syria in the middle of March 2016. The refugees will remain there, however, if they don't continue on to Western Europe. Turkey's assumption at the beginning of the war that the Syrian refugees would soon return to their homes hasn't materialized.

German chancellor Angela Merkel visited President Erdoğan in October 2015. It wasn't to be the last visit in these troubled times but the beginning of a series of consultations. This visit, though, was, of all things, two weeks before the Turkish parliamentary elections. The mood in Germany was highly charged. Angela Merkel was feeling the pressure at home and was prepared to make serious concessions to Erdoğan in order to better cope with the refugee crisis in Europe. She offered an easing of travel restrictions on Turkish citizens, €3 billion of EU funds for the refugee camps, and new dynamics in negotiations for Turkey's entry into the European Union. It was quite a bouquet, and it arrived just at the right time for the president, who was hoping to—and eventually did—secure unlimited power. It was bad enough that the Kurdish conflict hardly played a role in the negotiations. Instead, the chancellor tacitly accepted a political reevaluation of the Islamic, conservative Erdoğan, all but financing the launch of his election campaign.

THE END OF OPEN-DOOR POLITICS

Up until then, Turkey had pursued an "open-door" policy on refugees. This did not change after Merkel's visit, but Turkey didn't want to be the new home of the refugees—it referred to them as "guests," and guests move on. These ones, however, cannot. With Turkey under pressure at the negotiating table with the EU to improve border controls, Turkish border officials increasingly resorted to excessive force. They used live ammunition against the refugees and, according to Amnesty International, beat them and actively forced them back across the border. On top of this, Turkish soldiers arrested hundreds of refugees at the western border, taking them over 600 miles away to distant detention centers in the south and east of the country. There, again according to Amnesty, the refugees were held against their will. The report *Europe's Gatekeeper* documents cases of refugees being directly sent back to Syria and Iraq where they faced persecution, torture, or death.[8] This conduct is a clear contravention of international human rights.

Several refugees were held for up to two months in centers in the provinces of Osmaniye and Erzurum. During detention, their cellphones were confiscated and they were refused access to legal advice or to contact with members of their families. In order to be released, they had to sign many papers that they couldn't even read, as they were only in Turkish. Thus, the refugees agreed under pressure to "voluntarily" return to their homeland. The Turkish officials repeatedly told them, "Either you go back to Syria or you stay here in prison." It is particularly ironic that these centers are run using EU funding: there was evidence of EU financing in some of the facilities' fixtures. EU representatives in Ankara also confirmed that the six "reception centers" for refugees were in fact detention centers, which the Turkish government fiercely denied.[9]

THAT WAS THE end of 2015—the "Year of the Refugees" in Europe. By the beginning of 2016, the €3 billion promised to Turkey by the Europeans hadn't arrived. Day after day, hundreds, sometimes thousands, of refugees still jumped aboard small boats off the Turkish coast in an attempt to reach the Greek islands.

It seemed as if the Turks were just waving them on. (The German chancellor, in 2016, was described as waving them *in*.) At the beginning of the first large wave of refugees, early in 2015, the Turks had done everything in their power to block the sea routes to Europe, but even then without success. Experts in Turkey claim that since that time, the police and coast guard have been simply overwhelmed. At the same time, motivation to hinder the refugees has also sunk, partly because the Turks feel that the burden of enforcement on them is unfair.

However, the effect of the coast guard along the 600-mile Mediterranean coast was better than that impression suggests. Over 45,000 people were picked up on their way to the Aegean Islands. On the internal routes, especially the roads leading west—the routes known to be used by many refugees trying to reach the EU countries of Greece or Bulgaria—buses, trains, and small trucks have been more stringently controlled.[10] With tank traps, double rows of steel fencing, barbed wire, and infrared cameras, the militarized border with Greece seems secure, but the refugees are not deterred. Turkish officials and their controls only make access more difficult. Those refugees arrested on the Turkish side are, as a rule, sent to one of the two immigration detention centers near the Greek border. Kirklareli, the larger of the centers, holds around 1,000 people. One would think that fleeing was itself a crime.

IN THIS SPECIAL year, 2015, during the negotiations in Brussels and Ankara and the talks between the German chancellor and the Turkish president, there was much talk of the "readmission" agreement. Since the 1990s, Germany has made a multitude of such agreements with other countries. The agreement with Turkey, which came into effect on October 1, 2014, committed Turkey to readmit third-country nationals and stateless persons who had irregularly entered the EU via Turkey. In return, the EU offered Turkish citizens the prospect of eased visa requirements for short-term stays in the Schengen Area, that portion of Europe within which there are no passport or border controls.

But as Turkey also had several readmission agreements with the refugees' countries of origin, the whole process could prove disastrous for them. Now there was an acute danger of chain deportations without refugees ever having the opportunity to state the reasons for their flight, which would clearly contravene the non-refoulement principle of international law: that a person should not be returned to where they might face persecution. Not one person, however, has ever brought charges.

Although Turkey ratified the Geneva Convention on Refugees, it restricted its application to European refugees—with disastrous consequences for refugees in Turkey. This restriction was possible through a ruse, the so-called geographic proviso, in which non-European refugees only have the right of temporary residence in Turkey, for as long as their asylum applications are under review by the UNHCR. Once an application has been recognized and refugee status granted, then as part of the resettlement program, the UN body will look for a country prepared to accept that person. The UNHCR can make recommendations, but the final decision about whether to accept a refugee lies with the individual country. Refugees from war zones are seldom granted temporary residence in Turkey, as they are beneficiaries of "subsidiary" protection, which means they are considered victims of war or other serious threats.

The registration of refugees by the Turkish authorities has thus, as a whole, been fragmentary. And the majority of refugees manage to reach Turkey while deliberately avoiding reporting to the authorities. They know that the long-term prospects there are uncertain at best, and instead try to travel on, if possible, to Europe—"they," in 2015, being mostly men: fathers, brothers, elder sons. The others—the women and children—remain behind in Turkey.

A NUMBER OF Yazidi mothers in the refugee camp near Diyarbakir told me that they would try to get away by following legal channels, with applications to the UNHCR. Their aim was and remains to get to and stay in Europe, a safe haven—preferably Germany. They realize, however, that this can take months. With resignation, experts helping the refugees in Turkey admit that these applications can actually take years. Ten years of waiting without the long-term prospect of even being allowed to remain in Turkey and, if so, in a refugee camp—what sort of a future is that?

Furthermore, the living conditions of those seeking better shelter in Turkey are precisely regulated but not exactly characterized by humaneness. During the asylum process, people in flight are sent to one of fifty satellite towns in the interior of the 300,000-square-mile country. There they have to remain until their emigration. They are not allowed to leave the towns without permission from the police. If they do, all ongoing asylum requests and resettlement procedures with the UNHCR are shelved. Even so, in spring 2016, barely 220,000 of Turkey's 2.8 million refugees were accommodated in government-run camps. The vast majority of refugees are left to their own devices, without financial or material assistance.

Those wishing to work have to pay not only for basic supplies but for residence permits, too. The charges for these permits amount to $180 per person every six months. That is a pretty brutal measure, and can quickly drive refugees out of the country. Making it even more difficult, refugees who have received a resettlement slot are often not allowed to emigrate until they have settled debts to the state. So, as a result of lack of financial support, most refugees live in ruins or crowded accommodations for which they pay exorbitant rents.

Attending school is also more than difficult for refugee children, first because of language—most speak Arabic, not Turkish—and second, because they can hardly afford the school fees. Most refugee children don't have their own identity cards, yet another hurdle for those wanting to go to school.

Turkish law generously allows refugees to buy work permits, but this does not mean that they will be granted them. In her talks with Turkey, the German chancellor was keen to change the requirements for work permits. First, a refugee has to prove that a job is being offered; second, the potential employer has to prove that the position cannot be filled by a Turkish citizen. The Turkish state also demands that the employer finance the refugee during the processing period. These are hard administrative obstacles to overcome. The result of all these regulations is that most of the refugees work for low wages, illegally earning on average $250 per month, half of the Turks' minimum wage. Refugee children are particularly hard hit: a minority go to school; the rest beg for money on the streets—a hopeless situation.

So it is hardly surprising that hundreds of thousands of refugees from Syria, Iraq, and Afghanistan consider Turkey only a transit country. If they want to reach Europe, they have to leave the circumstances in Turkey behind them as soon as possible. And this will continue to be the case until peace returns to their homelands or humane conditions for a future in Turkey are possible. At the moment, both are distant prospects.

It is becoming ever clearer that for a solution to the refugee crisis, Turkey needs Europe and Europe needs Turkey. In Ankara, there were a whole series of state visits by EU heads of government. Turkey no longer demands €3 billion but €6 billion—roughly $6.5 billion—in aid to improve conditions for refugees in their own country. But the biggest hindrance to European concessions to Turkey is the lack of visible peace within Turkey. After three months of fighting between Turks and Kurds, Sur, the old quarter of Diyarbakir, was reduced to rubble. At least 200 civilians died in eastern Turkey during fighting between the PKK and the Turkish army. Freedom of the press throughout the country is in total disarray, and the borders to Syria shut. No more refugees are allowed in, not even the people stranded in the besieged city of Aleppo. This is why, day for day and night for night, up to 2,000 people get into inflatable boats heading for Europe. People who must flee cannot be held back, and so it is evident to the Europeans that they need to find a solution with Turkey.

A NEW AGREEMENT

After further horrific attacks in Istanbul and Ankara, an unexpected—and by no means simple—agreement with the EU was ratified: a deal in which Turkey had to be a "secure third state" for refugees. This now meant that Turkey had to enforce the Geneva Refugee Convention for Syrians and Iraqis, not only Europeans. Regulated asylum procedures had been unavailable in Turkey, so the only chance those seeking a legal route had had was to appeal to the UN refugee agencies in Ankara, where applications from Iranians, Pakistanis, and other refugees seeking asylum in the West had piled up. The waiting time was often years. That, however, was now to be a thing of the past. With a "one-to-one" agreement and €6 billion in aid in place, European countries would absorb the same number of Syrian refugees as Turkey would take back from Greece, provided that those refugees hadn't already applied for asylum in Turkey. Furthermore, it was agreed that the hundreds of thousands of refugees in Turkey outside this system could go to Europe. For Turkey, this was a great step toward accession to the EU. Now all it needed to do was make it work. It was debated whether the agreement would actually help the refugees; the larger aid organizations were highly critical of it. But first the deal's provisions would need to get started; we will know in the years to come whether it proved to be a humane solution.

IMAGES WE WILL NEVER FORGET

It is always pictures that touch us, reach our souls, and arouse empathy: the photo of 3-year-old Alan Kurdi, after the inflatable boat he was in capsized, washed ashore by the tide on the beach of the fashionable Turkish seaside resort of Bodrum—discovered with his face in the sand, arms and legs stretched out, dead. His mother and brother also drowned on the tragic trip across the sea to the Greek island of Kos, but the sea did not return their bodies. Only the father survived. How will this Syrian from Damascus, who at least managed to get his family as far as the Turkish coast—almost to Europe—ever manage to cope?

Or the photo of desperate children from the town of Tell Abyad looking for holes in the barbed-wire fencing, looking for a way through to Turkey. The grinning henchmen watch them without signs of emotion and force them back. Soldiers operate water cannons and fire warning shots. Eventually, two children managed to get through, but only with the help of Turkish civilians who take pity on their plight from the other side of the fence.

And, finally, the UNICEF Photo of the Year for 2015, by Georgi Licovski, of two despairing refugee children stranded on the

Greece–Macedonia border behind a cordon of police officers, separated from their parents. They are holding each other's hands, a crying boy and his screaming older sister; the boy stretches out his other arm helplessly. Behind them the crowd of refugees tries to surge forward. Who sent these children to the front—in the vanguard, as it were? Have they now lost their parents? They seem to have been completely abandoned in the middle of the soldiers. How will they one day be able to deal with these experiences? Where will they end up?

According to UNICEF estimates, between January and November 2015, children accounted for approximately one-quarter of the 730,000 refugees arriving in the EU through the Balkan states—182,500 children. How will they get over the long, strenuous, harsh trek? How will they sleep in the "safe havens" once they arrive?

In northern Iraq, 500,000 children were forced to leave their towns and villages with their parents—almost as many as the population of Nuremberg or Sheffield or Tucson. Now they are all fleeing, searching for refuge in quieter regions near the borders—children who cannot go to school, who have lost their friends, who suffer from the traumatic effects of bombs, artillery fire, and sniper fire.

Syrian women and children in the Kara Tepe refugee camp on Lesbos wait to join their husbands and fathers in Europe. (Photo: Maria von Wesler)

Volunteers in wetsuits prepare to jump into the cold water and help refugees ashore. (Photo: Maria von Wesler)

The final resting place of many refugee children is the cemetery on Lesbos. (Photo: Maria von Wesler)

Warm socks, a warm cardigan, a cup of tea, and a teddy bear make for a warm welcome in every sense on the beach on Lesbos. (Photo: Maria von Wesler)

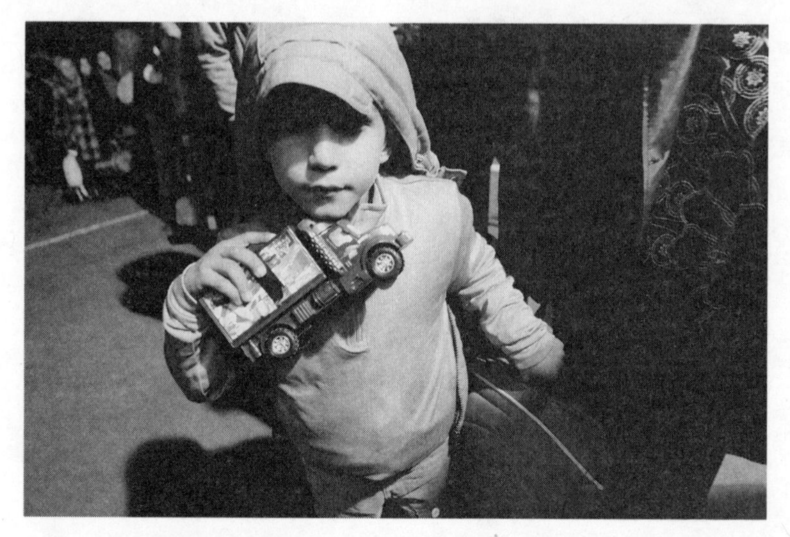

A present from volunteers before departure: this toy truck will be useful on the long voyage to Athens. (Photo: Maria von Wesler)

Finally, the ship to the mainland: 1,800 refugees board at Mytilene. (Photo: Maria von Wesler)

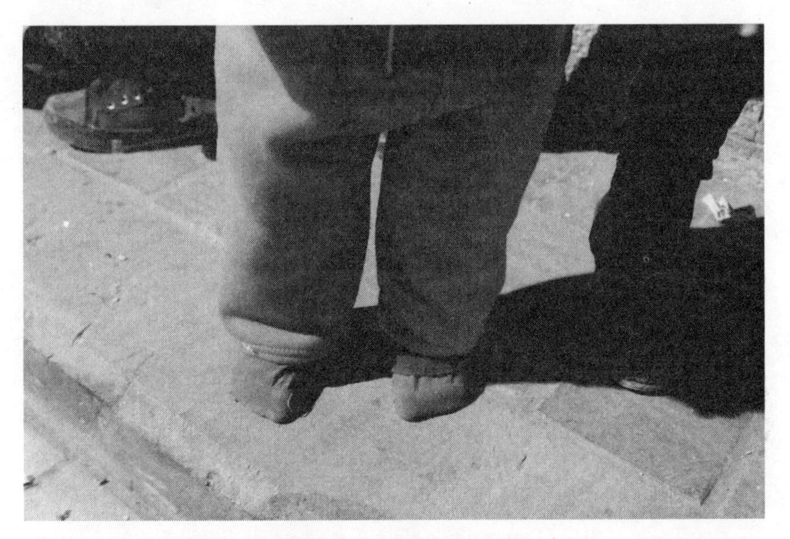

Her shoes lost overnight at sea, this little Syrian girl walks through Mytilene in her socks. (Photo: Maria von Wesler)

These women are part of a group of twenty knitting for small children on Lesbos. There are some 400 similar groups throughout Greece. (Photo: Maria von Wesler)

THREE

LEBANON

IN THE BEQAA VALLEY

Lebanon is a small country, just half the size of New Jersey, with a population of around 4.5 million plus, since the beginning of the Syrian Civil War, 1.1 million registered refugees. Aid organizations reckon that a further 900,000 unregistered refugees who are here illegally—although my fingers are reluctant to type the word *illegal,* as no human being is illegal, anywhere. In January 2015, Lebanon closed its borders. The country has long been hopelessly overwhelmed—not only by about 2 million people from a war zone, but also by an ongoing economic downturn. Especially overwhelmed are the Syrian refugees who used to work in Lebanon on the land as seasonal helpers but who now seek refuge here.

Try transposing this situation to Germany, or wherever you live: imagine nearly half the population being refugees. Taking the same ratio of population to refugees, Germany, with a population of about 83 million, would have to absorb and integrate some 35 million refugees. The aid organization Oxfam calculated that Lebanon, and likewise Jordan, have achieved sixty times (600 percent) more than could be expected based on their economic performance. Lebanon and Jordan surpass by far the cooperativeness of the United States (76 percent of a "fair share" in funding, 10 percent in resettlement) or Germany (152 percent in funding, 118 percent in resettlement; Canada sits at 248 percent in resettlement, Australia at 95 percent, the UK at 18 percent, and New Zealand at 3 percent).

It is no wonder then that the economic, political, and demographic pressure within Lebanon is increasing—the bounds of endurance have been crossed. Because of the rise in demand, water is scarce, food prices have risen horrendously, rents have quadrupled, schools and hospitals are overcrowded, and competition for the few jobs available becomes more intense by the day. Furthermore, the Syrian civil war is being exported to the beautiful country of cedars; there have been fighting and assassinations in the port of Tripoli, in Sidon, and in the Beqaa Valley, and bomb attacks in Beirut in 2015. It's a dangerous situation for this politically and religiously complicated country, which is bravely just managing to find its feet after fifteen years of civil war. In addition to the Syrians, an estimated 400,000 Palestinian refugees have been living here in camps and sealed-off slums for some sixty years, as well as tens of thousands of refugees from Iraq and 300,000 migrants from the poorest countries of Asia and Africa. The current peace here is very brittle, which is why the government prevents the Syrian refugees from establishing permanent camps, fearing that, displaced by war, they might remain for good—like the Palestinians who now live here in isolated townships under extremely harsh conditions. Altogether, it's dynamite for Lebanon's multicultural society. The new refugees from Syria have to suffer the consequences of the wars of 1948 and 1967. What's more, since 1990–91, latent conflicts have been brewing between Syria and Lebanon. Syrians had been unpopular in Lebanon as Syria had, in effect, occupied the country. The last Syrian soldiers left Lebanon only a few years ago. And now there is war in that neighboring country.

All this can be read in newspapers. But how do the people there experience life, the women refugees and their children? I have heard that it is principally women and children who are stranded there. The men are fighting the war in Syria, have been killed, or are being held in the torture chambers of Assad's regime.[1] But this year, 2015, the majority of the men tried to reach Europe. So I get into a cab on a sunny late afternoon at Beirut airport, my destination Zahlé, a mountain town on the eastern side of Lebanon's mountain range, high above the Beqaa Valley. It is here that most of the Syrian refugees are supposed to have found refuge. What will it look like? The Lebanese government has refused to supply the refugees with tents, to prevent the setting up of proper settlements. The country worries that a situation similar to that of the Palestinians who have been firmly established here for decades now could develop. Those Syrians who still have money live in apartments in Beirut, which are expensive. Others find accommodation in mosques that have organized soup kitchens and beds. Most, however, are housed in the shells of buildings, in storage depots, and in the Beqaa Valley.

IT IS A beautiful drive over the mountains, with peaks up to 10,000 feet, and into the green valley. In winter the mountains are white; they used to be famous for their exclusive ski resorts, but snowboarders slaloming through the cedars are a thing of the past. It is these snowcapped peaks that give the country its name, which is derived from the Semitic root *ibn*, meaning "white."

After just over an hour we are there. Zahlé is only 12 miles from the border with the refugees' homeland... so near, and yet so far. The Beqaa Valley is the "Garden of Lebanon": the whole country lives on the products cultivated here—the vegetables, the fruit, and the wines. Everything thrives here in abundance. The wines pressed here fetch high prices in Europe's luxury restaurants. But now the refugees are housed here, in makeshift tents, huts, settlements—I don't know the word to describe this hodgepodge of plastic sheets, wooden boards, and discarded building materials. The first time a member of the UNICEF staff showed me around, I could hardly believe my eyes. The settlements are termed "informal tented settlements" (ITS)—with the emphasis on "informal." The living conditions are horrendous, even inhumane. Neither plastic sheeting nor wooden boards nor cardboard wards off the summer heat, let alone the icy storms and snow at the onset of winter in November. Around the pretty, small mountain town of Zahlé are seventy such settlements; in the whole valley, 75 miles long and 5 to 8 miles wide, there are a total of 1,278 settlements.

The Syrian refugees pay the landowners monthly rent for the small pieces of land where they are allowed to build their new homes. The rents are 50,000 to 100,000 Lebanese pounds (U.S. $45 to $90), money that the refugees don't have. On top of this, in the summer of 2015, the UN's World Food Programme (WFP) cut the support payments to refugees from $26 to $13 per person per month because the international community failed to pay enough into the pot. It is a scandal. (Germany has transferred its contributions to New York every year so far, thanks to the commitment of Minister for Economic Cooperation and Development Gerd Müller.)

Who lives in these desolate dwellings? How do people survive summer and winter here? The emergency shelters made from paper, cardboard, and a little wood and plastic are hardly recognizable as tents. The first thing I learn is that the missing men have just left for Europe, at the same time as the WFP halved the monthly payments. From that moment, the families were not sure what to do—the money available was no longer enough to live or even die on. They scraped together their last reserves, borrowing when possible from other members of the family. Everyone wanted to go to Germany—I hear this everywhere. And, it became abundantly clear from the first meeting, even the elderly wanted to leave. But there is only enough money, if at all, for one person. And that means the fathers, the sons, the brothers—the "stronger" ones. The mothers, daughters, and sisters also want to leave, as soon as possible, in part because once the men have gone, they are easy prey for landlords, employers, police, and soldiers. Time and again, Amnesty International has highlighted this, and I also hear it in many of the women's stories.

THE FIRST STORY from the Beqaa Valley is a heartening one. Sixteen-year-old Eman has been married to a young Syrian man for one and a half months. She tells me proudly that both of them are setting off next week, with a plane ticket, legally, from Beirut to Turkey. Eman is a very attractive girl, with heavy makeup, her headscarf bound tightly so that no hair sticks out. How do they plan to get from Turkey to Germany? Illegally, she says hesitantly, along the smuggler route to Istanbul. How exactly, she doesn't want to say, and I fear she doesn't even know herself. Her husband has made all the arrangements; his parents have lent them some money. What is she expecting in Germany? "Work, security—above all for her future children." Her husband's parents are still in Syria, in Homs, which has been half destroyed. Her own father is already in Germany to greet them. And her mother? Staying in Lebanon, in a makeshift, windy, rickety tent with Eman's siblings, all girls. Does Eman have a guilty conscience? "No. I hope that they will all join us once we have applied for asylum." Wearing a long black dress with high-heeled shoes, she turns confidently to go, a little bit unsteadily on the uneven concrete floor of the women's center in the village of Sifri near the main road that winds through the valley.

Thirty-eight-year-old Laila is also stranded here in the Beqaa Valley with her children, her husband long gone on the way to Europe. They are waiting to join him. Laila's husband worked for three years here in a printing shop; she helps out as a teacher in the women's center. She and her four children live in a unit with a single room, kitchenette, and bathroom—five people crammed into the smallest of spaces. She is trying to get out of here on the UNHCR program, as a "quota refugee." But she realizes that her chances are slim. "If that doesn't work out," she says, "then we will have to go the illegal way." But she too has only limited funds. For each member of the family, she needs $3,000, a total of $15,000—an unbelievable sum. I listen to her in despair, as I know that Laila with her four children will probably have to endure a long wait in Lebanon—summer and winter, with an end to the war in Syria still a distant prospect.

Chaza, on the other hand, tells me that peace will soon return, she is fairly certain. The 30-year-old Syrian and mother of three fervently hopes she is right. After the war is over, she and her husband, who for the time being has found a job in Lebanon as a carpenter, want to return to their home. "What's the good of everyone staying away? Who can rebuild Syria?" she asks me. Every month for the four years since they fled across the border and arrived at the Lebanese border town of Majdal Anjar, surrounded by snowy peaks, just a hour's drive from Damascus, the small family has paid $200 for a single room with a kitchen. They had to abandon the car on the way, Chaza explains with a smile, and adds that the small town used to be a well-known smuggling center. Today it is a kind of reception camp, the first stop after the border. Chaza belongs to that group of women who don't give up, who never lose hope. She seems courageous and dedicated, and hugs the two smaller children tenderly. The older boy, about 9 years old, even kisses her on the cheek in front of me and then shuffles off somewhat bashfully. Chaza laughs and gazes at him dreamily.

Thirty to forty women come to the Women's Rescue Center in Sifri every day. They comfort and support each other. Thirty-year-old Amal, a mother of three, comes here regularly. She is a strict Muslim with a black hijab and doesn't want to be photographed. She tells me that the family held out for three days and nights in their apartment in Qudsaya, a suburb of Damascus. They were under continuous fire, shells exploding nearby and snipers shooting at anyone moving on the streets. As her husband cautiously tried to sneak out of the house in search of provisions, he was shot by a Syrian soldier. For Amal, then, there was no other choice—she had to get the children to safety in Lebanon. The four walked to the border, and have been living in the Beqaa Valley for three years now. Her future? She too hopes for peace, for a chance to go home: "I want to finally give my husband a proper funeral."

DATA AND FACTS: LEBANON, SPRING 2016

- Lebanon has a population of 5.8 million.
- Lebanon has been a republic with a parliamentary democracy since 1926.
- There are 18 recognized religious communities in Lebanon, the largest being Maronite Christians (21 percent) and Shi'ite and Sunni Muslims (27 percent each).
- The four highest state offices are reserved for four religious groups: the Maronite Christians, Shi'a Muslims, Sunni Muslims, and Roman Catholics.
- The national debt in 2015 was U.S. $51.5 billion—based on economic performance, one of the highest in the world.
- The country houses 1.172 million registered Syrian refugees, plus an estimated 900,000 unregistered "illegal" Syrian refugees.
- Since the wars of 1967 and 1990, it has housed 1.2 million more Palestinian refugees, adding to those displaced in 1948.
- Over half of the refugees in Lebanon are children.
- The main languages spoken in Lebanon are Arabic and French, with English also taught in schools.

- The literacy rate of people over 15 is 87.4 percent.
- The first Lebanese civil war lasted from 1970 to 1990 against a background of conflicts with Palestinians and increasing social disparity.

INFORMAL TENTED SETTLEMENT (ITS) NO. 004

The last stop on this first day of research is ITS 004, where 85 huts, or "tents," house 800 people. It seems to me to be almost comfortable. There are chickens, doves flutter in an eye-level cage, and black cows chew on their hay in a wooden enclosure. White plastic stools have been placed in front of lovingly planted decorated flowerpots. I am moved.

But there is also trash, trash, and more trash. Here too people throw everything away—not only on a heap but everywhere. If Lebanon and its inhabitants have a dramatic problem with trash, then the refugees seem to have copied the behavior of their hosts. Refuse collection doesn't exist. The municipalities in Lebanon apparently just don't have the money for it. The landfill sites are in the hands of a few rich people who charge ever-increasing fees, and now all the country's litter is left on gigantic mountains of waste. Luckily, no epidemics have spread yet. On the way from the airport up into the mountains, all I could do was shake my head at the sight of these illegal dumps. But in Lebanon, this is just a side issue.

THIRTY-FIVE-YEAR-OLD SYRIA HAS been housed in this ITS, between wooden boards, plastic sheeting, and a small concrete wall, for two weeks. She moved here with her nine children and her husband in the hope that the two older children, her 16-year-old son and her 13-year-old daughter, could find jobs, but they have had no success. Syria claims that they receive $70 total a month from the UNHCR. I do some sums in my head and reckon that they must get at least $143, but she says no. They can just about afford to buy tea and bread. The family fled Al-Raqqah three years ago. The ninth child was then a baby and had to be carried on Syria's back.

Her hometown, population about 180,000, was captured by ISIS terrorists, and after that, Syria explains, the cost of living became exorbitant. And it was dangerous. On top of this there was no more bread to eat and no gas to cook with, and the children were eating grass. For the family there was only one option—to flee... in the middle of the night, following a secret route, as Lebanese security was becoming increasingly tight. In Syria, her husband had earned enough money as a cab driver, but here in the Beqaa Valley he can't get a job. He also suffers from backaches and has breathing problems. He lies on a thin mattress and appears depressed. Syria organizes the household, demanding, like her husband, that the children find work.

"What about school and education?" I ask. Not worth mentioning at the moment. It seems to be a bitter chapter for them. In most dwellings I find far too many children taking on all sorts of tasks—they work and help their parents. Or they simply while away the long hours. But they don't attend one of the tented schools set up, equipped, and run by dedicated aid organizations. At least schools exist, even if there are too few of them.

In the evening sunshine we drive back south through this beautiful landscape, to Zahlé, full of conflicting impressions and thoughts. The valley lies so peacefully between two mountain ranges that we feel and hear nothing of the nearby war in Syria. To the west the sun sets over Beirut, sinking into the Mediterranean. People could live so well here—everything grows and flourishes. At the moment, grapes, tomatoes, and zucchinis are in season. All of these are unaffordable for most refugees. Tomorrow, Cecilia, our Lebanese interpreter, will take me to another tent settlement in the north, near the once thriving Roman metropolis of Baalbek.

FEAR OF WINTER

I sit for hours on end this day, on the floor or on thin mats in the dwellings of women and their children. I listen to them and drink their generously offered cups of tea. My knee is beginning to rebel; I'm simply not used to sitting cross-legged, unlike the Syrians, who are visibly pleased by the distraction of a visit. The question that haunts me is how on earth people can survive winter in these drafty dwellings. In the Beqaa Valley, it snows in November. The snow will be more than a couple of feet deep, and for weeks on end there will be icy Levantine winter storms. Then I consider what the big spring thaw's masses of melting snow will do to the mattresses and blankets on the floors. With these thoughts, I forget about my knee—it is insignificant compared to the stories I hear and everything else I see and experience.

Twenty-seven-year-old Amira invites us into her tent with a friendly gesture. She lives here with her three children and husband next door to her 50-year-old mother. They fled here four years ago from near Aleppo, at al-Bab, where the rebels and the Syrian army were fighting for control. Bombs were exploding everywhere, even during their flight. They had to pass through countless checkpoints, often having to pay $100 or $200. The bus broke down and they were forced to complete the trek on foot. This, she says, was without the children—all three were born in Lebanon. I think to myself, *That's pretty courageous.* I later learn that the women in the Beqaa Valley have hardly any access to contraceptives. One tells me, "None of them work."

Amira and her husband have managed to make their tent/hut, with its concrete floor, a bit homey, with a TV set that picks up Syrian programs and a small wood-burning oven that doesn't give off much heat in winter. Their greatest fear is that the roof will collapse under the weight of snow, as it did last year. Sleeping is then no longer possible. "We were very worried that having survived the flight, we'd be buried under a mass of snow," Amira says while waving her hands at the cardboard-lined wooden roof. The children are always ill in winter, but the little money that her husband earns as a coffee vendor is not enough to pay for doctor's fees and the necessary medications. Everything is so difficult, so hopeless, especially as the children haven't been properly registered. "There's no evidence that they really are my children," Amira explains in despair. She has birth certificates from the hospital in the Beqaa Valley, but in Lebanon they don't count as evidence of birth registration. She would have to go back to her homeland so that her three children could really become "hers" and get Syrian passports—a crazy world. On top of all this, they constantly worry about whether they can scrape together the $200 rent for the landlord. "If we can't pay him, we will be forced to leave," Amira says, visibly distressed. Amira's mother works for the landlord on his fields for 6,000 Lebanese pounds a day (about $4) but has to pay rent for her own dwelling, so she can't offer much financial help to her daughter and her family.

Amira talks us into having another cup of tea and begins to unwind. She says that women in Syria had rights, that violence against women was forbidden, but that now husbands beat their wives because they don't know what to do with their frustration, their depression. Sometimes she has to flee with the children to her mother. Her brother also lives there. Amira is distressed that so many girls marry young, in return for payment, and often as second or third wives. The 12- and 13-year-old girls then have to grow up very quickly, taking on housekeeping for the husband and the first and second wives, and bearing children. If there are no funds for the hospital, then the babies are born in the tents, as was the case with Amira's third child. She says, very concerned, that violence is widespread throughout the settlement. Older boys assault and rape girls, but the girls are too ashamed to tell their parents and then, all of a sudden, they are pregnant. People no longer look after one another; the people here are too scared of each other. "But we are all Syrians here in this settlement," she adds. It is a sad state of affairs.

Amira doesn't even hang out her washing on the line anymore after the time someone stole it. Now she dries the family clothes in the small space in front of her door. She points to where her children's pants and T-shirts are hanging. Although they are safe in Lebanon, although no barrel bombs are dropping on them and they are not being shot at, Amira has only one wish: to return to Syria, to go home. No longer to be a refugee, no longer to have to rely on charity. Why? "So that I can see laughter in the eyes of my children."

DREAMING OF OLD ALEPPO

At least Amira's children have not been directly exposed to the war in her old home city, unlike the people who remain there.

Aleppo: the very sound of it—after Mecca, the capital of Islamic culture; a former commercial hub, located at the most important intersection between India and the Tigris–Euphrates region, with Damascus to the south. The ancient city of Aleppo is a UNESCO World Heritage Site. Sixty thousand students attend the university. It has an impressive medieval citadel, gorgeous mosques dating to the Umayyad Caliphate, and the famous Al-Halawiyah Madrasa, a university founded in the twelfth century. In peacetime, it had a population of 2.5 million. The majority are Arabs and Kurds; about 20 percent are Christians.

As of spring 2016, some 1.5 million of Aleppo's citizens had found refuge elsewhere in their own country. Large sections of the city had been destroyed. Eastern Aleppo was dominated by the rebels, more or less radicalized, and the western sector was held by Assad's regime. Now that the Russians had joined the war, the dictator from Damascus hoped to gain full control of Aleppo. For Assad, defeat at Aleppo would mean a damaging loss of image and would be a bad omen. So Aleppo was anything but peaceful.

AMIRA HAS A cellphone. When she can get service in the ITS, she tries to reach her brother or his wife, who are still in Aleppo. It is becoming increasingly difficult to flee Aleppo. The Turkish border is just a stone's throw away, only 30 miles, but the Turkish border officials are stricter than ever, especially since the Brussels Agreement. Sneaking across the border is no longer possible—there are just too many people wanting to flee from the besieged city, having to flee to survive. The jihadists are waiting for them to the east; Assad has positioned his troops to the west, and the citizens of this once flourishing city certainly no longer trust him. His henchmen consider Aleppo's citizens to be disloyal to the regime, and those citizens can quickly land in one of the feared torture prisons. People with passports listing Aleppo as their domicile are sure to have a host of problems with security personnel at any of the countless checkpoints that the regime has set up throughout the country.

Amira's sister-in-law is restrained when talking about the daily routine in Aleppo. But both women know that the city has become one of the most dangerous in the world. It is difficult, they know, even to collect water and provisions because of the many roadblocks. Amira was distraught when she heard that the park near her old home had been destroyed and that her family no longer dared to venture into the streets, although they all had to work, to earn money to have something to live on. But her sister-in-law and her family are determined to stay, not to give up, not just to sit at home and rely on outside aid that won't materialize anyway. Before the civil war, Amira's sister-in-law studied English Literature; shortly after she graduated, the al-Nusra Front took control of the streets outside her house. That was in 2010. As a result, she fled to a relative in Lebanon, to Beirut. At that time, the borders between Syria and its smaller neighbor were open. But she couldn't stand being in the Lebanese capital, and after six months she traveled by bus and a shared cab back to Aleppo.

Since then, she has lived in the middle of a war zone and has to come to terms with it, as have her husband and children, enduring a daily struggle in a city without electricity and often without running water. She boils a kettle not to make tea but to use the kettle to iron her blouses and dresses. She doesn't want to give up or to concede, to let herself go. When a bomb drops on a neighbor's house, she rushes out to help, relieved that the bomb didn't land on her house. All this she tells Amira on the phone.

Both of them are worried about winter—the sixth winter of the war. In Aleppo, many people cluster in ruins, shells of buildings, schools, or tents because of the ever-increasing destruction, because the bombs continue to rain down, the barrel bombs to explode. Rockets have long flattened the most beautiful buildings in the old part of the city. It doesn't snow in Aleppo in winter and it's not as cold as the Beqaa Valley, but with average winter temperatures of 50 degrees Fahrenheit (10 degrees Celsius), it would be nice to be able to warm up at least one room in the evenings.

Amira's sister-in-law's biggest worry is the snipers. As in the war in Sarajevo, snipers, irrespective of which side they are fighting for, aim at children and adults alike. She now knows all the balconies in her neighborhood that she can duck behind on the way to the well. But to run away because of it? No, it's out of the question. Her children still go to a school that, although partially destroyed, is still functioning. Amira's brother still earns around $100 a month from his job, though it's not much, especially since prices have risen dramatically during the war. But when she hears about how Amira lives with her husband and children in the Beqaa Valley, she wouldn't swap lives. In any case, it has become increasingly difficult to flee, to leave Syria.

THE MATTRESS DRIVER

The next day, the next ITS. Again, drafty, shaky settlements—huts, tents, whatever you wish to call them—where refugees from the Syrian Civil War try, with limited resources, to create a halfway homely atmosphere. Thirty-five-year-old Esme has eight children and a husband... but one that doesn't work, doesn't want to go to Europe. He is, as they say in Arabic, a "mattress driver," meaning he just lounges around doing nothing.

Two years ago they fled from al-Bab, with their youngest child, 3 months old at the time, on Esme's back. Her oldest works for 15,000 Lebanese pounds a week (about $10), a well-paid job. Another daughter has a part-time job earning 60,000 Lebanese pounds ($40) a month. This helps her, the other children, and Esme's infirm mother-in-law, who lives with them.

From the money, Esme can sometimes get provisions at the *shawish* shop. The *shawish* is responsible for the settlement; he runs a little grocery store, buying his goods from Lebanese businesses at reduced prices shortly before their shelf life expires. The store's owner is also the landlord: he owns the property, collects the rent, and pays the *shawish* a fixed salary. So far so good. The *shawish* has a list of all the families' debts, but he never collects the money. Some families have run up debts of 600,000 Lebanese pounds (around $400). The refugees will never be able to pay off such amounts.

DESPAIR AND HOPELESSNESS—I feel it in most of the women here in the Beqaa Valley, including 37-year-old Aischa, who lives in another ITS. Her husband died of a heart attack shortly after arriving in Lebanon two years ago. Since then she has worn black; since then she hasn't known why she gets up in the morning. She lives, as she says, on the goodwill of the people in Lebanon. As a registered refugee, she receives $39 a month from the UN for herself and the two children. When a UNICEF school is built in her settlement, she wants to send her 5-year-old daughter there so that she can learn to read and write, and so maybe she can make something of her life. This Syrian woman is a beauty with a deeply sad look.

The gatherings in the biggest tent of the settlement are one of her life's small highlights. There the women can iron their husbands' shirts and pants; there they can support each other. In this ITS, they claim, there is a great bond of togetherness, unlike in Amira's. Here, they help out when someone has little or no food. They laugh with one another. The children watch videos on their cellphones and dance to the music—happy moments in an otherwise anything but happy everyday life.

It's midday and too hot to work in the neighboring fields. Only a few older boys are out, rounding up some goats to milk for the owner. The settlements often encroach on the edges of Zahlé. I watch a father and son rummage through a trash can, loading their "treasures" into a supermarket cart. All of it can be turned into money, to feed the family for a few days. They don't want to be photographed; they are too ashamed.

The women's and children's stories are similar, yet each one marks an individual fate—like that of 70-year-old Chambi, who looks after her son's six children. The children's mother remarried and simply left the children with their grandmother. Chambi and her family live in a tent with her other daughter-in-law, Feriar, and Feriar's five children—thirteen people in all. The men? Not there, gone. Working? I don't get a proper answer. Chambi asks whether I would like to take one of the children back to Germany. She has the furrowed face of a hundred-year-old, and seems to be without hope and deeply despairing about the task of catering for all these children.

ALEMANIA

The magic word for everyone here, especially the children, is Germany, *Alemania*. They become starry-eyed and clutch onto me. It breaks my heart.

I regularly hear of men proposing to widows, but always on condition that any children from the first marriage are left elsewhere—they are not wanted by the new husbands. The beautiful Aischa had such an offer, but leaving her children behind was out of the question. I also often hear, especially from women, that they don't believe there will soon be peace in their country. They are preparing for a long period of being refugees. They watch Syrian programs on old TV sets, if they own one, and become dispirited with homesickness and worry. I often hear that UNICEF is a help—that helpers do drop by with provisions and clothing. Other aid organizations also show up, to help and bring necessities. But they remain just necessities. How do relief organizations actually help in tackling these immense tasks?

$289 MILLION

How does an aid organization like UNICEF operate in a country like Lebanon? UNICEF's total investment in refugee relief in Lebanon was $289 million in 2015. UNICEF's largest allocation, worldwide, flows into this small country.

Seventy-five UNICEF staff are based in the Lebanese capital, Beirut. As most of the refugees live in settlements in the Beqaa Valley, roughly twenty more staff members work on development onsite in Zahlé.

Development work includes the setting up and equipping of schools. UNICEF's objective in this is establishing, in conjunction with the Lebanese government, a proper school system, one that can be carefully monitored, as the government is afraid—and certainly not without grounds—of radical influences in the classroom. "Classrooms" here means somewhat bigger drafty tents.

Water is another important issue here. Water is precious. And in Lebanon, water is scarce. UNICEF pays $90 million for water here every year. One use of these water supplies is for the building of desperately needed latrines. In the early years of the settlements, human excrement and urine simply flowed into the neighboring rivers and streams.

The third important issue for UNICEF is the care and protection of children. Sexual assaults can be quickly identified or forestalled. "Assaults on girls and women occur, particularly in such dramatic situations, when people are fleeing and at the mercy of insecure life situations," Berta Travieso, head of the UNICEF field office in Zahlé, explained to me.

A fourth important task is winterization of the refugees' dwellings; $10.1 million was being spent on this in the winter of 2015–16. That seems like a lot of money, but with around 2 million needy people, it amounts to only about $5 per person. Unless the international community honor their promises and provide more funds and more materials, the refugees will once again have to put up with the cold.

CHILDREN BY THE NUMBERS

If you look at the refugee figures more closely, you will see that over half the Syrian refugees in Lebanon are children. These children have to be immunized if they are to have a healthy future; as of fall 2015, 570,000 had been, by UNICEF. But only 290,000 were going, more or less regularly, to one of the tent schools in the valley. It's not a particularly good number if you consider that these children not only lack good reading and writing skills but will later have little chance of a good education and will have problems in making a living as adults—a lost generation.

At least in the winter of 2015–16, 200,000 children were supplied with vouchers for clothing and shoes. But, as the UNICEF staff keep pointing out in despair, the Syrian refugees are not the only poor. In Lebanon, at least 1.4 million non-refugees live below the poverty line, on no more than $4 a day. All in, there are 3.2 million people in need there, more than live in Madrid or Greater Vancouver.

FEAR OF ISIS

On a Sunday we drive to the north through the fertile, pretty Beqaa Valley. The feared checkpoints are poorly staffed today; a smile and a friendly gesture are enough to have us waved on. After less than an hour we reach Baalbek, chosen by the Romans as an excellent place to live and above all a wonderful place to build an impressive temple complex. Once the largest sacred building of the Roman Empire, the temple was for decades a highlight for tourists interested in ancient history and remains incredibly well preserved. Nowadays, however, few tourists travel to Lebanon—the country is too close to the war zones in Syria. I am amazed to see a German couple wandering around among the immense columns and huge hewn stone blocks, busily taking snapshots. They remark laconically, "We wanted to see Baalbek before it's destroyed by ISIS terrorists—after all, they're not far from here." It's not strictly correct geographically, but maybe the feeling of proximity is right. At any rate, rolls of barbed wire and massive concrete blocks shield the largest mosque in Baalbek. It is difficult to grasp that Muslims here have to be afraid of other Muslims.

The term "Islamic State" keeps cropping up; people here in the Beqaa Valley fear the jihadists in their very skin. ISIS appears in everyone's stories, whether the refugees telling those stories have had direct experiences of the terrorists or are referring to others'. Sixty-year-old Esme tells the story of her late son's two children, the ones whose mother remarried and abandoned them. (Esme's other son works for the local authorities here, so at least there is a little money coming in.) In the late morning sun, she sits in the shade of a tree on the ground with her youngest grandchild. It is no longer so hot; fall is gradually approaching. She gently rocks the 8-month-old girl. I ask whether she wants to return when the war is over. Horrified, she shakes her head. "No, not to Syria—ISIS will soon be here in Lebanon, too." I see the panic in her eyes.

The farmer who owns the land on which the grandmother lives seems to treat Syrian women refugees kindly: he doesn't charge Esme any rent. The rest of Esme's family have found work. Soon a school will be opening nearby; the younger children will be able to go there, so she is looking forward to not having to spend the whole day caring for them. At the moment, however, things are not so good. The gas flask is empty and Esme has to cook on an open fire; she owes money to the little shop. "But the people here are friendly to us," she says. This comforts her and helps her put up with her grief over her son.

Later in the day, Cecilia, who has accompanied us as an interpreter, takes us to a small but, she says, "special" ITS where she previously worked for an aid organization. My first impression is that it is spotlessly clean. The mattresses in the tents are all covered in the same fabric, as are the pillows with fancy fringes. The tent tarpaulins stop 10 inches above the concrete floors, allowing the wind to circulate in the hot summers. Today feels cooler, 90 degrees Fahrenheit (32 degrees Celsius). A mosquito net protects 23-year-old Ferial and her husband, who are expecting their first baby. They have been here just six months. They, like others, were fleeing Assad's troops, not ISIS. Their in-laws had expressly forbidden them to flee, even to the point of threatening them, but secretly, under cover of night, they managed to reach Lebanon just before the government closed the borders in January 2015.

Now they have to prepare for winter. The main question: Which aid organization provides the right materials? They need plastic sheeting to protect their tent from the wind and snow, a small oven and wood for warmth. Ferial has formed a close relationship with three women from other tents; they help each other and, of course, talk about the news from Europe, where, everyone tells Ferial, "many Syrian refugees are being accepted." She scrutinizes me quizzically, almost as if she has difficulty believing it. Everyone here knows Angela Merkel; everyone has seen the latest pictures of her on their cellphones. But all four families lack the money to send the men on the long, expensive trek. And one thing is clear: only the men could or would go. So the women make themselves as comfortable as possible where they are and hope that peace will once more reign in their home country—they and many others.

OBEDIENT SECOND WIVES

Cecilia, our interpreter, is the daughter of Lebanese and Puerto Rican parents and lived for a few years in the United States. Her parents have run an SOS Children's Village in the Beqaa Valley for ten years. We travel there with our driver, Mohammed, to meet one of the SOS house mothers.

Nidal has, like the other women working here, four days off a month. On her free days she travels north to her hometown of

Arsal, near the Syrian border. She tells depressing stories about the lives and fates of the Syrian women in her village. Some Lebanese men buy Syrian daughters from their fathers to be second or third wives. One Syrian father, she tells me, shaking her head, even managed to sell his 23-year-old daughter to three different Lebanese men. He kept getting her back with the argument that he had overlooked that she was already married to another man. That seemed to work each time.

This is nothing but a form of slave trade. The Lebanese men who willingly "bed," as they put it, an obedient Syrian woman are usually older and have the money for buying and maintaining an additional wife in their household. Having multiple wives is permitted according to the Qur'an. And $200 for a new second or third wife is, in the eyes of the Lebanese, a very small price. Some men pay as much as $1,000 to $2,000. Syrian women are highly sought after, Nidal tells me, because they aren't as self-confident as Lebanese women; they do all the household chores without complaining, without ifs and buts. "This doesn't happen, however, without conflicts with the man's earlier wife or wives," she adds. That I can well imagine!

There is another, very different business relationship between Syrian women and the Lebanese. Syrian refugee women do housework for much less money than Lebanese housekeepers. As Nidal says, this is the only real contact most Syrian refugee women have with Lebanese women. The sad thing is that Lebanese former housekeepers are now unemployed, a development that affects many Lebanese men, as I learn later in Tripoli, the port in the north of the country.

IN THE AFTERNOON we drive back through the valley to one of the countless refugee settlements, this time near the highway. A young woman is waiting for us and directs us to a large square. She is the *shawish*—a kind of mayor of the settlement—and the only woman *shawish*, Cecilia informs me with some pride, in all the 1,278 settlements in the Beqaa Valley. How did that happen to someone so young?

Confidently, the woman invites us into her tent, placing her 4-month-old baby son in a modern Maxi-Cosi baby carrier, and brings us ice-cold orange juice in pretty glasses on a tray. Not long ago, Heya told the men in the nine tents here, "If you're not going to do anything for us, then I will!" And then she was promptly voted *shawish*. Since then, she has made sure that the tents are prepared for the winter, that the latrines work, that there's wood for the small ovens, and that there's contact with the aid organizations. She was hoping that an aid organization would bring exercise books, pens and pencils, and schoolbooks, but, she told me, unfortunately it hasn't happened yet. She added that she would love to teach the children herself; none of them attend classes because of the long distance to the school in the next village. During the day the children are alone while, in this settlement, all the mothers work for something to eat. *So it's possible for the women to find jobs,* I think to myself.

I am very impressed by this young woman and her involvement, and ask how far it is to the nearest stationery store. Only fifteen minutes by car, she answers. The idea of buying school materials for the children came to me while I was listening to her. Heya promises to teach the children at least how to read and write—her husband can take care of the baby.

We jump into Mohammed's car and buy twenty exercise books, twenty schoolbooks, twenty erasers, twenty pencils, twenty lunch boxes, and other necessities. Afterward, Heya happily lugs the red plastic shopping bags into her tent. We arrange for Cecilia to monitor the project and, from time to time, to send me photos. For $100 I have supported a good cause—at least, I hope so.

LAILA'S HEADACHES

Though during my visits the Syrian women refugees all eagerly absorb any information they can receive on old TV sets or cellphones, and though, enthralled, they read friends' and relatives' updates on WhatsApp or want to hug them through Skype, not all like talking about the war happening in their homeland. It seems to be too near to where they live now. They do know that as of now, 470,000 people have died—men, women, and children. They're conscious that there's little chance of finding secure places for their friends, parents, brothers, and sisters who remain in Syria.

Laila is 23 years old and came here alone from Aleppo. She is young, brave, and very pretty, with dark hair casually covered by a headscarf. When describing Aleppo, she speaks of it as beautiful: once the second-biggest Syrian city, the traditional center of the rich Sunni art dealers, creators, and patrons. At the time she decided to flee, her whole family had been forced to sleep outside. The building they lived in had been bombed and was just a crumbling ruin. Their freehold apartment had been on the third floor. The cold at night was her greatest problem; the sinister flyers regularly dropped by Assad's helicopters warned of further airstrikes. Laila tells me how the news was coming in thick and fast, how Assad's troops, supported by Iranian special forces and elite units of the Lebanese Hezbollah militia, were advancing. This was before the Russians began fighting for the regime as well.

Unlike the rest of her family, Laila decided to flee. Her parents wanted to persevere, as did her younger sisters. They all live in East Aleppo, where the majority of so-called rebels were fighting against Assad. Locals helped her with preparations, and her parents gave her money—a lot of money, she says. Hesitating, she tells me about her adventurous flight, of the bus trips and checkpoints, how she hid in a friend's car that finally got her to the border, where, at night, with the help of a guide, she slipped into Lebanon. Now we sit on thin mats in her austere tentlike construction. Laila studied history and wanted to be a teacher. Now her only hope is to be able to leave the region, leave the Middle East. She tells me, "Aleppo is symbolic in this war: if Aleppo falls to Assad and his troops, then all is lost."

I asked her why she didn't flee to the Turkish border, which was much nearer, and she tells me that it was more difficult to cross that border as it was much more strictly controlled. This was before the February 2016 mass exodus of refugees from Aleppo, but Turkey has always been very strict at this border crossing.

"Those who tried to flee to the east," Laila continues, "fell into the hands of the jihadists." So the only option was the west—Lebanon. She stresses that she only got through the area controlled by the Syrian army with a lot of luck. But the bleak life in the settlement is wearing her down. She has ended up living with friends, but it's very cramped. Eight of them live in this dwelling, sleeping on thin mattresses that they clear away during the day. She believes that Turkey would be a good destination, preferably by ship, but she would have problems getting a visa, as she entered Lebanon illegally.

By restricting its borders, Lebanon has forced many Syrian refugees like Laila into the underground and, on top of this, entry regulations have been tightened. Furthermore, people who enter the country secretly are vulnerable to exploitation. Without the proper papers, they need expensive smugglers to reach Turkey; the going price is $1,500 to $2,000. People with the right paperwork and a Syrian passport with an entry stamp need only $170 for ship passage. Budget airlines from Beirut charge $450—one way. But Laila can't take a standard flight from Beirut. How does she plan to move on? Laila smiles pleasantly but doesn't want to tell me. She just stresses that she wants to get away. She shows me photos from her past on her smartphone: the house she lived in, the nearby park, her sisters as babies, her parents' wedding—mementos that she managed to scan in time . . . all that is left for her.

She asks me whether I have any painkillers on me. Laila has been suffering from severe headaches for some time and hopes that the mobile clinic will be back at her settlement some day soon. "Every two weeks they stop off with a doctor, two nurses, and a midwife." I have some ibuprofen in my backpack and give it all to her. But I think her headaches are caused by her "illegal" status in Lebanon. Many refugees have told me they suffer from headaches and heartaches. When adults or children become sick, they rely on the mobile clinics' free services. Aid organizations' tight funding isn't normally enough to pay for medication, let alone visits to a doctor. In Lebanese villages, every visit to the doctor costs $2 plus any needed cab fares. So UNICEF, like many other aid agencies, operates mobile clinic teams throughout Lebanon. A unit can offer free care, including medication, immunizations, and ultrasounds, to about eighty people a day. At least the Lebanese government contributes to staffing costs.

TRIPOLI, GATEWAY TO EUROPE

The port of Tripoli has a population of 500,000, with, now, an additional 50,000 Syrian refugees. In the evening I watch a CNN report about Syrian refugees who apparently paid $2,000 for passage on a Turkish ship docking in Izmir. The next day I want to have a look around Tripoli so I can form my own impressions of the situation.

The drive there is magnificent: up to the highest peak in the Lebanese mountains, over the pass, and down toward Greater Beirut, population 2 million, and along the Mediterranean coast on a well-made highway all the way north to Tripoli.

First we head down to the harbor complex in El-Mina. Another checkpoint—we're not allowed to continue right down to the harbor. Seven men, Syrians, sit at the side of the road, along with a family with two children. The soldier at the control point doesn't allow us to talk to or photograph the refugees. One pretty young Syrian woman, in a tightly bound dark blue hijab made of the finest materials, tells us that she is waiting for her parents and that yes, they really paid $2,000 per person for a ticket to Turkey. Now she wants to buy them a few presents for their journey. She is studying law in Beirut and wants to stay in Lebanon—evidently a wealthy family if they can finance Beirut's high rents for their daughter. Why can't they emigrate legally? Why do their tickets to Turkey cost an incredible $2,000 when normal ones can be bought for $170 to $200? Probably, I reason, her parents fled without passports and don't have entry visas, so they've been staying here illegally like Laila.

We drive along the harbor, past countless fishing boats. Farther away, a few rusty hulks rot away, some because they have been abandoned, others because they've capsized or run aground.

I hope the crews were saved, I think as I view the beach. In former times, before the Syrian Civil War, wealthy Syrian and Lebanese holidaymakers took the ferry from here to Turkish resorts. Nowadays, the Syrians fleeing to Western Europe are often those who have first spent time in Lebanon or neighboring Jordan eking out a meager living.

Today, all along the beach, I see nobody resembling a refugee looking for ship passage or for an amenable fisherman with his boat. I feel like a *chai*—a strong, black tea—and Cecilia, the interpreter, and Mohammed are looking forward to a Turkish coffee.

I ask the man who brings our drinks whether he knows where we can contact some Syrians. "Very simple," he says, laughing. "I'm Syrian. We fled Syria three years ago. We're all Syrians here—I'll introduce you to my whole family!"

And so we learn that most of the Syrian refugees in Tripoli live in houses or small apartments, but that many live in unfinished buildings or dilapidated ruins. The official Lebanese statistics reckon that 60 percent of Syrian refugees live in these circumstances. They are, apparently, better off than the some 180,000 women and children in the drafty, rickety dwellings in the Beqaa Valley.

Twenty-year-old Ismael tells me that a lot of the refugees here in Tripoli are now worried about traveling on to Europe. They've heard about the many people who have already died en route—particularly about the boats capsizing between Turkey and Greece—and about the strong winds, the huge waves, and the leaky inflatable boats. This is why they are very pleased that a Lebanese landlord allowed them to stay, rent-free, in rooms here in the harbor. They were told they could do whatever they wanted with the rooms. This all happened at the beginning of the wave of refugees, when the Lebanese treated their neighbors from the war zone cordially and openly. Since then the climate has changed. But this Syrian family has settled down well here, and has managed to open a café—though at the moment, in the off season, we're the only guests here.

The men tell me that many Syrians are trying the legal route, with applications to the UNHCR, as so-called quota refugees. "It's safer," says Akic. "Safer than crossing the sea in a storm." Akic doesn't want to take risks. Like all the other twenty Syrians here in the café, he is from the city of Idlib and fled from ISIS terrorists. His destination? Western Europe, sometime in the future.

THE SYRIANS WHO STAY

Other Syrian families have also made themselves comfortable in Lebanon. It is the women in particular who want to stay put. Some families have found accommodations near the university, in a building that was formerly a student dorm. Here we are lucky in our search for women refugees from Syria.

Thirty-two-year-old Maha invites us into the two-room apartment where she lives with her husband and six children, and a TV set with an antenna. Both adults work for the building management and in return live there rent-free. Maha communicates with her parents in Homs via WhatsApp and has learned that the war is getting worse and worse, that no one can get out of there and into peaceful Lebanon. I ask her what her children do all day. Unfortunately, they, like hundreds of thousands in the Beqaa Valley, don't go to school. The school is too far away, Maha tells me. "How far?" I ask. "Forty-five minutes, and it's a very dangerous route." I've often heard this, and it surprises me. Is forty-five minutes a long time to get to school in a safe country? Maybe Tripoli isn't as safe as it seems.

The UNICEF staff know these arguments and have a hard time countering them. Another mother, 34-year-old Zeinab, also from Idlib, would love to send her three school-aged children to school. "But it costs too much," she tells me. Furthermore, it is difficult for her children to follow English or French classes: they can only speak Arabic. So the children sit around at home all day, without education, without learning to read and write. What kind of life is that? What future is there? Zeinab never wants to return to Syria. She's already lost two brothers in the war, and her oldest son has found a job in Lebanon. This helps them all, though her debts to the corner grocery store are still rising daily. The store-owner, a small, friendly Lebanese man, understands her situation and says nothing—part of the Lebanese culture of welcome.

Zeinab's neighbor, 36-year-old Heba, will soon no longer be able to send her three daughters to school because they will have to work. She complains, "My oldest daughter is just 11 years old." She lists other reasons why she will soon come to an arrangement with a trafficker, at least to get away from Tripoli: "The Lebanese want to get rid of us; everything is expensive; we're not allowed to work; they force us into the black-market economy." And then there are the increasingly strict regulations, like curfews, prohibitions on working, travel bans, and high administrative fees. If, for instance, a Syrian refugee wants to keep his papers valid and, as prescribed, report to the registration authorities every six months, he will have to pay, sometimes up to $20 (U.S. currency is common). Heba thinks it's daylight robbery, and I tend to agree.

Heba's husband has found a job as a porter. His earnings: $10 a day. Heba admits that they still have some of their savings left. Once the family has scraped together $4,000, they all want to take the risk of heading for Western Europe.

Not far from the university's towers, a group of some twenty-five Syrian women sit on small benches in the waiting room of the Islamic Medical Association. They explain that for only a little money, they can get treatment here. Dressed in hijabs that match their dresses, all with cellphones in their hands and elegant purses, they—unlike Maha and Heba—seem to be doing well. Their husbands, they tell me, have found jobs in Lebanon: in construction, at the harbor, some at a joinery. Their children go to private schools, for which they can afford the $100 monthly fees. None of them want to leave Lebanon. They live in peace and no longer have to be afraid of the various warring parties in Syria.

This all sounds encouraging—a successful new life. I want to learn more about this outpatients unit. Just by showing my business card, I'm allowed to speak to the Lebanese doctor on duty. How does he assess his role? He's interested mainly in getting the importance of hygiene and nutrition across to the Syrian women. And what about contraception? I ask. To my astonishment, he tells me the subject is never raised, and goes on to explain why: "Syrian women who attend our clinic don't want to use contraceptives. In fact, the very opposite: they want to have as many children as possible, so that one day they can make up for the casualties of this terrible war." What an argument! Many of the Syrian women—here in Tripoli, anyway—are expecting their tenth or eleventh child. None of them are worrying about the future.

At the end of this sunny late summer day in the port of Tripoli, another thought-provoking issue is raised: the doctor tells me that nowadays it's not Syrian men waiting for passage to Turkey but Lebanese men. Syrians work here for lower wages than the Lebanese. Unemployment among the Lebanese has risen steeply. Now the Lebanese want to emigrate, especially the young ones, because it's hard to find a job to feed their families. This saddens the doctor and highlights one of the drawbacks of the generous intake of Syrian refugees.

A SMALLER CIVIL WAR

Far from the medical center near the university district, in the heart of Tripoli, a grim and bloody conflict is being played out: a microcosm of the Syrian Cvil War, just as gory and dramatic. Here, in the districts of Bab al-Tabbaneh and Jabal Mohsen, the Lebanese state is fighting against Islamic militia, opponents of the Syrian president Bashar al-Assad. Added to the mix are Alevite groups, supporters of Assad, who are shooting at the Islamic militia. Experts on the bloody strife claim that this conflict has gone on far longer than the uprising and war in Syria. That war has, of course, aggravated the situation in Tripoli and, according to Lebanese government representatives, the influx of Syrian refugees to Bab al-Tabbaneh has further complicated the situation. Now 20 to 30 percent of the quarter's inhabitants are Syrians, including, one must presume, many combatants from the rebel forces involved in the armed conflict against the Assad regime. One man, who we stopped to ask for directions out of the labyrinth of tiny alleys and streets, tells us, "We're prisoners of the situation in the Middle East." I think that gets to the heart of the problem.

IT IS LATE afternoon and we are desperately trying to weave our way through Tripoli's rush hour, turning left here and then right up a small street until our driver, Mohammed, exasperated, brakes suddenly. "Here and no further—we have to go back, and quickly." Somehow we've ended up in Jabal Mohsen. Mohammed is a Sunni, but Jabal Mohsen is run by the Shi'ites. A glance at the houses reveals hundreds of bullet holes; many houses have fallen into ruin, and apparently nobody dares to go out into the streets. So we reverse quickly up the narrow street—a screeching turn and we're away.

Later we finally hit the "orderly" traffic jams of the Lebanese capital, Beirut. Here everything seems to follow a normal pattern, but it's an illusion. While in the Beqaa Valley the refugee crisis is clearly visible from the multitude of settlements, the Lebanese authorities and the relief organizations say that the majority of Syrian refugees have found shelter in the capital. The rents can be horrendous—for many, after five years of war, money brought from Syria is disappearing like water down a drain. There's nothing left, to the point that Syrian children in Beirut can no longer go to school.

There's also a government decree that no more than half the children in a classroom can be Syrian. Admittedly, the school authorities have reacted flexibly to the large refugee numbers: in state schools some afternoon classes consist solely of Syrian children. The Syrians also don't have to pay for lessons at the state schools, in contrast to the very expensive private schools. But one thing applies to both systems: the children don't understand a word of the lessons. In Syria, classes were held in Arabic, not in English or French as in Lebanon.

GREAT HOPES FOR A YOUNGEST SON

In Beirut we meet with Sahla, a 15-year-old Syrian who works as a hairdresser. At least she has a job—her two sisters are desperately trying to sell long-stemmed roses to customers in bars and cafés for $1 each. Sahla looks like a young businesswoman in her high-heeled shoes, makeup, and a gray suit with a white blouse. Her outfit doesn't match her surroundings in any way. She shares a windowless room in the middle of the city with ten other members of her family. She notes, rather sadly, that she has already missed three years of school. On the other hand, her job helps to feed the family: "If nobody works, nobody has anything to eat."

In Sahla's family, all hopes are pinned on 5-year-old Khalid. He understands English and should stay in school, although the refugee family in the Beirut ghetto has hardly any money. Their savings are gone, Sahla's father has no job, and her brothers and sisters are all younger than her, which is why she has to keep on working hard, in the hair and makeup salon where wealthy Lebanese women come to be prepped for parties and weddings. Sahla can only dream of such things. She will never be able to dance away the weekend in Beirut's trendy clubs like her chic clientele. But her meager wage of $125 a month helps the whole family survive and ensures that Khalid receives a good education. Flight to Europe? Out of the question for her—after all, she's responsible for all of them, the only one with a job. But after work, she smiles pleasantly, standing proud and upright outside the salon before catching the bus home.

After a long day of research, we drive back over the mountains near Beirut to Zahlé in the Beqaa Valley. It feels like the return journey takes four times as long as the journey out had. As the sun gradually sinks into the sea, Mohammed, our friendly driver, asks me whether it is difficult to get a visa for Germany. At 22, he has a bachelor's degree in business management and has been desperately looking for a job for three months. I can only advise him to get into contact with the German embassy—I don't see any other option.

The heavy weight on his mind is shared by all the young people in this country, a generation that sees no future prospects, partly because their country is suffocating from the sheer numbers of refugees: proportional to its own population, Lebanon has absorbed more refugees than any other country in the world. Other countries should follow this example. Yet Lebanon doesn't provide accommodations or food; the refugees have to cope as best they can. I have witnessed this in the Beqaa Valley, in Tripoli, and in the capital. Only the relief organizations and UNICEF provide necessities, and even these are becoming scarcer, partly because the war in Syria is dragging on and partly because donations are decreasing. On top of this, after six years of war there are more government restrictions on Syrian refugees in Lebanon—curfews, employment and travel restrictions, high fees. But at least the country opened its borders for four years, and up until January 2015 didn't even fence the border.

JUST ONE BOOK?

It's our last meeting with women refugees in the southern Beqaa Valley. The *shawish* meets us with a child in his arms. He knows the score: we don't want any men present! He adds, "There aren't that many here anyway."

Fifteen Syrians, aged 15 to 55, are sitting on narrow benches—very unusual, and unlike any of the receptions in tents at other settlements. This time there's no taking off shoes and no sitting cross-legged on thin mattresses. Cecilia, as always, explains who I am, what I want, and why I want to talk with them. I feel a lot of goodwill toward me. The women all wear hijabs, some colorful but mostly black. The younger girls also hide their pretty hair under the headscarves. I can already tell the difference between Lebanese and Syrian women by the way they bind their hijabs. The Lebanese women wear them loosely, creatively, but by no means properly—not in accordance with the Qur'an as the Syrians interpret it. The Syrians are stricter; they bind their scarves tightly around their heads and are very careful that not a single hair sticks out.

The ITS where we meet today consists of forty-three tents housing over 200 people. They all come from a suburb of Damascus where they were surrounded by Assad's troops right at the beginning of the war. They had nothing more to eat and hardly any water; fleeing was their only chance at survival. When they hear that I'm planning to write a book about their fates, they are amused and laugh: "Just one book? Not nearly enough to tell all our experiences and stories!" We will see.

Unlike so many of the women I meet, these all fled with their husbands. None of the men are heading to Europe, either. Most of the families have taken the proper path and applied for exit permits and UNHCR recognition of war refugee status.

Only one of the girls at this gathering goes to school. It's too expensive, say their mothers—about $100 a month. I don't press them further, but I know that this applies to only private schools; Lebanese state schools are free. The government even runs afternoon programs especially for Syrian children. But the mothers prefer to keep their sons or daughters at home—probably because the children can then work in the fields for landowners and bring in a little money.

Later, in our very cordial round of talks, I learn that some of the daughters are apparently being molested by Lebanese boys. This might be another reason that the girls are no longer allowed to attend classes. Is this really true? Berta Travieso from UNICEF doesn't know for sure, but she does know that her school team is desperately fighting to get more Syrian children to attend schools. At the moment, 500,000 children live in the valley, of whom only 40,000 attend one of the tent schools. Why? The mothers, as in this settlement, name a number of reasons—high school fees, the danger of the girls being molested and teased. But nobody admits that children are working in the fields, that they have to work so that their families can survive. The situation is dire.

One of the women, Rimas, has been living in this ITS for only nine months. She fled Qalamoun with her husband and three children when Assad's troops requisitioned their house; there was fighting all around them. Her husband, she tells me, walked over the mountains to Lebanon while she grabbed the children and the necessary papers—nothing else—and jumped into a cab. She managed to get here before Lebanon closed its border.

If my suspicions that the children don't go to school because they have to work to contribute to the family upkeep are right, I ask myself, *What about the job situations for the adult women?* What are *their* chances of finding work? I ask them. They are slightly taken aback. It emerges that of this group of fifteen women, only one works. She's employed by a Lebanese family in a nearby village. Only a quarter of the men in this ITS work, but most of the children—both boys and girls—work in the fields.

LEBANON IS A country of high mountains, and in winter there's a lot of snow—especially in the Beqaa Valley, where the snow gets to be a couple of feet deep for several weeks. Now winter is approaching. For many people here, it is their fourth winter. They shiver at the thought. They tell me that winter alone deserves a book of its own. In winter the children are sick, dwellings collapse on families under the weight of the snow, and the small heaters or ovens are not nearly enough to keep twelve to fifteen people warm. They shiver and freeze, waiting, distraught, for morning and the first rays of sun, which will hopefully warm them up a bit. Some choose to sleep in the open, in the snow in front of their dwellings, as they are panic-stricken that their rickety, thin roofs will collapse and bury them in snow. They pray that they will soon receive notification from the UNHCR allowing them to leave the Beqaa Valley, even just to another secure place, somewhere they don't have to freeze. The women talk all at once, animated and furious as they try to depict life here in winter.

But, I ask myself, what happens when there is no mail from the UNHCR? Some families have been waiting nine or ten months. Then—and all the women agree on this—they will convert all their possessions to cash to raise the necessary $2,000 or $3,000 to send a "strong" man on the tough, dangerous trek to Europe. The women will just have to put up with life here, wait, and hope, just as many of them already are.

I ask them whether it is dangerous here without the protection of men. No, they reply, shaking their heads. They look after each other—nobody is left alone. One of the young women says that she once wanted to take her sick young boy to hospital by cab but the driver turned suddenly onto a dirt track leading to a vineyard. Only by screaming loud and long was she able to escape, she tells me, which is why, since then, the women have always traveled together.

Women whose husbands live in the Beqaa Valley are still adding to their families, year after year. Apparently, the contraceptive pills that they can buy for cheap are no good. "They don't help!" I'm told. This is news to me. The diaphragms are also no good, 39-year-old Alla tells me, laughing. She still became pregnant. She laughed even louder at my question about whether it made sense to have so many children when there's so little to eat. According to statistics, Syrian families used to have only 2.3 children on average. Nowadays, because of the war, things are very different. The children are their future, they tell me. I heard this in Tripoli too; the only new thing is the explanation: there's no TV, no entertainment—what else are they supposed to do? Love is the answer.

TO SAVE THE CHILDREN

The refugee children in Lebanon, as well as in Turkey and Jordan, are particularly vulnerable to the effects of war and their flight. They can't sleep; they scream at night, waking others in their tents. They dream of falling bombs, of snipers aiming at their feet. Everyone in the family suffers, alarmed at yet another sobbing child. The children of the Syrian Civil War will one day be able to live contented lives, but only with a lot of help from their parents and from specialists, even after peace has returned to their country.

And that is just one problem. A big one, admittedly, but there is another: these children will not have had a proper education, will be left by the wayside. This is true not only for the children in the refugee camps but for a whole generation of Syrians who cannot or are not allowed to go to schools in Syria. Only 40 percent of schools remain, more or less, in operation.

Earlier, even under President Bashar al-Assad, Syria was considered a model Arab country as far as education was concerned.

Assad raised the education budget to 15 percent of the national budget—an impressive commitment. School was obligatory for all children between the ages of 5 and 15, with enrollment rates of 98 percent for girls and 99 percent for boys. Two-thirds of all children went on to high school. The illiteracy rate was only 5 percent.

The school system was set up by the French during their 1922–43 mandate, when France governed Lebanon and Syria. French and English remained compulsory subjects. International agencies complained about corporal punishment still being practiced in the schools and about the apparently poor training standards of teachers, but still, before the civil war, the education system in Syria worked.

And now? Tens of thousands of schools have been destroyed; many others have been turned into hospitals or barracks. Only 40 percent of all children in Syria actually went to school in the fall of 2015; in besieged Aleppo, only 6 percent. Only in relatively safe areas is school an option. There's no chance at all in the regions occupied by ISIS: there, girls can't attend and boys are sent to madrassas—religious schools—where they are taught a variety of Islam that will later allow them to enter paradise as suicide bombers.

At least Lebanon managed, as early as 2014, to absorb 200,000 Syrian children into its school system—often, when nothing else could be done, by organizing afternoon classes with lessons in Arabic.

Since 2015, the school readiness of refugee children in Lebanon has been tested—not only Syrian refugees, but also Palestinians in southern Lebanon. Unfortunately, only half the refugee children pass the test, and children who no longer attend state schools can no longer learn: the private schools cost money—all the mothers in the settlements emphasize this—and in a vicious circle, it's money that the children have to earn.

One thing is sure: this war has cost more than the lives of 470,000 Syrians. It will also produce a generation of young people who cannot read or write, who have not been given an education. When they grow up, it will be two or three times as difficult to make up for the loss. And that's assuming that peace returns to Syria—yet another grim thought.

FOUR

JORDAN

A SMALL, SUFFOCATED KINGDOM

My next destination is Jordan, linked to Syria by a long border. It is hardly surprising that since the beginning of the war some 630,000 Syrians have fled there and registered as refugees. The country has a population of only 6.5 million. Jordan, like Lebanon, is hopelessly struggling to cope with the refugee crisis. The wealthy countries of the world have left the refugee host countries neighboring Syria alone with their financial burden. Between 2011 and 2015, Jordan's debts rose from 70 to 90 percent of GDP. In 2011, Angela Merkel's government halved Germany's already modest contribution, to the detriment of Jordan.

Early in 2016, King Abdullah II told the BBC that his country was at "boiling point" because of the influx of refugees.[1] His country now shelters more than a million Syrians, a considerable number of them there "illegally," not registered. Aid organizations confirm that at least 1.4 million refugees have found sanctuary in the neighboring kingdom. In 2015, the UN had to cancel all aid to people living outside the refugee camps.

King Abdullah told the BBC that Jordan spends 25 percent of its national budget (some U.S. $12 billion) on refugee aid. This has had a heavy impact on the education system and health services. Abdullah warns, "Sooner or later the dam is going to burst." One has to marvel that a country absorbing over a quarter of its own population in refugees was able to bear this burden without complaint for as long as it did.

However, refugees here often live in the most squalid conditions imaginable. As in Turkey and Lebanon, no more than 20 percent of refugees in Jordan live in organized refugee camps, in the desert regions. The rest languish in ruins, empty houses, and tiny, damp, overpriced apartments. Jordan is their sanctuary from Assad's troops, from the conflicts of the various rebel groups and attacks by ISIS terrorists, but what a price! In Jordan too, it is mostly women and children living in refugee accommodations. The men are either dead, fighting in Syria on one of the various fronts, or on their way to Western Europe.

ASMA IS ONE of these refugee women. The 32-year-old Syrian lives with her five children in a one-room apartment in the Amman suburb of Jabal Faisal. Her rent is 100 dinar a month, about $130. In winter the roof leaks, and at night it is freezing cold—she has no money to pay for heating. Wood is expensive, and on top of this the chimney doesn't draw, so thick smoke fills the room. The suburb where she has found shelter had previously been a settlement for Palestinian refugees. It was built decades ago, when the war of 1967 and the first intafada of 1987–91 drove hundreds of thousands of Palestinian refugees to Jordan. Jabal Faisal still has the cheapest rents in the city.

Asma's oldest son, Faisal, has a job that pays some U.S. $50 a month. But his work is risky, as refugees are not allowed to work in Jordan without permits. If he is discovered he will be deported, back to the war in Syria. Like hundreds of Syrians before him, the Jordanian military police will simply put him on a bus that stops in the middle of the desert, opens its doors, and ejects the passengers. A number of people who have experienced the ordeal say that for the men, there are two unattractive options: either they are captured by the Syrian army and sent to one of Assad's torture prisons as deserters, rebels, or refugees, or the rebels find them and, depending on the degree of the captors' jihadism, the men are either forced to fight or land in an ISIS prison. This information has spread to the Jordanian authorities, who are now a little more lenient with younger deportees. One of the reasons for the Jordanians' defensive stance is the fear that Syrians will take their jobs—first, because they work for less money, and second (and it has long been common knowledge), because the Syrians work considerably harder and don't enter into long discussions about extra vacation time. So Syrians have a realistic chance of finding work in Jordan, but more so if they have a work permit, which would cost Asma and the older children over $500 a year—an unaffordable sum for the young woman.

So, like hundreds of thousands of other refugees in Jordan, Asma relies on aid from NGOs, for instance, World Food Programme food vouchers. But the WFP was forced to halve its support to about 50 cents per day in the summer of 2015 when donor contributions fell short. One reason the WFP has run out of funds is that many industrialized nations haven't paid their promised contributions. Unfortunately, the WFP has no fixed budget at its disposal. Germany and the United States are among those that have neglected their payments. Only recently, with the hundreds of thousands of new refugees arriving in Europe, has Germany become conscious of its responsibilities and paid its contribution. The German chancellor announced at a London conference on Supporting Syria and the Region early in 2016 that Germany would contribute $590 million to the WFP, as much as all the other donors put together. One-fifth of the $16 billion pledged overall in London will also be covered by Germany. These funds were intended to go directly to the countries in need, to Lebanon and Jordan, and were in addition to the $6.3 billion that the EU is paying Turkey.

So at long last, there was money for Jordan. Hopefully, it will really be used to improve the refugees' lot—50 cents a day per person is hardly enough to survive on, Asma tells me, which is why she has only one wish: to be allowed to work in Jordan. There are enough job opportunities there.

AT THE BEGINNING of 2016, 630,000 registered Syrian refugees lived in Jordan, on top of the Palestinians with "old" rights. But both groups, according to the vice-mayor of Amman, Yousef Al Shawarbeh, are in fierce competition with Jordanians.[2] Black-market labor is flooding the market; water is scarce throughout Jordan; there are far too few drains, waste is seldom collected, and besides, there are no waste incinerators. It's hardly surprising that the country is groaning under the burden.

DATA AND FACTS: JORDAN, SPRING 2016

- Jordan has a population of 6.5 million.
- Its system of government is constitutional monarchy.
- 630,000 registered Syrian refugees live there, but the government estimates that there are 1.4 million Syrian refugees in the country in all.

- Half the Arab population stem from the million Palestinians who fled to Jordan and other countries after the wars of 1948 and 1967.
- 93 percent of the population are Sunni Muslims.
- The illiteracy rate for women is 14 percent; for men, 4 percent.
- Unemployment is at roughly 20 percent.
- Tourism accounted for 20.7 percent of the GDP in 2015 but is in decline due to the conflicts in the Middle East.
- In 2015, the GDP was U.S. $33.4 billion; government debt amounted to nearly 90 percent of GDP.

PRETTY SYRIAN GIRLS

Asma is the mother of one son and four daughters, each one prettier than the other. And that is a problem.

Asma is attractive too—a feast for the eyes, men in Europe might say. Sunni Muslims, according to Jordanian law, are allowed to have up to four wives. Syrian women are especially highly regarded by Jordanian men. Why not bring a third or fourth wife home? Without, of course, any of the children she might have had with her Syrian husband. Jordanian men want to have their own children.

Asma and her daughters regularly endure aggressive harassment in the streets. She doesn't even want to let her daughters out anymore. The small, overweight grocer who exchanges her food vouchers is always making advances. He specializes in collecting from food vouchers the names, addresses, and telephone numbers of refugee women and their daughters. When a pretty Syrian enters his store, he asks, as a matter of principal, whether she is interested in earning something on the side, for her own sake and for the sake of her children. If she agrees, he puts her in contact with other men. It's a lucrative sideline.

These are stories that politicians who travel to Jordan don't hear. When German Secretary of State Frank-Walter Steinmeier visits, he becomes acquainted with the traffic jams in the capital and drops in on orderly refugee camps. On their visit in the fall of 2015, Vice-Chancellor Sigmar Gabriel and President Joachim Gauck emphasize how important it is that little Jordan, with its estimated 1.4 million Syrian refugees, gets better financial support. They appear concerned about the fates of the Syrians in their containers and tents. In front of the cameras and microphones of the hordes of journalists, they call on Europe, the United States, and the Gulf States to each contribute $1.6 billion to support and stabilize the region. At the Supporting Syria and the Region conference in February 2016, it is suddenly $7.2 billion, backdated to 2015, and $8.96 billion for 2016, pledged to the three most important host countries: Turkey, Lebanon, and Jordan. Pledged: from my experience, these are above all declarations of intent—it is very often a long and rugged path until a government actually transfers money. These traveling politicians on their refugee camp tours seldom, of course, learn about the fates of the 80 percent of Syrian refugees living outside the camps.

Now, at last, the international community is guaranteeing billions for aid, to prevent starvation and protect people from freezing in winter. The money is welcome in Jordan, and desperately necessary. One in four current inhabitants is a refugee. But when German politicians raise the issue of work permits, it falls on deaf ears. The Jordanian government does not appreciate outside interference. Unemployment has risen to 20 percent as a result of the refugee crisis, which is why even the Jordanians are beginning to grumble—a fact that is not lost on the refugees.

Equally, the patriarchal social structures that prevail in Jordan are ever-present for the Syrian women refugees. Some who were able to work as a matter of course in Syria experience clear role divisions in Jordan. A girl here marries soon after completing her schooling, then stays at home to look after her children and husband and to manage the household. That is the social consensus. Furthermore, profound disadvantages for women are anchored in law. Even in the twenty-first century, polygamy is widespread in Jordan. According to the law, a man is allowed up to four wives and can divorce them quickly and easily; a woman, on the other hand, has great difficulty obtaining a divorce. The result is that the majority of women in unhappy or even violent marriages remain with their husbands, whom they often had to marry at the age of 15, especially if there were concerns about providing for them financially. In principal, any woman in Jordan can be married against her will. A male guardian makes the arrangements for her and her family, and signs the marriage contract. But it gets worse: a rapist, according to the law, need not be brought to justice—if he marries the rape victim and remains married to her for at least five years.[3] How inhumane is that? First a woman is raped, then she's forced to marry her tormentor. Admittedly, in these cases she can refuse to marry, but family and social pressure is usually so great that women often see no other option but to marry.

Other laws also prevent equal treatment of women. A woman who has had or is having extramarital sex can be severely punished and ostracized. In such cases the family honor is considered tainted, and women often fear for their lives. There are no women's shelters in Jordan, so to avoid death threats from male relatives, these women are forced into accepting long prison sentences—almost a form of administrative custody for their own protection. If a male relative actually does kill the girl or woman in question, he will very often be sentenced to only six months in prison, assuming that he is charged in the first place. Ten years ago, however, such crimes went unpunished. This reminds me very much of the position of women in Afghanistan. I was not, however, expecting such conditions in the Kingdom of Jordan, with the progressive Queen Rania at the side of King Abdullah.

CRUISING THE DESERT IN SUVS

It is hardly surprising that Syrian women and girls who have managed to find supposed safety in neighboring Jordan don't feel particularly safe. On top of the prevailing patriarchal and misogynist structures, Jordan has become a popular destination for men from the Arabian Peninsula. Their motto: "Find yourself a Levantine wife—your guarantee of an easy life."

They cruise the desert on a hunt for wives. The younger the better... and the more expensive. These men can easily afford to pay up to 8,000 dinar, about $10,000. Syrian women are considered hardworking and obedient, as well as pretty and graceful. The grocer already has two wives but is still on the lookout for wife number three. He wants to have yet more children, and if it all becomes too much for him, it's easy enough for men to get a divorce in Jordan, as it is in other Arab countries—quick and uncomplicated. All that will remain is a "damaged" Syrian woman with even worse prospects for the future than before. She'll have none at all if she tries to keep the children from that relationship—they remain with their progenitor. Men in Jordan are often heard to remark cynically, "Thanks, Bashar al-Assad, for sending us your beautiful daughters."[4]

Even in Internet forums, Jordanian men discuss their Syrian brides. A newspaper article quotes one Saudi Arabian man's chatroom comment: "The long drive through the desert was well worth it. The good things in life are becoming more and not less."[5]

Regional groups that freely describe themselves as charitable organizations seem to be acting as matchmakers. Syrian women regularly tell journalists about one Saudi organization supposedly concerned with caring for women and orphans, but with a catch: the mothers and daughters have to be pretty, and prepared to marry someone from the Gulf States.

For the men from the Arabian Peninsula searching for brides in Jordan, age is particularly important, and a candidate has to be a virgin. Thus, girls as young as 13 or 14 are getting married, even though it's against the law. Patriarchal Jordanian society has an escape clause standing by: men wanting to marry younger girls have to have a religious leader, an imam or sheikh, perform the ceremony. These religious marriages are quickly sealed and can be just as easily dissolved. In law, only the civil registration of a marriage with the courts is recognized. But in times of war and crisis, nobody asks whether this practice contradicts the will of the wise prophet Mohammed as recorded in the Qu'ran. A young imam serving refugee families in a suburb of Amman put it this way: "When times are hard, many people lose their dignity."[6]

Compared to the "free" life in the Jordanian cities, the lives of women and children in the refugee camps are relatively secure. One such place is Zaatari, 15 miles from the Syrian border. The camp is the largest in the Arab world, a collection of containers, huts, and more containers as far as the eye can see. It was set up in the desert two years after the outbreak of war in neighboring Syria, when Jordan was registering 3,000 to 4,000 refugees a day at the border. Nowadays, 80,000 Syrians live in Zaatari. It has adequate medical facilities, two supermarkets, and schools for the children. But one-third of the children can't attend school—there's not enough room. A lost generation is growing up here too, right in front of our eyes.

WHY SOME RETURN

In another worrying development, many refugees who sought shelter with Syria's neighbors are giving up. They have hardly enough to eat, aren't allowed to work, and live in abject conditions. So they return to where they came from, back to the war. In the summer of 2015, some 6,000 Syrians returned home from Jordan alone. Those tracking them in Jordan are not sure whether they return because they actually intend to stay in Syria or just to sell property to raise funds for fleeing to Western Europe.[7]

Take, for instance, a 47-year-old Syrian father who settled with his family of twelve in the Jordanian city of Ramtha. They lived on food vouchers, with the oldest son selling vegetables to help pay the rent. Then, suddenly, there were no more food vouchers, so the father wants to return to Syria. He gets some consolation from knowing that his two eldest sons and two of his other children are heading toward Europe. The saddest thing about this story, however, is that the mother and her daughters will be stranded, in a ruin for which they have to pay 200 dinar ($240). How is she going to raise the funds to survive? She doesn't know. In any case, the men have all gone, the father back to Syria, the boys on the way to Europe.

The eldest daughter keeps in contact via WhatsApp, and lowers her eyes when she is out on the street so that no one gets the chance to speak to her or to ask for her hand in marriage. School? Training? Future? Forget it. What a fate—but just one of hundreds of thousands.

BUT THERE ARE positive developments, too, even though the Jordanians don't see them quite that way. For instance, the Syrians have undeniable skills as businessmen, traders, and merchants. Hundreds of small businesses have been set up in the refugee camp at Zaatari.[8] The main shopping street has been dubbed the Champs-Élysées. Zaatari itself doesn't sound too bad—the name is derived from the Arabic word for "thyme"—but it was certainly resourceful to copy the most exclusive French shopping street name and lend the camp a hint of the big wide world. In the early days, Zaatari had no infrastructure; now there are concrete streets everywhere, power lines, and wells. The settlement transformed from a collection of tents and improvised living quarters to container housing. Two hospitals are in working order, along with nine health centers, seven playgrounds, and schools for 16,000 children—far from sufficient, but still.

There is only one snag: Zaatari is an enclosed settlement, surrounded by an artificial sand wall with watchtowers staffed by members of the Jordanian armed forces. A concrete wall topped with barbed wire reinforces the feeling that no one gets out of here once they are in. And no one gets in without registration.

It had become clear that the Jordanians have no interest in integrating refugees—not again, not after absorbing the Palestinian refugees from earlier wars.

Nevertheless, the Syrians have managed to set up a lively business center in Zaatari. And in addition to the hundred-odd stores along the main street with its elegant French name, there are said to be another 3,000 spread throughout the country. Officially, there isn't supposed to be a single one, but the Jordanian authorities have allowed themselves to be won over by the resourcefulness and drive of the Syrians. An American working for the UNHCR, Codi Trigger, enthuses, "These stalls give people responsibility and a footing. They are also social gathering points, places to forget that they live in a settlement."[9]

Where does the money refugees spend in the camps come from? The camp organizers explain that at first, the refugees have their savings. Everyday life in the camps—accommodation, medical care, clothing, food—is free of charge. Then there are plastic cards from the UN that refugees can use in one of the two supermarkets. But these stores are expensive, more expensive than the goods available on the free market on the Champs-Élysées. The traders there can offer their goods much cheaper because they pay no rent or taxes. Their wares come directly from the producers in Jordan and within the Syrian border region. And it will soon be possible to withdraw money from mobile cashpoints: that will then be the ultimate economic stimulus for free trade within the refugee camp,[10] and perhaps support the booming cab business desperately needed for visits to the doctor or shopping trips. Soon there will be even more chickens sizzling in the sun, the smells of falafel and tabouleh permeating the air—or wedding dresses, in colors far too garish for European tastes, with wild, flowing skirts that draw in customers. Even here in the refugee camp, families are prepared to spend serious money on a wedding dress; it is, after all, tradition—all fathers are ready to splash out, assuming they want to marry off their daughters and not sell them off outside the camp, in Jordanian neighborhoods.

The markets already open in the refugee camp are flourishing. The refugees spend $11 million a month in the Syrian stores in Zaatari—though this is a small sum compared to the $2 million the larger UN organizations spend daily in Jordan on office rent, living quarters, provisions, and the other essentials of everyday life. But everyone who has experienced this astonishing development and the proof of Syrian entrepreneurial spirit in Zaatari is impressed, especially the Jordanians. Many aid organization staff now say in amazement, "The Syrians, they just don't let it get them down."[11]

NOT OFTEN TAKEN into account when considering how to support the small kingdom in the refugee crisis is that Jordan's 2015 projected deficit was only half as high as 2014's, thanks to over $1.5 billion in subsidies. Researchers at the Konrad-Adenauer-Stifnung foundation say that as early as 2012 and 2013—the first years after the beginning of the Syrian civil war—Jordan experienced a spurt in economic growth, even though unemployment had risen. The nation has spent some $7 billion on providing for refugees but, according to experts, that's offset by $5 billion in additional revenue.

A look at the history of Jordan shows that this is not the first time the country has profited from refugees. A hundred years ago the country was almost deserted, and oil or other natural resources had not yet been found. Only with the arrival of Arab refugees, particularly from Palestine, did the country gradually become populated. So in the small country surrounded by Syria, Saudi Arabia, Iraq, and Israel, heated discussions are taking place about whether the Syrian refugees could offer a fresh opportunity for the future and might not be such a burden after all. It's a discussion that seems familiar.

This large family is happy about having a visitor to their windy dwelling in the Beqaa Valley. (Photo: Maria von Wesler)

A fertile valley, a beautiful landscape: almost 1 million refugees have found shelter in 1,278 informal tented settlements here, near Zahlé in the Beqaa Valley. (Photo: Maria von Wesler)

The main problem in the 1,278 informal settlements: no clean water. Almost everywhere lacks latrines, and small streams are contaminated. (Photo: Maria von Wesler)

Garbage is an unsolved problem throughout Lebanon, particularly in refugee camps where there is no garbage collection. (Photo: Maria von Wesler)

Instead of going to school, the Syrian refugee children work. These boys are loading vegetables to sell at the market. (Photo: Maria von Wesler)

Aischa lives only for her children; without them she wouldn't have the will to live. (Photo: Maria von Wesler)

Chambi's daughter-in-law left her children with their grandmother when she remarried. Now Chambi is left to cope with the little ones. (Photo: Maria von Wesler)

Amira is proud of her clean dwelling. She is expecting her first child in Lebanon. Here, a friend's children visit. (Photo: Maria von Wesler)

FIVE

ERITREA

HER BODY FOR HER FLIGHT

She didn't want a child yet, and certainly not like this.

Seventeen-year-old Almaz was brutally raped multiple times by three traffickers while fleeing. She doesn't know who the father of the child is. The baby boy was born in Munich after her flight through the Libyan Desert. Initially, Almaz couldn't even bear to look at him; she wanted to have him adopted immediately, wanted nothing to do with the baby, hated being continually reminded of the horrific days of her flight. But Almaz's aunt, who like many Eritreans lived in Munich, managed to persuade her to keep the baby and took the young mother to Condrobs, a housing project for young refugees. That was a start. The authorities, concerned about the child's welfare, came very close to taking the baby into care, because some days the African teenager was simply unable or unwilling to look after him. She's now cared for by the counselors, who are there 24/7 for the young mother and her baby. Almost all the young refugees here were raped while fleeing or felt they had no option but to "sell" their bodies to pay the traffickers.

Things are improving for Almaz. The day I was invited to have breakfast with her at the huge oval table was a good one. But there are also bad days, days when she can't get out of bed because of her headaches or nightmares. Almaz has these often. At times like this her small son, Jama, is cared for by one of the five women—social workers, psychologists, nursery teachers—employed to look after the eight mothers and their children. There are also two volunteers and a local student intern.

Sometimes Almaz talks a little, telling stories about her homeland, but never about the long flight. She now understands that her child needs a special diet. The pediatrician diagnosed malnutrition, so Jama has customized meals every two hours, which is a strain on his mother. But slowly, week by week, she is coping better. The Eritrean community in Munich provides the young mother with emotional support. They all know what refugees have had to go through during the flight. Almaz is always welcome there, to speak in her mother tongue, to talk about her childhood and her parents, how much she, like all the other women in the housing project, misses her home country.

WHAT DO WE in Europe or North America know about Eritrea, this small country on the Red Sea wedged in by the neighboring giants, Sudan and Ethiopia, and sharing a small border with Djibouti? After Syria and Afghanistan, most refugees applying for asylum in Germany come from Eritrea. In 2014, 360,000 people fled the country, and that out of a total population of just 5 million—7 percent of the population. That would be the equivalent of 5.6 million people leaving Germany, or nearly 23 million escaping the United States. They are fleeing the dictator Isaias Afwerki, who has led a brutal totalitarian regime since 1993. Few other countries have such a callous disregard for basic human rights. Human rights organizations have been refused entry for fear that they would report on the situation. Even the UN was forced to base its June 2015 report on the testimony of hundreds of Eritreans living outside the country. The Commission of Inquiry on Human Rights in Eritrea found that Eritrea "is marked by repression and fear" and that the regime is responsible for "extrajudicial executions, widespread torture, sexual slavery and forced labor";[1] Eritreans are confined "in prison camps, holes in the ground or ship containers,"[2] for weeks or even months on end. It really is a country of horrors.

Above all, it is the forced labor (the regime prefers to use the term *national service*) that frightens people to such an extent that young Eritreans in particular are fleeing the country. The refugees are between 18 and 50 and both male and female—women are also forced into national service. Almaz had the threat of national service hanging over her and had been terrified at the prospect. In Eritrea, all adults have been called up to national service since 1993. National service can mean anything from military service to road building to agricultural work. Initially, service was limited to eighteen months, but this hasn't been the case for a long time. Nowadays it can mean service of ten years or more, during which the Eritreans have to endure strict military discipline, mostly without pay and with little food.[3]

DATA AND FACTS: ERITREA, SPRING 2016

- Eritrea has a population of 6.3 million.
- Its capital is Asmara, with an estimated 500,000 inhabitants.

- Officially, Eritrea is a constitutional democracy. The president is the head of state and supreme commander of the armed forces.

- According to the NGO Freedom House, "Eritrea is not an electoral democracy."[4]

- The population is half Muslim (Sunni) and half Christian. In recent years the regime has systematically persecuted unrecognized Christian minorities.

- 75 percent of the population work in agriculture.

- Eritrea's main natural resources are gold, silver, copper, sulfur, nickel, potash, marble, zinc, and iron, and it produces large amounts of salt. These resources have long been exported worldwide. Other important industries include cement, textiles, and foodstuffs such as beer, liquor, and wine.

- The nine languages of the nine ethnic groups have equal status as official languages.

- Officially, schooling is obligatory for all children aged 7 to 13, but only 50 percent of school-aged children attend.

- The illiteracy rate is 35 percent.

- Life expectancy is 63.

- Almost 90 percent of women have been genitally mutilated even though it is forbidden by law.

- According to the German Foundation for World Population, only 7 percent of married women have access to contraceptives, a figure linked to the forecasted growth in population of 14.3 million by 2050.

- The war of independence in Ethiopia ended in 1991 after thirty years, with the Eritrean People's Liberation Front emerging victorious. The EPLF formed the new government and arranged the establishment of Eritrea as an independent state.

HUSBANDS NEVER SEEN AGAIN

Thirty-two-year-old Ashanti, from the capital, Asmara, lost her husband; he has now been missing for nine years. He was called up for military service then simply disappeared. Her father vanished in similar circumstances, never to be seen again. Ashanti decided to leave her two older children with her mother and try to escape. Later, on reaching safety, she intended to arrange for the children to rejoin her and to send money to make her mother's life more bearable.

She saved up, borrowed money from friends and family. She knew that she would need about U.S. $10,000 to get to Europe, preferably Germany. It took a while. She worked hard, day and night, until at last she could count enough bills, and hid them in small bundles close to her body. There were long negotiations with the smugglers about the price and route. Hard negotiations. The go-between walked away twice and twice he came back, until, at last, they reached an agreement and Ashanti jumped into a people-smuggler's rickety, rusty car for the first stage of the journey. The destination was Khartoum, capital of Sudan. But first they had to secretly cross the border.

At that time this was a new trail; previously, the Eritrean refugee route was through the Sinai Peninsula to Israel. Until recently, tens of thousands of Eritreans had escaped repression along that route, most of them remaining in Israel. Since then, however, the Israelis had built a fence at the border to stop the influx of refugees. It was finished in 2013, and after that hardly anyone could enter the country by the Sinai route. People like Ashanti wanting to reach the West have to travel through the Libyan Desert to the coast.

There are no problems crossing the border into Sudan at night. Ashanti explains later, from the safety of Germany, that she had heard from others that the first stage was the easiest. She had relatives in Khartoum and was able to stay with them for a while. Then it was on to a refugee camp in Shagarab, close to the Eritrean border to Libya. Hundreds of Eritreans live there, both women and men. It was there that Ashanti discovers, to her horror, that many of her compatriots were selling their organs to raise funds for their further travels. She is happy in the knowledge that she, at least, still has her money: it has remained undiscovered. After a week-long wait, the next stage was in a pickup with twelve other Eritreans and twenty Syrians, including two women and eight children. "We were far too many people," she tells me later. "The traffickers forced us to leave our luggage behind." They even took away vital bottles of water and her carefully prepared food supplies. Ashanti began to panic. How on earth was she supposed to survive a trip through the desert without water? Without food? Let alone without blankets or warm clothes—nights in the desert, as she well knew, could be icy cold.

After two days she began to understand the traffickers' evil tricks. They mixed the 60 liters of water carried in the truck with gasoline. Ashanti was appalled, but soon her thirst became unbearable. The traffickers passed around the water-and-gas mixture drop by drop, and everyone drank it even though it tasted disgusting. The traffickers' reasoning? Very simple: the fewer water containers they carry, the more room for people, and the more money they can earn. As simple as that.

Almaz shared and survived similar conditions, but she doesn't feel up to talking about her flight. After the trip through the desert, she ended up, as did Ashanti, in Benghazi, in a so-called safe house together with 180 other refugees, two toilets, and no showers. The stench was sickening. On top of all this Almaz was continuously sick, as she was already pregnant. The rapists had long since vanished; they were on another pickup, counting up their thousands of dollars for carting the next batch of refugees to the Mediterranean. Almaz could only sit and wait for the ship that would take her on the "short and safe" trip, as the smugglers described it, to Lampedusa, almost 200 miles across open sea and thousands of miles away from home. But to safety—safety in Europe.

THE OFFICIAL REASON for the Eritrean requirement of national service is, according to President Afwerki, the permanent threat of invasion by Ethiopia. Eritrea fought for independence from its huge neighbor for thirty years. In 1998, just five years after the long-awaited separation, hostilities between the two nations were renewed. Since then Ethiopia has occupied a strip of Eritrean land, leading Eritrea to declare a state of emergency. The Eritrean constitution, approved in 1997, has never come into effect; general elections have been repeatedly postponed and 200,000 to 300,000 people in this small country have been compelled to do national service at any one time. They guard the border to Ethiopia, build roads, and work in the fields of the elite, serving, at public expense, generals and leading politicians. While performing their compulsory duties, they are bullied and abused to such an extent that fear of the regime determines every aspect of the lives of families in this country.

Nobody dares revolt, in part because the country is brimming with informers. People who nonetheless dare to criticize the dictator disappear very quickly, overnight. There are no open trials: a person simply remains missing. This happened to a group of fifteen politicians who, in an open letter, pressed for free elections, demanding that the constitution, approved years earlier, at last be ratified. Eleven of them disappeared within twenty-four hours. The same fate awaited a group of some hundred rebels who stormed the Ministry of Information with similar demands. Eritrea seems to be a nightmare. But German development aid still flows into the country, supposedly to strengthen infrastructure and stop the flow of refugees, but that seems unlikely.

Ashanti tells me that in a short visit, it is difficult to notice this repression. Everything appears sweet and rosy. Italian colonial buildings, palm trees, and pleasant cafés line the streets. Twitter and Facebook are not forbidden—there's no need to ban them as Internet service is so slow that it hardly ever works anyway.

THE FAITHLESS PRESIDENT

The German minister for economic cooperation and development, Gerd Müller, visited Eritrea in 2015, in part because of the immense rise in the number of Eritrean refugees arriving in Germany. After all, Europe does provide over $200 million for "tackling the root causes of displacement" in the country. Among other things, the money is to be used to improve electricity supplies. With almost $2 billion in funding, the EU wants to support Eritrea and Sudan and, in doing so, to prevent even more Africans coming to Europe.

President Afwerki, in return, has promised to reduce national service to eighteen months, its original limit. The problem is that up to now the Eritrean president hasn't kept a single one of his promises, so there's no reason to believe that this time will be different.

In addition, expats—Eritreans living abroad—are an excellent source of cash for the country. The money the refugees send home from North America and Europe is one of the last reliable sources of income left to the regime. How does it work so reliably? Quite simply: with the help of a network of informers.

Every Eritrean living abroad is obliged to transfer 2 percent of his or her income to the regime in Asmara. Those who fail to do so receive no birth certificate or references when needed and are barred from claiming inheritances, and their families will run into difficulty if they try to join them abroad. It's pretty ingenious, this system. Up until 2011, Eritreans could deposit this "reconstruction tax" at embassies or consulates, but the EU has since forbidden it. Now expat Eritreans who are loyal to the regime gather the "tax" directly from their fellow citizens and personally deposit the takings in Asmara. Why, you ask yourself, does almost every Eritrean refugee pay so much money? Because they all still have relatives in Eritrea. Foreign secret services speak of a well-oiled network of translators and informers true to the regime and on the president's payroll. Nobody escapes their notice; nobody can hide from them.

Almaz's community in Bavaria pays the "tax"; they're too frightened of the power of the state not to. They still have family in Eritrea who would otherwise be left to the mercy of the president's henchmen.

Almaz doesn't have to pay yet, as she has no income and lives on aid. But she plans to take a German course and to finish school. She wants to repay the country that accepted her, maybe work for an aid organization and help other women find their footing. She doesn't mention Jama, her son, in her thoughts for the future at the moment, but her caring counselors tell me, "Everything will be fine. She just needs time. The long trek, the violence, the fears—nobody finds it easy to come to terms with them or to quickly brush them aside." The other women in the housing project help the young Eritrean. Together they are strong, they tell me on parting. And it seems to be true.

TWO ERITREAN GIRLS ALONE

Eritrean sisters Bien and Milena, who also live in the Munich center, made the dangerous trip from Asmara to Germany alone. How did they achieve this feat? They don't feel up to explaining. But the 15- and 17-year-old regularly participate in a biographical project launched by the Center for Victims of Torture and War. Some fifty other unaccompanied boys and girls take part in this program organized by the Youth Welfare Office in Munich.

Bien, the 15-year-old, wants to learn German as quickly as possible; she writes new words in her notebook and, believe it or not, after two weeks can say whole German sentences. She and her sister spend a lot of time on their cellphones, the only contact they have with their parents in Eritrea. Their father, a doctor, has an Internet connection from time to time and can catch up on what the girls are doing, like, for instance, three hours of German lessons a day. The girls do, of course, have other activities: talks about contraceptives and other important issues, movie outings, dancing to hip-hop music.

Everybody working with unaccompanied children agrees that the children have phases when they withdraw, when they can't talk, when they just want to do nothing. The girls in the house, especially after breakfast, go back to their rooms and hide beneath blankets; some later wipe tears from their eyes. They are, after all, in a strange country, alone and without their families. The girls with a better understanding of the language follow the German political debates on social media, often with alarm. The sisters prefer to link arms with their counselor, Uta, when they go out into the city, observing the people all around from the shelter of Uta's arms. How will they fare here in this alien country with its strange culture?

On public transit, Bien and Milena are the first to jump up and offer their seats with a smile when an older person gets on. It comes naturally to them. "In our culture, we learn early to respect older people," they tell Uta, who is delighted and encourages them: "Please, hang on to that in Germany... The kids here are very different." There is so much that is different here, so much that they will have to learn. But Bien and Milena, who managed to cross the desert and the sea alone to reach Munich, will adjust. They are strong, open, and bold. That will help them, and maybe it will help us, too.

HORROR ON THE HIGH SEAS

In the midst of all the news about refugee tragedies on the route from Turkey to the Greek islands, the western Mediterranean passage between the coast of Libya and southern Italy has been somewhat neglected. But this route continues unchanged. In 2015, some 154,000 risked the voyage from Africa to one of the European islands; 3,000 lost their lives in the attempt. The Mediterranean has become a gigantic graveyard. The Italian coast guard counts the dead it takes from the sea, but there are no reliable figures for the number of bodies washed up on the coast of Libya. But hundreds of scuffed, bruised black rubber inflatables languish in harbors large and small dotted along the thousand-mile coastline of Libya, mementoes of unsuccessful crossings. Most are missing motors, likewise any trace of migrants from Syria, Eritrea, Somalia, or Nigeria. They must all have died.

Wealthy migrants who pay thousands of dollars can board safer motorized inflatable boats to France. France is a good destination because it isn't usually monitored by the coast guard. The long distance across the sea is not a concern for those who can afford to choose safer transport. However, the majority of mostly poor migrants aim for the Italian island of Lampedusa, as it is only 200 miles from the Libyan port of Tripoli. This is the cheaper option, but they may not succeed in reaching Italy at all.

THE PRICE OF TRAFFICKING

The price of passage from Libya to Italy while dictator Muammar Gaddafi governed was $5,000, but has since sunk to $1,600—all inclusive, apparently. If traffickers manage to cram 200 migrants into one boat, they can make an unbelievable $320,000. It's a tidy profit, which, if they are pressed, they try to play down by citing the immense associated costs. The cost of renting "safe" houses as temporary accommodation for the refugees are $5,000 a month alone, and how long the refugees have to wait there varies. Then the smugglers have to pay at least $20,000 a month to the local chief of police to ensure that these premises are left alone. Then the boat to ferry the refugees to a larger vessel costs another $4,000. The boat for the actual passage with roughly 250 refugees is $80,000. The captains, mostly Tunisian or Egyptian, expect $5,000 to $7,000. The captain's satellite phone, important in international waters for emergencies, is an additional $800. Lifejackets are $40 apiece.

The trouble is that, according to the Red Cross, 80 percent of the lifejackets for the crossing from Libya are useless. Like those commonly used in Turkey, they pull people under water instead of keeping them afloat. Early in negotiations, most traffickers promise not only total security but also these life-jackets. The fact that most are missing even from the small ferries taking the refugees to the main vessel doesn't seem to bother anybody in a fragile country like Libya. There are no laws anymore; the country, the desert, the seas—all are free from governmental control. So, for the migrants, there is no protection whatsoever.[5]

ONE WEEKEND'S DEATHS

One April weekend in 2015, at least 700 people, possibly more than 900, drowned while fleeing to Europe, only 60 miles off the Libyan coast. Like all those before and after them, they had been squeezed onto and then trapped in an overloaded boat that eventually capsized. Where did they come from? No one will ever know. The traffickers hustled them aboard at gunpoint;

many were forced below decks into the ship's belly. Then the cargo hatches were sealed. When the ship went down, nobody below decks escaped. The Mediterranean swallowed them. Ships arriving at the scene of the catastrophe were able to rescue only twenty-eight survivors.

A second example, also in 2015, the Year of the Refugee—another of thousands. A ship left Zuwarah on the Libyan coast with about 370 refugees on board, including 12 women and 13 children. They had almost made it to safety and were very close to Lampedusa, which was clearly visible on this sunny day. Their rescuers, in the form of the Italian coast guard, were approaching them when panic broke out and the people on the hopelessly overloaded boat all surged to one side. Witnesses later reported that the ship began to list, keeled over, and, with its metal hull, sank fast. Because many ships had received the SOS and were quickly at the scene, everyone on board was saved.

Another case: 110 nautical miles from the coast of Lampedusa, a fully laden refugee ship sent out an emergency signal. It was the middle of winter and, supposedly, the motor was refusing to start—a ploy often used by the traffickers in international waters to get other ships to take refugees aboard. Two container ships docked in Malta couldn't leave the port because of the sea's heavy swelling. The coast guard at Lampedusa had also been notified, but it took them five hours in a speedboat battling against a storm to reach the sinking ship. By the time they arrived, seven refugees had died. They hadn't drowned because the ship had capsized: they had frozen to death on board. On the way back to Lampedusa, a further twenty-two people died of hypothermia. The journey in the coast guard boat took nineteen hours. It had no cabins—nowhere to shelter—and the glittering aluminum blankets fluttering in the wind were of little comfort. Only the tougher refugees managed to survive.

THE GERMAN NAVY

Two German ships operate in the Mediterranean Sea with a mandate to rescue refugees in distress. The area they cover is some 600 by 500 miles, but they mostly patrol off the Libyan and Italian coasts. The frigate *Hessen* and auxiliary ship *Berlin* have complements of 255 and 159, respectively. The *Berlin* is also equipped with a MERZ (*Marine-Einsatzrettungszentrum*)—an onboard mobile surgical hospital housed in a container. The *Berlin,* according to naval sources, can easily cope with taking on board an extra 250 people and the frigate another hundred, but in an emergency, they can manage larger numbers. The quarters are provisional, however, and only designed to be used for a maximum of forty-eight hours. The ships carry woolen blankets and supplementary provisions and have installed additional showers and sinks.

In 2015, more than 12,500 people were rescued by the German navy in its patrol area. Most were taken to the Italian ports of Pozzallo and Reggio Calabria and passed on to the local authorities there. The two ships can use other ports if necessary; these have been instructed to follow the directions of the Italians. The operation is based on Article 98 of the Law of the Sea, which states that the captain is duty bound "to render assistance to any person found at sea in danger of being lost."

SIX

LESBOS

GRAVEYARD OR BRIDGE?

It is only a one-hour flight from Athens to the beautiful island of Lesbos, the third-largest island in the Aegean with a population of almost 90,000. This tourist destination has now, in the wake of the floods of refugees from the Middle East and Turkey, become the center of a dramatic crisis, mainly because the Turkish coast, at the narrowest point, is only 6 miles away. A mere stone's throw, you might be inclined to think.

According to the UNHCR, in 2015 over 848,000 people from Syria, Iraq, Afghanistan, and Pakistan landed on the coast of this Greek island. But during the passage across the sea in flimsy inflatable boats, 3,695 others lost their lives.

Now, early in 2016, it doesn't look as if fewer people will be seeking assistance—especially if the storms don't whip up the seas too much and the unsound inflatables manage to complete the voyage without capsizing. By April 2016, 172,000 migrants will have boarded the rubber dinghies to reach Europe. As long as there are reasons to flee, people will take the risk. This revelation is nothing new.

In the winter of 2015–16, I looked for lodgings in Mytilene, the capital, on the eastern side of Lesbos. Nowadays, with the Internet, this is a simple task. First look at the map, then view the distance to the Turkish coast, and there it is. I want to find out how the refugees are actually doing, particularly the women and children, who in 2015 had still been in the minority. Early in 2016, the numbers increased considerably. Suddenly there they were, the women and mothers, the sisters and daughters, often with children and babies firmly pressed to their bodies, huddling together in the boats.

The hotel is well placed. Shortly after my arrival, on my first evening out, I happen across a Syrian refugee family just around the corner, in front of one of the many, and now much frequented, local travel agencies. These Syrians come from Idlib and have traveled for six months to get here—fleeing from bombs above and ISIS terrorists on the ground. They sold everything they owned: the house, the furniture, crockery, and linen. All they possess tonight is a backpack and a large Adidas bag, plus a single backpack for all the children. The parents show me what they packed—T-shirts, socks, a spare cellphone, and warm pullovers. It's a lot, but still far too little for a long journey. When I think of the temperatures in Germany at this time of year I'm apprehensive. I manage to reassure myself with thoughts of the well-supplied clothing donation projects. The parents have sealed their most important documents and a few family photos—their wedding, newborn babies—in plastic.

Two other married couples, each with two children, lean against the outer wall of the travel agency. The husbands are brothers. The travel agent does a bit of translating from Arabic to English. He comes from Morocco and ended up on Lesbos three years ago, also as a refugee. Today he is a successful business owner. *So it can work out well,* I think to myself. The youngest child, a 3-year-old girl with big, round eyes, is standing on the street in her socks. The father explains in broken English, "She fell in the water. We just managed to grab her, but she lost her shoes." They hope to buy her new ones tomorrow, sturdy ones so that she can walk long distances. Nowadays, many shops specialize in the needs of refugees, some selling cheap sneakers but also tough hiking boots in all sizes.

Tonight, the two families will take a cab to their accommodation; the Moroccan travel agent interprets for the Greek cab driver and the families before giving them their tickets to Piraeus, the port city for Athens. Tomorrow evening the longed-for ship will set sail, taking them deeper into Europe—a proper ship, not like the flimsy rubber boat that brought the two families from Turkey to Lesbos. Already in the early winter of 2016 the European border control agency, Frontex, has registered 45,000 refugees, 38 percent of them children and 22 percent women. When possible, the fleeing men now take their families with them. This is a new development: up until now, most of those risking the journey were the fathers, brothers, and adult sons.

THE HOTEL'S PARTICULARLY friendly receptionist, Stella, who is always prepared to help all and sundry and always with a dazzling smile, has found me a driver and a very nice interpreter. I agree to meet the driver at six in the morning tomorrow for the trip to the bay at Skala Sikamineas. Vangelis speaks good English and has already chauffeured a number of prominent guests around the island. I later discover that he went to the same school as my interpreter, Angela, an English teacher.

On this first evening, three friendly Frontex staff invite me over to their table in the hotel lounge. Frontex was founded in 2004 as the European agency responsible for controlling the Schengen borders. The EU has recently sent an additional 760 police officers to Greece's borders, including 60 from Germany. The three at the hotel come from Sweden and are assisting Frontex to protect the Schengen frontiers on two-month stints. It's not an easy job. They have to check the refugees' passports—are they forged? Is a refugee making a repeated attempt at entry? What is his or her story? Is it true? Where do they want to go? Where do they have the best chance of being granted asylum? Is the scanner/biometric camera/fingerprint recognition device actually working? Everything has to be translated. The three speak English fluently, but none speaks Arabic, let alone Farsi or Dari, to understand the Afghans.

The oldest of the three men recounts that today, for the first time in his experience, two Kurds applied for asylum in Greece. He's happy about that development but worried about the situation as a whole. The two Kurds have every chance that their applications will be quickly approved, but few of the other refugees want to remain in Greece. The previous year, only 14,368 migrants applied for asylum in Greece. It has quickly become common knowledge that Greece has enough problems of its own. The government in Athens has been struggling with its debt crisis for exactly as long as war has been raging in Syria.

Those registered as Syrian refugees by Frontex are granted freedom of movement in Greece for six months. Afghanis and Pakistanis are allowed to stay for only thirty days. But everyone has only one aim, and that is to reach Germany. *Alemania*—a word that I will often hear in the coming days on this island.

Some of the refugees want to go to Sweden because they have relatives there, which improves their chances of being granted asylum.

The TV set in the hotel lounge is on the whole evening. We learn that Macedonia has just closed its border—well, almost closed: Syrian and Iraqi refugees with official papers are being allowed through, but Afghanis and Pakistanis are being blocked. There is a traffic jam after the closing of the Austrian and Hungarian borders. So what do they do now? Are all the hundreds of thousands of refugees supposed to stay in small, poverty-stricken Greece? In this country of all places, which in the throes of a financial crisis has been struggling for so long for its very existence? Things seem to be coming to a head—the three Frontex policemen agree. Who is going to look after these people? Who will give them something to eat, tents and blankets, medication when they are sick?

The refugee issue dominates every Greek TV channel. Journalists talk about it with politicians, then switch to reporters on location at the Macedonian border, on Lesbos or Kos, in Piraeus or Kavala in northern Greece, to which many ships heading out of Lesbos are bound. Everyone feels the beginnings of panic in this small country that, with 8,500 miles of coastline and a vast number of islands, is completely swamped by the situation. The prime minister, Alexis Tsipras, even makes a plea for help to German chancellor Merkel, saying that Greece could provide only up to 50,000 places for refugees. Well, at least there's that—up until then, Greece had been quite content to just wave people through.

I SET OFF for Skala Sikamineas while the sky above the island is still dark. The bay lies in the northern part of the island, an hour's drive from the capital and, more importantly, just two hours away from the Turkish coast by inflatable boat. This is the shortest stretch to there, 6 miles—the reason why in just the last few days hundreds of boats have landed here. And the prevailing wind direction is right, too, blowing east to west, toward Greece. When storms are forecast, the traffickers offer "bad weather discounts." The price for the passage is then linked to wind strength and wave height. In these first few weeks of 2016, thirty-six dead refugees have already washed up on the coast of Turkey. In 2015, almost 3,400 people died in the Mediterranean between Greece and Turkey—drowned and washed ashore, despite the supposedly safe lifejackets. "Bad weather discounts"—what a grotesque concept.

DATA AND FACTS: LESBOS, SPRING 2016

- Lesbos (or Lesvos) is the third-largest Greek island and the eighth-largest island in the Mediterranean. According to the 2011 census, the island has a population of 86,436.
- About 38,000 people live in Mytilene, the island's administrative and economic center.
- Lesbos is in the northern Aegean Sea far to the east, near the Turkish coast.
- The island's economy is shaped by agriculture. The main source of income is high-quality olive oil. Other sources include cheeses (feta, *kasseri*, and *ladotyri*), ouzo, fishing, and salt extraction from the Gulf of Kalloni.
- The word *lesbian* is derived from the island's name, as the Ancient Greek poet Sappho wrote lyrical poems

about, among other things, same-sex desires, particularly between women.

A COAST GUARD INTERCEPTION

Slowly the sky in the east turns red, and after a picturesque drive across the island on narrow, curving roads, we reach the small bay. It is still completely quiet here; no boats have arrived during the night, although the sea, even overnight, was unusually calm for February. A crowd of young people are milling around, scanning the sea and grabbing their binoculars from time to time. Several wear reflective vests. I ask them where they come from. Many of them are Norwegian, some from Holland and Ireland; one, a doctor, is from the States; others have come from Great Britain. It is impressive that these mostly young people have used their vacation time to be here, at their own expense, to help. I'm sure that eventually I will find representatives from every country in the world here on this small island. Thousands of volunteers—it is simply beyond belief.

A Norwegian father, here to help with his daughter, is the first to see them: "Boat approaching with roughly twenty-five refugees on board," he announces. Everyone seems happy at the news. At the welcome stall on the beach, sandwiches are spread, tea and coffee prepared and decanted into flasks. A couple of men change into neoprene wetsuits to help people out of the slippery inflatable boat and through the water. But it's all for nothing. The Greek coast guard intercepts the boat on the open sea, takes the refugees on board, and leaves them at Petra, a port in the northwest of the island. From there they will be bussed to the Moria refugee camp in the middle of the island for registration. At the bay of Skala Sikamineas, the helpers would have given the refugees warm clothing, served them tea, and massaged their ice-cold feet before the bus journey, which is why these young people of all nations are disappointed. But it is probably better that the refugees boarded the coast guard ship—it's safer than getting out of the rubber boat and walking ashore on loose and slippery stones. So far, so good. The fifteen Frontex boats together with the Greek coast guard now have a single aim: to save lives. Previously, they went to the assistance only of people in distress; the rest were allowed to head for the Greek coast without interference, nobody stopping them.

Beginning March 2016, five NATO ships will patrol the Mediterranean. They're supposed to make the lives of the traffickers more difficult and deposit the refugees back in Turkey. In my opinion it doesn't make much sense: because the traffickers simply take the money, launch the inflatables, and vanish, there are hardly ever traffickers actually on board. Many aid organizations are incensed by these actions: people want to get out of Turkey and into Europe. During my visit, however, this is all at the planning stage. Greece and Turkey, though both NATO partners, are in no way acting toward each other as partners—rather, the opposite. So a joint operation with NATO ships should be less of a militarization of refugee politics and more of a trust-building exercise between Greece and Turkey. It certainly makes sense to stop the business of trafficking and to end the chaos in the Aegean; the NATO ships could at least defuse the refugee crisis here. But the flow of refugees will not end as a result: 2.8 million people are stranded in Turkey, most of them in shabby accommodations. Only from the middle of January 2016 have they been allowed to work, and then only if they had been in Turkey for longer than six months. All of them want to leave as soon as possible, and to beach their black inflatable dinghies at the crack of dawn somewhere on Lesbos, Kos, or Chios. Europe is so near.

ORANGE MEMORIALS TO THE DROWNED

On Lesbos everything is now working fairly well. Day by day, aid for the refugees seems to be better organized—nothing like the chaos of last year, when tens of thousands camped out on the streets, desperately waiting, freezing and wet, for a ship to take them to Athens. In 2015, half a million people arrived in the EU through this small island. By late summer everything here had collapsed. The stadium near the port became an open-air waiting room. Water, food, medication, even simple basics like socks were all lacking. People ended up marooned: nobody was registering them, nobody taking fingerprints, let alone helping them with daily needs. Even though everyone on the island did what they could, the refugees were simply too many. "We were completely and utterly overburdened," Angela, my interpreter, tells me later.

We drive back to Mytilene. Vangelis, my driver, is keen to show me a garbage dump—a very special dump, he stresses. Curious but skeptical, I agree to a detour up into the mountains. A stony road leads us up a steep slope and beyond a curve to a gleaming, bright orange mountain: a massive heap of old lifejackets and a backhoe scooping more lifejackets from the back of a truck onto the ever-growing mountain of plastic. The lifejackets come from the island's beaches, where people drop them as soon as they reach land—lifejackets for which they paid handsome prices, and which we now know don't save lives because they are filled with substandard materials that become saturated and drag people under instead of keeping them afloat. In my view, these are not lifejackets but deathjackets. The unforgettable orange mountain is, I realize, a memorial.

The Chinese artist Ai Weiwei also recognized this. Vangelis is proud to have driven him in his cab. Ai Weiwei created an installation in Berlin from 14,000 orange lifejackets salvaged from Lesbos. His temporary art installation on the five columns of Berlin's Konzerthaus was created for the Cinema for Peace gala. The artist is now planning to erect a monument on Lesbos to draw attention to those who have drowned on the way to Europe. It is hard to imagine a more poignant memorial to the refugee drama on the high seas.

I CAN'T GET the image of the dump out of my head. We drive back in silence to Mytilene, where I have a meeting with my interpreter, Angela. I would rather have gone to the hotspot in Moria, but we can forget about that: first an email application had to be made and approved in Athens. This is a recent development. The bureaucracy is functioning now, and that's certainly not a bad thing, especially with so many journalists, hailing from the United States to Japan, all here on Lesbos to research and report on the Greek island.

In the harbor, a Frontex ship is docking with refugees on board. About 200 more refugees have landed with their inflatable boat on the southeastern tip of the island near the airport. They squat next to the lifeboats or below the radar mast; their orange lifejackets stand out against the dazzling blue sky. I am reassured to notice that here too things are well organized—the officials have allowed women and children to disembark first, then the fathers, and finally the younger men. They all board a UNHCR bus, which will transport them straight to Moria.

On the docks, hundreds of outboard motors are neatly lined up, and a Frontex man explains that these are just half, if that, of all the motors that have been retrieved. Frontex and the Greek authorities plan to auction them off. Vangelis tells me that the rest of the motors—the ones left behind on the beaches—will be sold back to Turkey. Vangelis, it turns out, is well informed about everything that happens to the refugees on his island. To begin with, I find it difficult to believe him about the motors, but then I read that in Turkey the production of outboard motors is booming because the traffickers are running out of them, so some secondhand motors are simply being sold back to the Turks. I myself have witnessed how quickly the boats are dismantled and carried away after the refugees have landed, and I find it highly plausible that a new secondhand market is emerging—yet another side effect of the refugee crisis in Europe.

Now we drive to the local hospital. Last year 100,000 women and children were treated here, at a cost to the clinic of over U.S. $1 million, as I learn from the senior duty physician. Treatment is free of charge, just as it is for the Greeks. The ear, nose, and throat specialist tells me that many children arrive with throat and ear infections, often severe because during the long journey they received no treatment at all. Some refugees have been traveling for a year or two, often including long stays in Turkey in conditions far from humane.

The head of the maternity ward dejectedly tells me that many women give birth in the inflatable boats or on the beach right after landing. Vangelis recalls the time he drove the husband of one of those women and their other children to the hospital. The husband told him in broken English that his young wife hadn't wanted to board the boat in Turkey as her contractions were coming at increasingly shorter intervals, but that the trafficker had held a pistol to her head and forced her in. Both mother and child were healthy, which must have been a relief. The doctors kept them in the clinic for ten days, although the family wanted to press on as soon as possible, first to the Macedonian border, then through the Balkans to *Alemania*. The resolute doctor, however, says that she managed to put her foot down for the sake of both mother and child.

She goes on to tell me that she just couldn't understand why, sometimes just one day after birth, they *needed* to move on, despite exhaustion, despite having been wet through when they got to the clinic. "They endanger their own lives and the lives of their babies," she says. But the experienced obstetrician can do nothing to stop it. In her thirty-five years of medical practice, she has never had anything like this refugee drama. "You just have to do what you can to help," she says ruefully. The likely plight of the young mother and her baby on their travels through Europe to Germany weighs on her. "All pregnant women require special care," she adds. Toward the end of our talk she tells me with a smile, "Some of the babies are now little Greeks—the parents name them after their rescuers." It's one of many such pleasant gestures.

FOR THE SAKE OF HER CHILDREN

PIKPA is one of the smaller reception camps for refugees on Lesbos. It consists of ten wooden huts, a number of large white tents, and thirty to forty volunteers from all over the world. Previously it was a summer camp for children. The volunteers, mostly men, are busy setting up further accommodations—huge white tents made of a thick material intended to withstand wind and rain but also to offer protection against the strong sunlight. It is almost as if they know that the refugee drama on Lesbos isn't over yet. Today is a quiet day in this peaceful spot.

Here I meet Janna, a 54-year-old Syrian from Helab. Our interpreter is a young Palestinian with a *keffiyeh*—a checkered black and white scarf—draped around her shoulders as a political statement. She has an Israeli passport and is here to help out during her four-week vacation.

Janna sits at a round table in front of her wooden hut. Smiling cordially, she begins with her most important message: "If I'd had no children, I'd never have left Syria." As if to confirm this, she shakes her head then rearranges her headscarf, which sits loosely on her head. She and her family lived for three years in Turkey, in Mersin, close to the border with Syria. Her husband managed to find a part-time job—or rather, a starvation job. Money, which they could have used, was not involved: his Turkish employers paid him exclusively in goods. The rent for their small house with two rooms, without water or electricity, was $475 a month.

Janna's eldest son, in Sweden, decided that they must join him there. It would be a long, expensive trek. The first stop on their journey was Izmir, where one of her other daughters was living. Then, after an arrangement with traffickers and some last-minute packing—only one backpack was allowed—they were taken to a beach in the north. There they had to wait for two nights, in a minibus without seats, huddling on the floor with fifteen other adults and ten children. Finally, silently ducking and weaving through the undergrowth, they made their way to the water and jumped quickly into the inflatable boat, their destination Lesbos. Janna's husband agreed to skipper the boat, although he couldn't swim and had no experience of steering a rubber boat with an outboard motor. Later the couple show me photos that a friend took on the boat with his cellphone. The smugglers quickly pocketed the money for the passage and lifejackets—$950 per person, no reductions for children, plus $75 for the lifejackets (yes, the same deathjackets previously mentioned)—and disappeared.

Janna, her husband, and the three children still with them made it to the south coast of Lesbos, ending up at the hotspot in Moria, where they were registered. Then it was on to the PIKPA camp, which they are now hoping to soon be able to move on from, to Athens and from there to Sweden, to join their son. They don't want to take the Balkan route; they believe that their son will manage to get them visas for Sweden, enabling them to fly from Athens to Stockholm. But that is all in the distant future.

While we talk, Janna slices cucumber and potatoes, preparing lunch for the family and speaking of her hope that they'll be permitted to leave the camp soon. PIKPA is the third stop on their journey but infinitely better than being stranded in Turkey. The children play on the floor and Angela draws some objects, writing down the English words for them. She's clearly passionate about teaching. Janna's youngest daughter is certainly enthralled, and quickly grasps the meaning of the words and repeats them.

AT EIGHT O'CLOCK in the evening, the huge ferry *Ariadne* will depart Mytilene bound for Piraeus. The ferry takes eleven hours to reach Athens, stopping off at Chios on the way. With room for 1,800 passengers, it is not much smaller in capacity than the *Queen Mary 2*. It is, however, considerably cheaper. Tickets for the passage are $48 to $75, depending on whether you book a lounge seat or a cabin berth.

Two hours before departure there are already long lines of refugees, the migrants, the displaced. Many families have tiny children; some younger women hold hands; I see a lot of unaccompanied youths. Everyone is beaming, laughing, making V-for-victory signs as they swagger up the gangway into the belly of the ship. The few belongings they have left after long journeys are stuffed into backpacks or carried in new suitcases. I read on my phone the latest news about Macedonia allowing only Syrians and Iraqis with valid passports across the border.

Tonight I especially notice two very young women here, one holding a baby, the other a huge backpack. They hold hands and are full of happy anticipation. I hope that they both have valid passports with a record of the baby. Behind them now is the flight through the war zone to Antakya, then on to Lesbos via Izmir. Before embarking, the young mother has been given a small teddy bear for the baby by one of the volunteers, and the baby has been given a pill so that he can rest calmly. The two sisters and the baby have been traveling for twenty-five days so far. It's yet another of thousands of stories that deeply touches me.

On Lesbos a rumor is circulating that people from Afghanistan, Pakistan, and Eritrea are being sent to camps and then being deported as quickly as possible. The situation in the camps is grim—hardly any food supplies, far too few tents, and all this in winter too, in the cold and rain. Idomeni is now the destination to head for. The drama that will beset the small town close to the Macedonian border has not yet begun. The refugees are still full of hope, persevering in their thin tents and certain that they will be setting off on the Balkan route the next day. They don't yet know that this will come to nothing.

But now, I stand next to the gangway, watching the stream of people board. "Good luck!" and "Have a safe trip" is all I can say to them. I'm choked—1,800 migrants and refugees, most of whom have lost their homes or left them behind in the rush to flee. What awaits them on the long and hard trek through the Balkans? Will the border even be open? Or will they be forced into the hands of yet more traffickers in an attempt to find new routes through Albania or Italy? One thing is sure: none will allow themselves to be held back. They have been on the move for too long, and the living conditions in Turkey were too dire.

On the way to the ship earlier today I witnessed another admirable example of the selfless commitment of the international volunteers. They set up a long row of boxes filled to the brim with warm clothing, better backpacks, umbrellas, and cozy caps so that the refugees could be better equipped for the next stage of their journey. Now women distribute bottles of water for the almost twelve-hour voyage to those waiting in line. Games and stuffed animals are pressed into children's arms.

A 20-year-old Pakistani man asks me about his chances of being granted asylum in Germany. I didn't dare to say "zero"; instead I ask him if he has a passport or ID. Answering my inquiry—or rather, if I'm being honest, my diversion—he tells me that he has neither but assures me that his parents could send them on from Pakistan in no time at all. However, something is not quite right about his story: without a passport or other ID, he wouldn't have been able to buy a boat ticket, but he had one. He showed it to me proudly. Regardless, on parting I wish him too "Good luck."

A HUGE, RED full moon rises in the dark sky above the Turkish coast, illuminating everything, as at eight o'clock sharp, the *Ariadne* sets sail full of people in hopeful anticipation—finally, Europe. I, however, am heavy-hearted, and tears well up in my eyes. My God, what else lies ahead for these people? They will disembark tomorrow, early in the morning, in Piraeus, the famous port of Athens, joining thousands of others already stranded there. The Greek authorities used to organize buses to the Macedonian border, but the crossing is now closed. These refugees will all have to wait at the border. Barbed wire and tear gas, even against women and children, is all they can expect there.

Greece, reeling from the austerity after almost six years of a debt crisis, is the first country to collapse in the refugee crisis. The 1,800 from the *Ariadne* will join the roughly 10,000 refugees who have been waiting there since the middle of February, all desperately hoping to move on, preferably along the Balkan route—hoping against hope that it will again become accessible, walkable, that it will reopen. All those not wanting to head for the Macedonian border are camping in the passenger hall in Terminal E7 in Piraeus, on bare floors without beds, not even for children or the elderly. Some manage to make improvised beds by pushing metal benches together, but most just sleep on the floor. Athens's Victoria Square has long been home to migrants who sleep in the open air. The Greek government intends to host 50,000 refugees, but Greece no longer has any money and is hoping for emergency funding from the EU, as Greece's immigration minister, Ioannis Mouzalas, points out frankly in a TV interview the next day.

SOMBER AFTER SEEING the ship off, I return to my boutique hotel in downtown Mytilene. I don't dare think about what is brewing up in Idomeni. The weather forecast on my iPhone displays rain, wind, and a high of 50 degrees Fahrenheit (10 degrees Celsius).

I've planned an early start for tomorrow, this time heading to the east coast, south of the airport. If the wind is in the right direction and not blowing from the west toward Turkey, boats will land there—at least this is what a Dutch volunteer told me earlier this morning in Skala Sikamineas. Now we bump into each other again on the harbor promenade. He's on his way to his aid organization to find out whether there is any new information from the Turkish side. "Okay, then, see you in the morning."

PROFESSIONAL VOLUNTEERS ON THE BEACHES

At four on the dot, I get up, shower, and download German newspapers onto my iPad, so that before I leave I'll have all the latest news, especially about asylum policies, Greece, and Turkey. Vangelis arrives punctually and we head south. When we arrive we see the first of the countless volunteers and the huge white truck belonging to the Boat Refugee Foundation, a Dutch organization. Dave, one of the volunteers, tells me that yesterday he was on a boat in the bay of Skala Sikamineas helping the Greek coast guard pick up people from the refugees' boat. They were all Yazidi women and children, and were conspicuous as they were not wearing headscarves. The coast guard dropped them off in Petra, on the west side of the island, from which they were transported by bus to the hotspot in Moria. It was certainly a good decision to take the women and children on board at sea. It's always safer and drier than an unsteady landing on a stony beach, even though the sandwiches, hot tea, sweaters, socks, and foil wrappers (for warmth) prepared by the volunteers are not then used.

While Dave and I are talking, one of his colleagues sights a boat heading straight toward us, despite a hefty headwind. The Spanish, Dutch, British, and Greek volunteers organize themselves quickly and professionally. The men climb into their wetsuits, as the boat has to be pulled closer to shore. They can usually expect about sixty people on board a boat. The coast here is extremely stony. Another ten minutes, five, and the helpers begin to wave to the refugees, a warm greeting after a long, dark night on the sea.

Then everything happens quickly. The volunteers pull the heavy, black inflatable boat as near to shore as possible, placing large stones next to it to make disembarking easier. Women and children first: here too the old maritime rule is upheld. They are pale and drenched to the bone. A young man from the boat surreptitiously and modestly wipes away tears with his hand, turning aside as he notices me. Two babies are crying; their father presses them close to his body so that they don't fall into the water during the beaching maneuvers. Everyone seems exhausted and scared. On the shore, a tearful mother hugs her two children, who bravely watch the volunteers remove wet socks and replace them with warm, dry ones. Gray blankets are spread out so that the women and children have somewhere to sit. They're all deeply relieved: they've made it. Most of the people on the boat have come from Afghanistan and Pakistan. The volunteers briskly place thermal foil wrappers beneath the pullovers and jackets of those who are freezing cold. I forget to take photos or write notes. Instead I join in and learn how to knot the corners of the foil, thread it behind their outer layers, and pull it over their heads and back down the front so that they're protected back and front. A new jacket on top, and the new, warming "rescue package" is complete. A friendly Brit hands out cups of warm tea in plastic beakers. The UNHCR bus is already standing by. The lines of communication are working. Everyone is relieved and happy—refugees as well as volunteers. A young doctor hands out bandages and painkillers and urges people with more serious complaints to go to the outpatient clinic in Moria. Those afflicted nod in appreciation.

But at the same time something else is happening: the locals, like vultures, swoop down on the boat, taking everything—the not-so-effective lifejackets, the outboard motor, harnesses, even the boat's slatted wood floor. Everything gets packed onto their pickups and into trucks. Recycling has attained new heights here.

As forecast, it has begun to rain. I hope that other rubber inflatables will not arrive now. "Our" refugees, at least, are now sitting in a dry bus on the way to the reception camp 5 miles away, one of five hotspots or registration centers planned for Greece. On Lesbos, these are surrounded by double fencing 10 feet high, topped with barbed wire, but, Vangelis tells me, the fences are remnants of Moria's time as a military camp. Inside the fences are tents, plastic huts, and containers. Any migrant who wants to get to Europe has to pass through one of these centers. While I was on the island, 2,000 refugees were registered each day. Often as many as ten UNHCR buses arrive at Moria in the morning. The refugees then wait on benches in front of a container until their number is called. Frontex officials examine the submitted documents particularly critically, in daylight, and maybe that's not such a bad idea. Ten international NGOs have permanent access to the camp. They prepare breakfast and bring lunch and supper. Nobody has to sleep outside—1,300 beds are prepared and ready for use.

THE WOMEN AND CHILDREN OF KARA TEPE

When there's no room in Moria, refugees are directed to Kara Tepe, a municipally run camp to the north of Mytilene. During my visit there, not all the tents and containers are occupied. A friendly man gives us a guided tour. He is called Aimar, and comes from Libya. He fled here three years ago via Turkey and has been granted asylum in Greece. He works now for ActionAid, an NGO based in England that mostly cares for unaccompanied women and children.

We meet Amal from Homs, Syria, who on Aimar's request has stopped to talk to us, her two children clasping her hands. She seems open, enthusiastic, and positive, which she has every good reason to be: last year her husband got to Saarbrücken, Germany, with their third child. Now she's just waiting for her permit to join them with the other two children. Aimar translates that things are not looking too bad. We're allowed to take photos of her, and she assures me that she'll learn German as quickly as possible. Her son in Saarbrücken can already speak German pretty well, she tells us, before setting off to town with big, jaunty strides. We're left to cross our fingers that the family reunion really does takes place.

At noon, Linda, from Syria, awaits us at the PIKPA camp, where we previously spoke with Janna. Before the meeting, Angela and I buy some cookies for the children. The store owner is curious why we're buying so many, and when we tell her about the refugees we're planning to meet, she crams another huge bag with goodies for free. It's amazing how kind and friendly the islanders are.

Then we're off to our meeting with Linda. She's 42 years old and grew up in well-to-do circumstances in Latakia, on Syria's Mediterranean coast. She tells us she never had to work. Angela can translate everything directly this time because Linda now speaks fluent Greek. But the war changed everything for the attractive, fun-loving young woman. Her brothers and sisters left Syria long ago, her friends too. Latakia became home to a Russian airbase with over fifty bombers—Antonovs and Tupolevs—supposedly deployed on missions against ISIS terrorists. Observers confirm, however, that the Russian pilots mostly drop their bombs on areas controlled by rebel groups, thus supporting President Assad. Anyway, Latakia is anything but a quiet city. It's been stuck in the middle of a war. But Linda had already decided to flee. She packed away U.S. dollars in her money belt; for the cab ride to Beirut, a trip costing about $30, she used the rest of her Syrian pounds. She aimed to reach Turkey via Lebanon and the Beirut airport before the Lebanese–Syrian border closed in January 2015. She flew from Beirut to Mersin, in southern Turkey, close to the Syrian border. From there she took a train to Izmir, where her brother lives. Everything up until then ran smoothly. After three days in Izmir, she had even managed to contact some traffickers. Two days later she was sitting in a dark inflatable boat at midnight with too many other people. It was supposed to be twenty in all, but that's always what happens—as many people as possible are crammed into the small boats, often forcibly. This time it was almost fifty. She couldn't count them all, she tells me later. The people-smugglers demanded $1,300 for the crossing. "Everything's perfectly safe, no problems," they said. That's what they all say. I hear it time and again on Lesbos.

But then there *was* a problem, in the form of the Turkish police. No one had heard them, let alone seen them in the dark. Linda is still panic-stricken as she tells me how the police attempted to destroy the boat with stakes and rifles. Then chaos breaks out among the refugees—people screamed, fearful for their lives. Water was swamping the boat and already up to her chest. All the bags, backpacks, duffels had long since sunk or floated off. Linda grabbed her phone from an upper jacket pocket and in desperation contacted Médecins Sans Frontières—and they came. They warded off the police and helped the refugees to get the flooded boat shipshape. It was successful. After midnight, slowly and still frightened, the men, women, and children glided out to sea and headed for Lesbos. Linda was exhausted and could only hope there was enough fuel to get them to the coast. At dawn they found themselves in luck: the motor had held out, the boat hadn't leaked, and they hadn't been intercepted by the Turkish coast guard. The Greek Red Cross was waiting for them on the beach, welcomed them all, and took them away for registration. Since then everything has been fine for Linda.

She recounts her story with sparkling eyes and spirited gestures, saying how happy she is now to be here in PIKPA—how she wants to repay the kindness, to give something back, especially to the Greek Red Cross, whose members treated them so well right from the start on the beach. Linda, who has since learned Greek (Arabic is her mother tongue), is sure that she can help in some way. Her asylum application in Turkey was, believe it or not, processed in one day. She has already filed her application for a work permit. Once that's been accepted, she wants to lend a hand and to show her gratitude. And she already is. "I love Greece," she says, beaming at Angela, which makes our interpreter visibly happy.

THE NEW UN High Commissioner for Refugees, Filippo Grandi, visited Lesbos on one of his first trips, in late February 2016. This pleased and encouraged the people here, as the Italian had been in office only since January 1. On the island he was shown everything: where the refugees land at night or at dawn, how they are registered, then provisioned, and finally taken on the huge ferry to Piraeus, Kavala, or Thessaloniki. "I will be your ambassador," the impressed commissioner pledged to the people of Mytilene. "If Europe tolerates what is happening here, what kind of Europe have we created?" Grandi seemed angry as he added, "Europe has not shown much solidarity, but here we see the best face of Europe."[1]

This has also been my experience here. Greece, already reeling from its financial crisis, now has to cope with tens of thousands of refugees. How is this supposed to happen without European assistance? Chancellor Merkel is banking on Turkey, but everything I hear on Lesbos about Turkey from Syrian, Afghani, and Iraqi refugees didn't sound too promising. People—and after all, it is all about people—have not been treated humanely in Turkey. Why then are we shoveling billions of dollars there instead of supporting the afflicted Greeks? At least Brussels, together with the governments of individual European nations, announced €700,000 in emergency aid in the winter of 2016, available until 2017. It is to be hoped that these funds will actually be used to help those in need on the Macedonian border and in the already existing hotspots and refugee camps in Greece.

BURIED

After *Bild*, a German tabloid newspaper, describes Lesbos as "The Island of the Dead," I decide I must visit the cemetery in Mytilene to see how many refugees are actually buried there. It's not all that easy—we're allowed access only with written permission from the cemetery office. This can be collected at the administrative offices, but only between 10 and 11 a.m. It's too late now, so I'll have to try again tomorrow.

Instead, I meet up with a couple of hard-working Lesbians in a small bar near to the harbor—and yes, the islanders of Lesbos really are called Lesbians. In the fall of 2015, the two women started knitting small caps and scarves for refugee children, always in pretty matching colors. Now twenty women meet every Sunday and exchange ideas. The rest of the week they knit caps. They show me plastic bags bulging with their little works of art.

At the start of the project, they went down to the beaches trying to help the freezing children put on their caps and scarves. The women quickly recognized that the aid organizations were far better equipped to help, so now they take bags full to the brim directly to the camps to be distributed there. They manage to make 150 sets a week, which makes the women happy and gives them the feeling that they're making a useful contribution. At least 400 women's groups all over Greece knit for refugee children. They're connected to each other via Facebook, and give tips on YouTube on, for instance, how to make a pom-pom. This may be a small initiative, but it's a good example of the compassion of people in Greece.

I'M TOLD THAT another 2,000 refugees were registered in the hotspot at Moria yesterday. Afterward they trekked downtown with their papers and letters of confirmation, waiting on park benches or the quay walls for the ferry to Piraeus or Kavala. What I see on television doesn't seem to have reached the refugees yet: the numbers of refugees stuck in Idomeni on the Macedonian border, the demonstrations on the highway to Thessaloniki, chaos at the port of Piraeus—testimony that, as of now, Europe has not yet found a common course out of the refugee crisis.

When I arrived on Lesbos in February 2016, there were said to be 22,000 refugees in the country. But here on the island I know that 2,000 arrive every day. The people-smugglers won't stop sending inflatable boats to Europe—it's far too lucrative a business: 60 people per boat each paying $850 yields over $50,000 per trip. With 2,000 refugees on Lesbos alone, that amounts to over $1.7 million per day.

That is scandalous. And the situation hasn't improved with the deployment of five NATO patrols between Turkey and Greece, taking refugees on board and depositing them back in Turkey. In fact, just the opposite: the refugees have lost their money but they haven't lost their will to flee. Displaced people never do.

At least here on Lesbos, they are well cared for by hundreds of relief workers, who provide them with clothing, water, food, bandages, and medication at the military base at Moria. Small-scale commerce has developed too, with kiosks and stalls selling SIM cards or backpacks. Downtown, some people are doing a roaring trade selling sleeping bags, umbrellas and raincapes, and phone chargers—not the kinds of items that used to be sold in the heyday of tourism here. The absence of tourists is a worry that touches everyone on the island, a bitterness in this chapter, because people made a good living from tourism on Lesbos. Now both the local tour operators and hoteliers claim that reservations for the summer are down by 70 percent, especially for package holidays. On the other hand, hundreds of Frontex police officers and many European volunteers occupy rooms in hotels and guesthouses. This must be profitable in the otherwise quiet month of February, but the fear of a slump in the summer to come, the summer of 2016, remains.

THE NEXT DAY we actually succeeded in getting a permit to visit the cemetery, using photocopies of Angela's ID card and my passport. We wander silently through the imposing Greek cemetery. Way back, at the edge high above Mytilene, we find the graves of the Muslim dead, some of them nameless, hastily buried. Around the graves are mud and dirt and even a garbage heap. I find the names of two children, side by side, 2 and 7 years old; their 30-year-old mother is buried nearby. I learn later that the father was the only member of the family to survive. His wife and children drowned: how on earth will he ever come to terms with that?

It is especially sad for the Muslim relatives of the deceased because in Greece, graves are cleared after three years. This is not so among Muslims; according to the Qu'ran, they are not allowed to be reburied. With thick, heavy clods of earth on our shoes, Angela and I trudge back to the entrance. Some hundred drowned refugees are buried in this small graveyard alone. How many more will it be before finally nobody else has to flee?

Dramas play out all over the island. The locals are suffering too. They suffer along with the refugees. We take a final look out to sea, to the run-down fortress, to the beach where, as on almost all the beaches, are scattered lifejackets in all colors and sizes. Where, I ask myself, are the people who wore them? I watch the evening news and I see that angry Afghani and Pakistani refugees have blocked the highway to Thessaloniki because they are not being allowed across the border to Macedonia; the traffic jam stretches to Austria. It's raining; it's cold. How will this drama unfold? I worry about these people, people who have fled war, assassinations, insecurity, and bombs, not because they're dreaming just of a better life. Nobody leaves his or her home willingly—I'm convinced of it—and Angela, my worldly-wise interpreter, agrees with me. They flee because they want to live in *peace*. Is that so difficult to grasp?

CHAOS IN GREECE

On March 20, 2016, an agreement between the EU and Turkey to secure the Schengen borders came into force. From this point on, all refugees who survive the dangerous passage in a flimsy boat and land on a Greek island must declare whether they want to make an application for asylum in Greece. Two Syrians die of heart attacks on the beach on arriving on Lesbos after a stormy passage. Did the hopelessness of their situation and the thought of life in a refugee camp overstrain their hearts? Who knows.

Now if refugees don't apply for asylum in Greece—for instance, in the camp on Lesbos—they will be sent back to Turkey, where they will be received together with €6 billion from the EU. The repatriation, as it is officially called, began two weeks later, on April 4. In this "one in, one out," deal, for every Syrian deported, another Syrian who had tried to reach Europe but through legal channels is granted access to a European country. Other deported nationals—Afghanis, Pakistanis, or Iraqis—have to remain in camps in Turkey for the time being. The whole process is intended to stem the flow of smuggled refugees entering Europe illegally—to ruin the businesses of the traffickers. But migrants from countries other than Syria, whether fleeing from civil war or out of financial necessity, will also be deposited back in Turkey. Is this not just another form of trafficking in people? Is Europe simply paying a ransom? And, above all, what about people's rights to asylum? That is the key question about this agreement. Germany is not the only country with the right to asylum firmly anchored in its constitution, but all other European states have come to an agreement about EU rights of asylum. This means that every single refugee asking for asylum has to be heard and to have his or her individual case considered.

Another critical point is linked to this agreement: in order to send refugees back to Turkey, Greece has to first recognize Turkey as a safe third country. The government in Athens plans to get the process started in April 2016. It is interesting to note that for this acknowledgment, Turkey does not need to fully ratify the Geneva Convention on Refugees; it merely has to offer protection to refugees in accordance with the convention. It is precisely this point that Greece should scrutinize.

In any case, asylum-seekers are entitled to have their individual cases examined by Greece. They could avoid deportation by proving that in their case, Turkey isn't a secure country. All asylum-seekers must have the opportunity to present their concerns in a court of law—such are the terms of the agreement. In the first weeks after this agreement was ratified, some 8,000 refugees landed on the island of Lesbos; they are now stranded, some of them living in inhumane conditions, especially those at the former registration hotspot at Moria, which is encircled by high fencing with barbed wire on top, and which nobody can leave.

The aid organizations have scaled back their operations in protest against the EU agreement. The UNHCR no longer ferries refugees from the beaches to the camps. The highly efficient rescue system is in disarray. Once more, it is the refugees that suffer the most.

Although Greece was represented during the drafting of the agreement in Brussels, the country and its infrastructure were in no way prepared for the outcome. Now they are desperately juggling to find space for 50,000 refugees, the number they promised the European heads of government they would take. But it's a slow process. Europe sent 4,000 experts from Brussels as quickly as possible, but they don't plan to visit Idomeni, where, since spring, 13,000 refugees have lived in thin tents, in mud and dirt, and without proper provisions. How is this possible, when after every earthquake or other environmental catastrophe emergency structures are set up within hours? Are the Greeks deliberately doing nothing? A number of refugees speaking to international TV journalists say that they will not yield—that after their long flight to the Macedonian border, they would rather die here than turn back. They plan to ignore the EU agreement and press on to "Europe," not to apply for asylum in Greece. Who can blame them? Not after all the hardship and fear they've experienced. And the refugee drama is far from over: as long as wars rage, people will flee.

A CHANCE AT EUROPE?

When this book first goes to print in Germany, most of the refugees I am meeting on Lesbos in the early spring of 2016 will still be stranded in Greece, in the tented settlement in Idomeni . . . in the mud and the dirt and the freezing cold. It rains so much there that you would think the good Lord is crying for the poor souls stuck there. The numbers in the camp fluctuate—sometimes 12,000, sometimes 14,000, mostly Syrians but also many Afghanis, Pakistanis, and Iraqis. The Syrian group, in particular, includes many families. The children feel the cold very quickly in this situation. They lack medical care.

Two thousand desperate refugees tried to wade across the river to reach Macedonia, but at the end of the fence, the Macedonian police were waiting for them and sent them back. Three drowned in the river on the way back. This information didn't even make it to the TV news.

The fact is that in March 2016 there is no chance of anyone continuing on the Balkan route by crossing into Macedonia from

Idomeni. All they can do is to take a bus back to the middle of Greece, to one of the refugee camps recently established there. Since the closing of the Macedonian border, about 50,000 refugees have been stranded in Greece. And despite the agreement between the EU and Turkey, hundreds, sometimes thousands, join them every day. In Turkey the traffickers are apparently making "last-minute" offers to smuggle people across the sea at even higher prices—utterly beyond contempt.

In March and April 2016, the refugees in Idomeni certainly don't want to give way. The settlement has been left to its own devices, as officially it doesn't exist. A few aid organizations provide for the people there. The air, according to radio and TV reporters, is pungent. Everyone tries to generate a bit of warmth by building little fires in the open air. Is Idomeni the last chapter in the refugee story of 2015–16, a story so rich in human drama?

Now the great bureaucratic machinery is cranking up. All refugees arriving in Greece after March 20 have to register and to say whether they want to seek asylum in Greece. Those not wanting asylum in Greece are bussed to camps and sent back to Turkey as quickly as possible. Asylum applications will be judged in high-speed processes and either accepted or declined. According to EU regulations asylum-seekers are allowed to appeal rejection. This sets in motion a long legal procedure that also has to be handled in Greece. So in addition to all the other problems, Greece is facing immense administrative tasks. Germany and France were the first European countries to offer Greece assistance and are sending officials. In spring 2016, 4,000 EU experts arrived in Greece to help. The other signatory states in Brussels agree that Greece cannot be left alone with this Herculean task. And everybody hopes that soon the refugees at Idomeni will back down, accept the closed border, and apply for asylum in the country of entry in Europe, as planned in the Schengen Agreement. In any case, in March 2016, the first steps were taken to solve the refugee crisis in a European, democratic way—in a way that corresponds to European values.

NEW ROUTES...FOR MEN

It is the closing of the border that offers the people-smuggling business its big moment. In the blink of an eye, new routes are being forged. The first runs from Turkey across the Mediterranean to Italy by fishing boats or small merchant ships. They set out from Antalya, where European holidaymakers get their suntans. A second route begins in the port of Mersin near the Turkish–Syrian border. Where will the refugees land? Apparently, they only learn that once they are on board, once they have paid $3,000 to $5,500 for the passage. There are supposed to be two trips per week, each with 200 people crammed together on board—average takings of $835,000 per trip.

Business, in spring 2016, isn't yet in full swing. Too dangerous, say many, especially for families with women and children. But by summer, when the EU agreement begins to bite and the refugees deported from Greece begin to arrive in Turkey, the traffickers will be able to finalize their million-dollar business, using ships where the whole crew knows the score and shares the profits.

A third route goes from Greece through Albania then either the north by car or across the Adriatic to Italy by ship. The journey through Albania, however, is arduous, especially for families with women and children, as the borderlands between Greece and Albania are mountainous. There are no trains, and people making it as far as Montenegro or Bosnia run the risk of treading on the mines that still plague these countries.

One thing is certain: people will continue to try to reach Germany, but for women and children the routes will become more dangerous and more difficult. Those attempting to enter through Bulgaria have to get past the infrared cameras and cleared forests at the border. Romania is protected by the Carpathian Mountains; Serbia is a dead end as all the Balkan countries try to seal off their borders.

Another route being discussed in Turkey is by boat across the Black Sea to Romania, then cross-country by land and up into the almost impassable mountains. This route is exhausting and hard to overcome for women and children. On top of the other hindrances, Polish border police patrol the border with Slovakia because Poland has very clearly stated that it won't accept any refugees. The bottom line is that there are routes, but they are expensive and long, and often cannot be undertaken by families with women and children. These will have to remain in the camps in Turkey, Lebanon, and Jordan. As in 2015. As always.

SEVEN

EUROPE

MIRYAM'S STORY

PART 2

ALL'S WELL THAT ENDS WELL?

The Italian police are kind to the woman with five children. They all receive warm clothes, like all the rest of the 150 refugees in the boat. They are given something to eat—Italian cuisine, she later tells me with a sparkle in her eyes. Her only complaint is that she has to have her fingerprints taken. She tries to refuse, but hundreds of other refugees are in line behind her, the sun burning their faces while they wait for registration. Back in Syria, Miryam's contact helping her to flee had cautioned that if she wanted to stay in Germany, she should give information—her name, her passport, her fingerprints—only to German officials. But the Italians continue to exert pressure, threatening her and the children with prison. Miryam speaks neither Italian nor English. How did she manage to understand the Italian police then? I ask. By using her hands and feet, she tells me. So there is a sign language that works all around the world.

In Lampedusa, she reluctantly dabs her fingers on the blue ink pad, presses them down on the card, gives her name, and shows her passport, which, as her most precious possession, she has wrapped in plastic and kept close to her body. The officials then try to reassure her: "Just one more night in the camp, in a six-bed room with bunks, then off to Milan by plane." Sounds good, sounds hopeful.

The small children and Miryam's older daughter are brave. None of the children cry and the older ones are in a good mood. They all know what is at stake—their future. They are allowed to take a shower, and after the weeks in Libya and the days and nights on the open sea, they feel as if they are in paradise.

Early the next day they are taken by bus to the local airport—the one small airport, with an extremely short runway, for the tiny and, since the influx of refugees, anguished island. In 2014, 170,000 people from North Africa, Syria, and Afghanistan flew out from here; in 2015, three times that.

It is only 700 miles by air to Milan, but the plane made a stop in Palermo, arriving at Milan four hours later. The refugees are given drinks on the Alitalia flight—cola for the children, their favorite. Miryam just drinks water. She leans back and looks down at the "boot" of Italy, which she's seeing for the first time in real life. What will the following days bring? How will they travel on now that they're registered in Italy, even though she insisted that she wanted to go to Germany?

She can't know what is happening in Germany at this very moment. "People seeking asylum in Germany need luck. If out of luck, they end up in tents, bus depots, or living containers on the water," wrote the *Süddeutsche Zeitung* newspaper back in September 2014.[1] Its readers didn't know that this was just the beginning. In Neumünster they're planning to erect tents for all the refugees; in Munich the migrants will have to sleep in a bus depot. There's not enough room in the reception centers. At least they should have known this in 2014. German Minister of the Interior Thomas de Maizière spoke of an "extremely tense situation."[2]

A method using population figures and financial standing as guidelines for calculating the capacity of each state within Germany to accommodate refugees, called the "Königstein key," seemed a reasonable solution, and German politicians seriously thought that they had solved the problem. In practical terms, it meant that populous North Rhine–Westphalia would have to absorb 21 percent of Germany's refugees, and tiny Saarland just 1.2 percent. But when measles and chicken pox broke out in the overcrowded quarters in the month of Miryam's arrival, both North Rhine–Westphalia and Bavaria announced that they were stopping their intake of refugees. This will not be possible in 2016 as there will be not 16,900 people applying for asylum but double that.

AT THE AIRPORT in Milan, a man holds a sign saying "We will help you" in Arabic, and Miryam, with the children in tow, approaches him. He seems trustworthy; besides, what other option do they have in the huge airport? Other refugees join them and they are all taken by bus to, again, refugee quarters on the outskirts of the city. Miryam throws the tiny backpack on the bottom bunk, which she will have to share with Amir. It's now lunchtime. Food? "Across the yard is a canteen. You can get something to eat there," says a friendly Arab man who helps refugees on behalf of Milan's Muslim community. First, feed the children, then mull over what to do next. How on earth are they going to get to Germany?

This question is cleared up that very evening. Some North African men amble through the corridors, popping into the rooms. "Germany? No problem," says the small fat one with a moustache. His offer is, for $600, everyone, in a private car, through Switzerland to Frankfurt. This sounds promising to Miryam, but it means using the very last of her savings. She agrees, and plans are made for setting off the next morning—departure at eight o'clock, after breakfast. And now straight to bed, especially the little ones. They're tired and grumpy today, which is hardly surprising as they have been on the move for four weeks now. That night Miryam sleeps soundly. They have a solid roof over their heads, unlike the nights on the boat. No noises or explosions like there were at home during the war. Tomorrow they will reach Germany. *Wunderbar!*

The journey of around 450 miles is expected to take seven hours, plus time added for breaks, for both adults and children. There's enough room in the vehicle for everyone. The driver is as strict about seat belts as possible. Two of the girls, Djamila and Kalila, laugh while securing them: They'd never used seat belts in Syria. Different country, different habits. They've traveled far enough to know this now.

WE'RE SITTING IN Miryam's living room in the container settlement in Hamburg, a year later, laughing over the story. "Once we got to Frankfurt, things really started going wrong," she tells me, though. I find it hard to believe her. She seems to be implying that compared to Frankfurt, the whole trip up until then had been a piece of cake. In Frankfurt, they were yet again registered. The police then carried out a "total search," as Miryam phrased it. She means a complete body search, including all openings—a demeaning experience for her and her daughters. Okay, it was a policewoman who carried out the search, but for a Syrian woman, this ordeal was nonetheless simply horrific.

I ask her where she hid her money during the flight. "In my bag," she tried to make me believe. "And nobody thought of looking there?" I ask her skeptically. "Believe me or not, but that's the way it was!"

AFTER "TREATMENT" BY the Hamburg policewoman, the police take the last of her money, just over U.S. $50, and buy food for the whole family. Then they take the mother and children to a platform, between two trains. Miryam and the children are supposed to lie down there and spend the night. Miryam is stunned. No blankets, no mats, nothing—just stretch out on the bare platform. The train to Hamburg is supposed to depart at six in the morning. That is her destination, and that is where she wants to go. Even the people-smugglers in Syria drummed that into her. So, at almost midnight, they lay down their weary heads; the mother, her four daughters, and Amir have no other choice.

It is quiet now on the tracks of the main Frankfurt rail terminal. They cuddle together, cover themselves with their jackets; the mother giving hers to the two smallest children so that they will be well covered. It's one o'clock in the morning, and in the distance the drunks are brawling and rampaging. The children fall asleep quickly, even though the platform is rock hard. Miryam doesn't sleep a wink. On top of everything else, she's worried about Akilah, who clasps Amir tightly in her arms.

At five o'clock Miryam wakes the girls and sends them to the washroom two at a time then finally goes herself with Amir. Before she does, an official brings them free train tickets for Hamburg. Now she hasn't a single euro left, not even in her pockets. Hundreds of other refugees get on the train with them, including some who were on the same boat. They greet each other sleepily. Then they're on their way again. Last stop—or new start: Hamburg–Harburg... wherever that is. Later she shows me photos on her phone of the children on the platform at Frankfurt. "That's where we lay down; that's where we slept."

FIRST IMPRESSIONS

The six of them sleep soundly during the trip. The night was short and uncomfortable. But the InterCity Express is fast. After just four hours, they alight at the main terminal at Hamburg. Miryam looks around inquiringly. She, with her headscarf, and the five children are immediately recognizable as refugees. Two women approach her, one asking in Arabic where she wants to go, what's written on her papers. The volunteers take the children by the hand and walk them through the station hall to an area where at least 250 other refugees have spread themselves out. Unlike Miryam last night, they've been given colorful blankets to place on the tiled floor. They sit cross-legged in circles. Miryam is afraid that she too will have to wait here, another night on another station floor. One of the volunteers fetches an Egyptian woman to interpret then she tells the disconcerted mother that these refugees have been there since the weekend and are waiting to go on to Sweden. Riots near the station, traffic jams, and train delays had driven the people back into the station. Miryam notices that a number of them are holding train tickets tightly in their hands; others are deep in conversation with security people. Bored children are dashing through the station and fooling around on escalators.

But Miryam's family, with the help of the volunteers, continue to the refugee tent. First they all get something to eat, and a few plastic chairs so they can rest their feet. A man inspects their papers from Frankfurt a little more closely. "You will have to travel on," he says. "You weren't supposed to get off at Hamburg—you need to go to Harburg." Miryam has misread her destination, an easy mistake in a foreign alphabet when just one letter is different.

The same thing, I think, must happen to many refugees. Harburg is the site of the first reception center, and in a strange country with a strange language, it's easy to swap an *m* and an *r*.

In the months following Miryam's arrival, thousands of other refugees will pass through the Harburg facility. By a year later, 1 million migrants will have reached Germany. According to the Königstein evaluations, Hamburg is obliged to take 2.5 percent of the refugees, but they take on more—35,000 in 2015, and political trends clearly indicate that it won't have been fewer in 2016. Certainly, not all of them wish to remain there permanently—not all of them can remain there permanently.

Hamburg, in any case, is prepared, and has tackled the stampede with admirable composure and professionalism. The average time for processing asylum applications in Germany is 4.2 months; Hamburg, however, manages to process them in just 2.7. Fördern und Wohnen (Aid and Habitation), a nonprofit that assists a wide range of groups, from the homeless to the disabled to refugees, is expanding, with thousands of Hamburg citizen volunteers, without whose help the project couldn't exist. Another example of popular commitment: in one Hamburg neighborhood, 800 migrants had to leave their thin tents to be rehoused in wooden huts in time for winter. Local carpenters and joiners put in extra shifts at night and the weekends, and in short order the first huts were erected on the island in the River Elbe—with proper double beds not camp beds, central heating, and electrical outlets, one per person—vital for recharging phones... a masterpiece of organization.

Just down the river, ships providing living quarters for more than 2,000 refugees are also fully occupied. "Ships Not Tents" is the motto of the governing Social Democratic Party in Hamburg, whose representative for social issues has stated, "We're standing with our backs to the wall." He'll soon have to be even more creative in finding accommodation for thousands of refugees. But the politicians are loath to tie up more ship berths, which are much in demand where luxury cruise ships can anchor near the high-end shops, office blocks, and busy jogging trails. What about the inland ports outside the city, or on tributaries to the Elbe—wouldn't they be suitable? All options will have to be studied. But the ships have to be docked near a school and where there is public transportation to towns and cities. There is plenty still to be decided in September 2014, but Miryam knows nothing of these background maneuvers.

Harburg's refugee facility and initial reception process seem like paradise to Miryam and her children. Miryam affectionately recalls a year later, "It was so beautiful there, the support staff so friendly and loving, I never wanted to leave." She was allotted a room with six beds. A bed of her own! That was quite something. Men and women were in separate quarters, which meant the situation with the showers and toilets was a little more relaxed. She fondly remembers the abundance of clothing.

They were allowed to stay there for two weeks. Then it was made clear: next stop, Alsterdorf. "That was a shock for us," Miryam says, of Alsterdorf. "No comparison to Harburg. My daughter immediately had a bladder infection. It was anything but clean there." She is still shaken by the experience.

Her daughter's infection worked in their favor. Miryam and the children were granted preferential treatment and they moved to the Fördern und Wohnen facility in Hamburg-Stellingen, where they live now. It was a stroke of luck: three rooms plus a kitchen, a shower, a TV set; shared laundry next to the building offices; mentoring for the whole family; and a bus stop right outside the front door. The girls don't have far to go to school. Amir can stay at home with his mother. He needs her the most, and nestles up to her while we sit on the floor enjoying Miryam's homemade hummus with pita bread . . . and cola, of course—it's impossible to live without it.

Akilah is also living here, reunited with her husband. Their first baby is expected in two weeks, and they're better off here as they can reach the hospital quickly when the time comes.

Akilah, is a gentle, slim (despite being heavily pregnant), and extremely beautiful young woman. She got to know her husband in the canteen at Stellingen. "Love at first sight?" I ask, being typically direct. She laughs and looks aside bashfully. But it really seems to be the case between the young woman and Hassan. They'll be moving into an apartment north of Hamburg after the baby has arrived.

How is Miryam coping a year and three months later in Hamburg, in Germany, in Europe? "All the children go to one school. We're safe here. It's peaceful, which is great." But—and it's a big "but"—they're still waiting for recognition of their asylum status. The German officials initially turned down Miryam's application because she had her fingerprints taken on Lampedusa for registration. That's how the Schengen Agreement works: those entering Europe have to register their asylum applications on entry at the border. Miryam didn't do this, as she wanted to go to Germany. Now a lawyer is working on her case, and she can stay in Germany through that. But she desperately wants to be *properly* accepted here, to have her asylum status made official, with all the rights and obligations that go with that.

I suddenly realize that Miryam hasn't talked about her husband for a long time, and I ask what has happened to him. I seem to have touched on a delicate subject, one she doesn't want to discuss. She's always been prepared to talk about her flight and her children, but she doesn't want to talk about her husband. I later hear that he is in a reception center in Papenburg and visits occasionally. He too managed to flee Syria, but the couple seem to have separated. In any case, Miryam tells me later, she lives alone and that's the way she wants to keep it.

During our conversation the children sit captivated in front of the TV, watching cartoons. Does Miryam watch Syrian TV, like the women in the camps in Lebanon? "No, we don't have the right receiver here." But they do watch Arabic TV—they can tune in to Al Jazeera via cable. And other news? News from home, from family and friends? A shadow falls across the pretty face of the still young woman. Of the eight sisters, four are still in Syria, but they have nothing to eat, nothing to keep themselves warm; their homes have been destroyed. They live together now in a sports stadium. It's a terrible state of affairs. Tadmur, Akilah's husband's hometown, has been completely destroyed. None of his family live there now. He doesn't know where his parents or brother are. He too has yet to have his asylum status confirmed, although he has been living in Germany since 2013. But now he is about to be a father, and has a new family with his wife, Akilah, with Miryam and the children. At least that's something.

COCOONING TO SURVIVE

Miryam and her family didn't follow a lot of what was happening in Germany, even in Hamburg, in the first year there. They sealed themselves off, protecting themselves somehow, after all their bad experiences in their home country of Syria. Did she have contact with other Syrians, other Syrian women? I ask. Miryam nods but adds that they don't have any *close* contacts. Everyone seems to be busy with their own lives. They go shopping near the refugee facility, where, fortunately, they can buy many of the familiar things for Syrian cuisine, things the children like. They like the head of the container village, with the funny name Lila; she is friendly to everyone and looks after them. She's handing out calendars now because the refugees often have trouble keeping appointments.

Miryam knows nothing about the German newspapers being full of stories about refugees, that day after day and night after night people are dying in inflatable dinghies while trying to flee. Since she phoned her sister, she's had trouble sleeping. She can't get the images conjured up by her sister out of her head, and she's very concerned about her family. The lawyer who was recommended to them and is appealing the rejection of her application tells them time and again that she is not the only Syrian woman refugee fighting for asylum and that Syrians are the largest group of refugees, ahead of Afghanis and Iraqis. But for the time being, that's not important to Miryam. She just longs to be recognized as an asylum-seeker. "And then we will dance the whole night long, here in the apartment." She smiles, adding, "But only once I've recovered from fainting at the decision."

Like all asylum-seekers in Germany, she receives €149 a month under the Benefits for Asylum Seekers Act. Multiplied by six, that's €894 for the whole family. She pays no rent for her unit in the container village and nothing for heating. Still, I can feel the cold creeping up through the floor after two or three hours of conversation sitting cross-legged on the floor. On top of this they receive a regular "hygiene package" of $85 from the German authorities. Finding clothing for the whole family is not a problem, either: thanks to the generosity of the people of Hamburg, the depots of donated clothes are full, and as winter approaches, there are enough warm coats, underwear, caps, and gloves for all. "We didn't need any of these things in Damascus," says Miryam with a sigh. Well, maybe sometimes, she adds. Is she homesick? If so, only for the good times—the times before the war that has dragged on for five years now.

HAMBURG HAS BEEN good not only to Miryam. The city is friendly toward refugees. In 2014, Hamburg spent about $70 million on aid for refugees, almost $250 million in 2015, and in 2016 the figure is expected to rise to $273 million, which will pay for the accommodation and support for the arriving refugees, for security officials and organizations, language classes, and extra lessons for the children. The huge clothing depot, with its stacks of boxes of clothing weighing many tons, is expanding. The times when over 1,000 people were housed in a single massive hall are over: conditions are improving, with more, smaller reception centers. The portable toilets have been returned. Hamburg and its volunteers are managing. However, after the closing of the Balkan route, it's not clear how the next wave of refugees will reach Germany. But they'll find a way—maybe via the Black Sea and Romania, or through Italy, or via Lampedusa, like Miryam and her family.

Two-thirds of all refugees in Hamburg are from Syria, Afghanistan, or Iraq—65,000 of them came through here in 2015; 22,315 remain, not including an additional 1,400 unaccompanied minors. The minors receive particular care and attention.

At the end of 2015, however, heated discussions arose in Hamburg about refugee housing. Small container villages, like Miryam's in Stellingen, don't bother anybody, but in two other neighborhoods, the city had plans for living quarters for 950 and 700 refugees. Courts agreed with the residents that the numbers were too high. Now community groups are negotiating with the municipal council about smaller facilities, which, the plaintiffs say, make integration easier. The burning issue in the city remains, however, the thousands of refugees living in precarious conditions—in large complexes, gymnasiums, even army tents, albeit with heating.

But there's also good news coming out of Hamburg. The first refugees have started apprenticeships combined with language courses: 80 percent of Hamburg businesses are admitting refugees on internships, and 70 percent of all Hamburg companies want to include refugees in other training schemes. That's an impressive confirmation of the humanity of civil society.

But the Hamburg hairdressers take the cake. Under the banner "Free haircuts for refugees,"[3] the Hearty Hairdressers of Hamburg, with 330 members, believe that looking after the migrants' hair and beards has "something to do with self-esteem," as one of them put it so nicely. The hairdressers come from salons all over the city every weekend because they want to do something positive, and many consider it their chance to show Germans in a different light. Their first customer was a 16-year-old Syrian who sat beaming on the barber's chair and wanted his hairstyle to be "a little more German." They all broke down laughing, including the interpreter, without whom they wouldn't get far. Back to the essentials: learn German quickly!

WHEN MIRYAM AND the children are a bit more settled, maybe one day they'll go to the theater that, in the afternoons, becomes a "language café" and meeting place for Syrians, Afghanis, Somalis, and Eritreans to speak and learn German with the Germans of Hamburg. They talk about their troubles and worries, and for many it's the only place they go outside the refugee camps or official buildings. There is also free wifi—very important for many of them.

Six other "welcome cafés" have opened in Hamburg, and they've gone down well with the refugees. Miryam, however, lets her daughters out alone only for the trip to school; the rest of the time they're in her sight. She's too steeped in Syrian culture, which ordains that pretty girls have to be guarded, not to do this. Akilah is now being looked after by her husband, so at least Miryam has one daughter less to worry about. She's more concerned, though, about the health of her children—that they eat good food, rich in vitamins. The cafeteria serves plenty of fruit and vegetables, which is not part of their traditional diet. There are many news reports of warnings by Hamburg pediatricians that refugee children, in particular, suffer from a lack of vitamins and are underweight. But other than that? Miryam's life seems to be taking a smoother course, even though every day she eagerly awaits the decision that she will no longer be tolerated but properly recognized, be granted asylum. Until then the children go obediently to school, their German improving by the day. Miryam, unfortunately, isn't attending integration courses and hasn't started taking German lessons yet. "Too much work to do at home," she tells me every time we meet, even though the two older girls are always busy helping her out with the housework.

AKILAH HAS GIVEN birth to her baby, a girl. For the first couple of weeks after the birth she and her husband will stay with Miryam. It's now pretty cramped in the container apartment. They'll just have to squeeze together and spread out mattresses on the floor. It will work out somehow, and for the young mother it must be reassuring not to be far away at first with the new baby. The father of Miryam's children has announced that he plans a visit with them during the Easter vacation. Space will be even tighter, but he'll have to return to his own place, which seems to put Miryam's mind at ease. She still doesn't want to talk about the reasons for separation, but they must be serious for a Syrian woman with five children to say that she doesn't want to live with her husband anymore. After all, she planned her flight without him, followed through without him, and, thank goodness, survived the ordeal without him.

We stand together at the front door as I put on my shoes, Miryam laughing her warm, young laugh. Christina, our interpreter, says that she is also separated and getting a divorce next month. We women understand each other, especially regarding men. Miryam seems to be bearing a heavy load that she hasn't yet dealt with. But she has found some peace, and that's a start. No more bombs, no war, a steady life with the prospect of a better future: Miryam has arrived.

Seve's large Yazidi family live in two tents in the Kurdish camp in Fidanlik. (Photo: Peter Müller/BILD-Zeitung)

The Turkish army provided and erected tents for Syrian refugees in twenty-five camps dotted along the border. (Photo: Peter Müller/BILD-Zeitung)

A mother and daughter despair. ISIS terrorists murdered Sari's husband and two of her sons. (Photo: Maria von Wesler)

Their goal: as little movement as possible. When the thermometer climbs to over 100 degrees Fahrenheit (38 degrees Celsius), life becomes unbearable. (Photo: Maria von Wesler)

The once beautiful city of Kobanî, destroyed by ISIS, sits on the Turkish–Syrian border. (Photo: Peter Müller/BILD-Zeitung)

Resmis wants to leave Turkey as soon as possible and rebuild her house in Kobanî. (Photo: Peter Müller/BILD-Zeitung)

As always, children make the best of the situation and play between the tents. (Photo: Peter Müller/BILD-Zeitung)

These Syrian Kurds want to return to Kobanî and have been waiting at the Turkish border since five in the morning. (Photo: Peter Müller/BILD-Zeitung)

EIGHT

GERMANY

2015–16

There are dates, years, that are fixed in memory. For Germans, 2015 will always be the year of the refugees. That year, 1.3 million asylum-seekers arrived in Germany; 1.1 million of these were officially registered, while the rest entered the country as "illegals," as they say. It was the biggest wave of refugees since the end of the Second World War seventy years earlier. Syrians, Afghanis, Pakistanis, Iraqis, Eritreans—all of them applying for asylum. Politicians have spoken of the refugee influx as the greatest challenge since the reunification of Germany, almost as if the nuclear disaster at Fukushima, the 2008 financial crisis, and the Greek threat to leave the EU were child's play in comparison. But they aren't, and never were.

Foreign people in our own country, and with a different language and religion at that—this was too much to bear for many Germans, but, fortunately, not for all. Since 2015, there has been a cleft in German society: on one side, the welcoming culture, saying, "We can do it"; on the other, the worriers, who don't believe that 81 million Germans can cope with 1.3 million "foreigners"—even though the majority of Germans have migrant roots themselves, even though after the Second World War the state of Bavaria alone absorbed 6 million refugees. So what happened in Germany?

Part of what happened is Angela Merkel. No chancellor before her has polarized Germany like Angela Merkel. A rift appeared between men and women, regardless of political affiliation, dividing families and marriages, and separating society as a whole. Heated debates flared up around the question of how we German Christians should deal with the mostly Muslim refugees, all sparked by Merkel's stoic and often-repeated sentence "*Wir schaffen das.*" With this remark, she cast her protective mantle around all the refugees arriving in Germany. In a book about women and children in flight, the role of this one German woman cannot be underestimated.

In November 2015, *The Economist* called Merkel the "indispensible European." For years she has topped the *Forbes* list of the most powerful women in the world. But in Germany, the headlines in *Stern* in January 2016 read, "Angela against the Rest of the World." The news magazine *Der Spiegel* declared that "the clock's ticking," meaning that Merkel's time as chancellor was nearing its end. In the capital, Berlin, augurs murmured about "Merkel's dusk."[1] How can a single politician cleave a country to such an extent? What's more, a woman not from the extreme left or right but from the center-right?

What follows is a chronology of the most important events in Germany's year of the refugee, in an international context and highlighting the crucial role of Angela Merkel over those momentous months.

UNICEF'S 10-POINT PLAN TO PROTECT CHILD MIGRANTS IN THE EU*

1. Recognize and treat all migrant children always, first and foremost as children with rights as set out in the UN Convention on the Rights of the Child.

2. Apply existing laws and policies to safeguard and protect the rights of children affected by migration, including monitoring and enforcing the consistent application of the EU Anti Trafficking Directive and Strategy, with special focus on prevention, reduction of demand and prosecution of those who exploit and abuse child victims.

3. In all decisions, authorities should be guided fundamentally by the Convention on the Rights of the Child—the best interests of the child—including in decisions on international protection, granting or refusing applications for residence as well as decisions regarding transfer or return.

4. Protect migrant children by reinforcing integrated national child protection systems and taking EU-wide action to drive up protection standards and address cross-border protection needs as proposed by the European Commission guidelines on "Integrated Child Protection Systems."

5. Children should not be put in detention centres and should not be separated from their family for migration purposes.

6. In search and rescue operations at sea, uphold International Maritime Law and long-held custom to save and protect lives.

7. At all times during and after search and rescue operations, children and pregnant women must receive special care and attention.

8. All children—regardless of their or their parents' legal status—must have equitable access to quality education, health care, including mental health, social protection and justice.

9. All children should receive equal and consistent protection, without any discrimination based on their or their parents' nationality, residence or migration status, or race.

10. Invest in tackling the root causes for people fleeing their homes through comprehensive approaches addressing risk reduction, emergency response and development.

---

*Source: UNICEF, "Put migrant children's rights on EU agenda, urges UNICEF," press release, May 12, 2015, https://www.unicef.org/media/media_81876.html.

APRIL 2015

Aydan Özoguz, German commissioner for migrants, refugees, and integration, complains that Germany, Sweden, and France bear most of the burden for feeding and accommodating the refugees, and criticizes other European countries for doing nothing. German Minister of the Interior Thomas de Maizière follows a similar line shortly afterward, criticizing Greece and Italy for releasing refugees into the Schengen Area without registering their asylum applications. "They're just waving them on," he says—a sentiment we will hear often. By spring it has become clear that the situation is complex. The UN High Commissioner for Refugees declares that in the long term, Germany and Sweden alone cannot absorb the majority of refugees.

MAY 2015

Angela Merkel, de Maizière, and center-left Social Democratic Party leader Sigmar Gabriel meet with the heads of the German states in the Chancellery for the first summit on refugees. At the press conference afterward, the chancellor declares: "We are determined to find a solution."

One is needed. By the end of the month, ISIS has seized Palmyra and destroyed pre-Islamic monuments. ISIS now controls 50 percent of Syria.

JULY 2015

German politicians desperately look for ways to speed up asylum processing, with a goal of deporting claimants from Serbia, Bosnia-Herzegovina, Macedonia, Kosovo, Albania, and

Montenegro, who account for around 46 percent of applications. The first three have been considered "safe countries of origin" since 2014; the last three will be also after October 2015. People from these countries no longer fulfill the requirements for asylum in Germany, and their applications are given priority so that they can be removed more quickly. Applications of asylum-seekers from other countries—Syria, Iraq, Afghanistan, and Eritrea—are pushed back. At the same time it is decided that asylum procedures for refugees from the Syrian war zones and for Christians and Yazidis from Iraq should be simplified, and asylum for these groups should be granted without the usual hearings. The so-called revocation procedures are dropped.

But resistance grows. The staff of the Federal Office for Migration and Refugees (BAMF) claim that this fast-track process is unconstitutional. Without identity being established in person, there is no certainty that someone who claims to come from Syria actually does. Recognition is to be conferred when an interpreter identifies a refugee as a Syrian, but the interpreters don't necessarily come from Syria and are not under oath. The requirement to grant status to refugees with Syrian passports is also hotly debated by the public, especially after reports emerge of forged Syrian passports—passports that ISIS troops stole during their military campaigns. The situation in Germany, in terms of both the flood of new information and the national mood, becomes more critical.

AUGUST 2015

An average of 3,000 people a day seek refuge in Germany. In July 2015, it is announced, BAMF received 37,531 applications for asylum. The government releases new refugee forecasts, now speaking of 800,000 migrants.

In this summer of 2015, Europe has been trying to abide by the Dublin Regulation. Since it came into force in 1997, the Dublin Regulation (also called the Dublin Procedure) has determined the country responsible for assessing an asylum application lodged in an EU member state by a third-country national: the country in which the asylum-seeker first enters the EU is responsible for processing the application.

But with the sheer numbers of refugees now entering Europe, especially via the Balkan route, the governments of Hungary, Austria, and Germany are at loggerheads. Government actions correspond in no way to the Dublin Regulation. Sometimes it is applied for a while only to be abandoned later. At least half the refugees landing in Italy travel on to other European states without having been registered or applying for asylum. In the first quarter of 2015, Germany registered 40 percent of all asylum applications in Europe; Italy over the same period recorded only 8 percent, and the same for Greece. Chancellor Merkel is forced to admit that "the Dublin Regulation no longer reflects the circumstances we once had."[2] But this isn't only about other countries: Germany no longer sends asylum-seekers back, not even to Italy or Greece, and certainly not Syrians. During the German summer of 2015, the situation becomes increasingly more dramatic.

On August 25, a BAMF press release announces that the Dublin Regulation has been suspended for Syrian refugees. The consequence: Angela Merkel is inundated with messages of admiration from Syrian refugees. The next day, Merkel speaks to refugees and refugee workers at the emergency hostel in Heidenau, where there have been serious anti-immigrant clashes.

Then, on the last day of August, the chancellor makes the statement that will go down in history: "*Wir schaffen das*"—we can do it. She speaks of a great national mission. German TV, day after day, shows thousands of refugees trudging along on the Balkan route in the summer heat, often barefoot or just in socks. The August sun burns them mercilessly.

"WORLD CHAMPION OF HEARTS"

SEPTEMBER 2015

The first rumors circulate on the Internet, particularly on Facebook and WhatsApp, reaching the refugees: "Germany is granting entry to all remaining refugees." The chancellor declares on September 1 that Dublin III (the most recently amended regulation) applies. But the flow of refugees on the Balkan route is ever increasing.

The next day, the photograph of drowned toddler Alan Kurdi is seen around the world. It sparks a worldwide movement in favor of refugees. In the UK, "Refugees Welcome" becomes a viral slogan. The UK pledges to bring in more refugees, but it will opt out of the EU distribution plan. U.S. president Barack Obama's White House announces that the country will accept 10,000 Syrian refugees by 2017, and New Zealand prime minister John Key adds 750 to the country's quota. Australia will take an additional 12,000 refugees from Syria and Iraq, in spite of controversy over the treatment of refugees who arrive by boat and are held in offshore detention centers. The photograph has particular strength in Canada in the middle of a federal election:

the Kurdi family hoped to find a home there. Syrian refugees become a key election issue.

The day after the death of Alan Kurdi, Merkel defends German refugee policies against attacks by Hungarian prime minister Viktor Orbán. Orbán claims that the refugee problem is a German problem and has ordered the erection of a border fence between Hungary and Serbia. Thousands of refugees are stranded in Hungary, sleeping in the Budapest train station, on the streets, and along the railway tracks. Merkel's reply: "Germany does what is morally and legally necessary—no more and no less. Isolation in the twenty-first century is not a solution."

On September 4, the Dublin Regulation is suspended again—this time not just for Germany. Merkel and Austrian chancellor Werner Faymann agree, after consultations with Hungary, on a departure from the Dublin agreement. The suspension is termed an "emergency measure" in an "emergency situation." Refugees are now allowed to pass through Hungary to Austria or Germany without being registered. This is a moment many people will never forget—certainly not the refugees who, after weeks of exertion, no longer have to endure closed borders.

In the fall of 2015 Germany becomes the "World Champion of Hearts."[3] The reception of refugees in Munich and Hamburg, Berlin and Düsseldorf, and many other places in Germany is touching and impressive—inspiring, even. It is a signal against xenophobia, against resentment, hateful tirades, and violence. Hundreds of thousands of Germans become involved, standing by their country that had seemed to be impotent on its own. Germans knuckle down at train stations and in schools, in nurseries, in clinics, in mother–child facilities. And not just for a few days, no: for weeks, months, against all predictions that they would quickly run out of steam. People who were once themselves aliens in Germany also pitch in—immigrants, political refugees, civil war refugees from the Balkans, Russian expatriates. At local, state, and national levels, something outstanding is being accomplished. Fully 40 percent of the population want to actively help refugees; 34 percent are willing to donate. Chancellor Merkel declares, "This country can be rightfully proud and pleased with itself. I say: Thank you, Germany!"[4]

In September 2015, the EU heads of state and government decide "to allow 160,000 people temporary residence in a European Union with more than 500 million inhabitants. Initially Slovakia, the Czech Republic, Hungary, and Romania were strongly opposed" to higher refugee numbers, but it was only "a matter of time before they would buckle under pressure of the powerful North and West Europeans."[5]

A week later, Merkel visits a reception facility in Berlin-Spandau. A selfie of the chancellor and a refugee, cheek to cheek, goes around the world. For this image she is berated for months by a growing number of political opponents. In the refugee camps, particularly in the Middle East, the picture is a big hit.

Then, just nine days after the "emergency relief" opening of the border, controls are temporarily restored. In September alone the number of refugees crossing the German–Austrian border into Bavaria has exceeded 135,000—more than the previous eight months combined. Driven by the sheer numbers and by news media, the German government has permitted at least eight trains a day from Salzburg directly to German reception centers. Increasingly people are saying, "Close the borders, it can't carry on like this." But reintroduced border controls cause no noticeable drop in the numbers of newcomers—only longer traffic jams.

By mid-September, center-right politician Horst Seehofer is heading for confrontation with Merkel. He demands a cap on the number of refugees and the closing of the borders on the Balkan route. Merkel counters explicitly: "If we start to apologize now for showing a friendly face in an emergency, then this is no longer my country." She witnesses incredible vigor among the refugees: "It's worth looking after every single child," she says while visiting a "welcome" class where refugee children are learning German. But a majority of Germans are beginning to doubt the chancellor's crisis management.

At the end of September 2015, Russia's first airstrikes fall in Syria.

OCTOBER 2015

The chancellor decides that the refugee issue is a matter for the boss, and on October 7, the Chancellery takes over responsibility for coordination of refugee policies. Rumors abound that the Minister of the Interior will be toppled. Journalist Heribert Prantl notes "fears about Merkel's courage... The speedy first reading of the already concluded new asylum package was a prelude to a cascade of demands for resistance."[6] Men in the main parties, in particular, are fearful of their chancellor—and she, in turn, worries about voters.

Pressure is mounting on the chancellor. Male news columnists in particular foresee the end of her time in power. The planned hotspots for registering refugees on the outer EU borders are not yet functioning. Refugees in Jordanian and Lebanese camps are increasingly heading for Europe. A former mayor of Hamburg defends the chancellor: "People want to come to

Germany because there are jobs here. What is she supposed to do? Let them stay in Austria?"[7] He too believes that Germany, with its high degree of volunteer involvement and decentralization, will be able to cope with the refugee problem.

In a government statement on October 15, five days after suicide bombs killed 100 at a peace rally in Ankara, Turkey, Chancellor Merkel declares, "With the Dublin III Regulation we, in effect, shifted control to Europe's outer borders. It was a leap of faith. Today, we have to say that these controls on the outer borders are not working. This is the reason we have to rely more heavily on a common European approach: it has to be made more effective, and we have to provide more personnel. The Commission has requested up to 1,100 people. Only a few member states have registered, among them Germany and Austria. But I count on—and this must be the outcome of this European Council—other countries making a contribution. It goes without saying."

The European Council meets again two days later but can't agree on the allocation of refugee quotas. The Germans have the impression that they have to shoulder the problem alone. But Chancellor Merkel has provided the solution: "*Wir schaffen das.*" She repeats this in parliament, on talk shows, and on news programs. Germans are divided. Some stand with Merkel. Others, and their numbers are increasing, side with the populist movements AfD and PEGIDA and the Bavarian head of government, Horst Seehofer. Seehofer wants stricter border controls and a firm cap on refugee numbers, and he is prepared to do anything to persuade the chancellor to change her policy. Merkel should also, he says, tighten asylum laws—something that was never mentioned before the wave of refugees. The chancellor strikes back: "Isolation and blockading are illusionary in the age of the Internet."

ASYLUM TIGHTENED

OCTOBER 2015

In Canada, the election of Justin Trudeau's Liberal government after a campaign fought partly on increasing refugee numbers from Syria and on opposition to the Harper government's announced hotline for reporting "barbaric cultural practices" will bring in a wave of tens of thousands of Syrian refugees, sponsored by private citizen groups, on top of the regular quota.

In Germany everything has changed. An expected 1 million refugees in a year—that is the new figure. Against this backdrop, the coalition government comes to an agreement on new legislation. The Asylum Procedures Acceleration Law decrees, among other things, that arrivals can stay up to six months in reception facilities, that cash payments should be increasingly replaced by non-cash benefits, and that only limited amounts of pocket money may be paid. Asylum-seekers who have had their applications rejected and don't leave will receive only a bare minimum. Deportations should be sped up. The list of secure countries of origin expands to include Albania, Kosovo, and Montenegro.

NOVEMBER 2015

The climate in Germany becomes bleaker. Right-wing groups become louder. The head of the Federal Office for the Protection of the Constitution, Hans-Georg Maassen, tries to calm the population: "Violent acts against refugees are not organized. There is no evidence that national structures are behind them. But violence against refugees is being committed by people who previously weren't associated with extreme right-wing groups. We see the danger that people who used to vote for democratic parties have become radicalized... people objecting to the rights of asylum but feeling that they have no possibility to influence them. They want to send out a signal and resort to violence."[8]

German president Joachim Gauck adds his own words of warning: "In an open society, it is not important whether a society is ethnically homogeneous, but whether it has a common foundation of values. It is not important where someone comes from, but where they want to go, which political order they identify with. Precisely because Germany is home to different cultures, religions, and lifestyles, precisely because Germany is increasingly becoming a diverse country, it needs the commitment of all to incontrovertible values... Our values are not up for discussion! They are what will and should tie us together here in this country. Here, the dignity of humankind is inviolable... Here, achievements like equal rights for men and women or for homosexuals are not questioned, and the inalienable rights of the individual are not curtailed by collective norms... There will be no tolerance for intolerance here."[9]

The leaders of the major parties agree on the setting up of registration centers at the border and on accelerated procedures for migrants who have little chance of being granted asylum. Yet uncertainty grows among the population. Merkel claims in a TV interview that she "has the situation under control." But the CDU and CSU present a muddled picture—nothing like unity, no joint communiqués, unlike during the bank crisis of 2008, when joint statements were released guaranteeing the security of people's savings. Such calming messages are no longer in sight.

On November 15, after a night of horrific coordinated terror attacks in Paris, the refugee debate flares up again in Germany, with new arguments. Did the terrorists travel through Germany before getting to Belgium? Without being registered? Proponents of "controlled and legal immigration" gain the upper hand. Merkel guarantees French president François Hollande European solidarity and consents to a German military contribution to the fight against ISIS. This is her first war—until now she's been able to avoid them—and its outcome is uncertain.

In addition to the discussions in Germany, Merkel has to present her position to the EU, with few willing allies. The EU decides on November 29 to grant Turkey some €3.1 billion for the care and provision of refugees in Turkey. The German press is now claiming that the chancellor is losing control of refugee policy. The first package of drastic changes to asylum rights is already in force, and party leaders are discussing more amendments. Communication between ministers is breaking down. Merkel is forced to express confidence in her Interior Minister, although it is apparent that she no longer has it. Her warm optimism and firm refusal to speak of a cap on refugees vanish when faced with the Herculean task that refugee politics has become.

DECEMBER 2015

Until year's end, the EU coalition discusses more stringent changes to the rights of asylum. The influx of refugees continues unabated. In Syria, Assad's forces have permitted evacuation of Homs and retaken it. Russian airstrikes have hit a market in Idlib. As of December 30, 1 million migrants have gone by sea to Europe, with about 4,000 believed drowned. In the United States, Republic primary candidate Donald Trump, who is rising in the polls, calls for an end to Muslim immigration.

In decades past, asylum law reforms usually ended in a tightening of asylum rules. But Germans can be proud of their constitution, which says: "Persons persecuted on political grounds shall have the right of asylum." Thus it was written in 1949, a reaction to the Nazi reign of terror that turned countless Germans into refugees. In Germany, a foreigner recognized as entitled to asylum is legally equivalent to an internationally recognized refugee, and as a rule, is granted a residence permit for three years. The exception to the three-year limit is those who have a right of subsidiary protection, meaning that they are not recognized as refugees but also that they cannot be deported to their home country because they are threatened there with "serious harm," such as death or torture. For decades the basic right to asylum was unrestricted in Germany. But while the number of applicants fluctuated, it typically remained fairly low: up until 1975, usually fewer than 10,000 a year.

NEW YEAR'S 2016

The mood in Germany will change dramatically in the new year. Everywhere people will be saying: "Before Cologne? After Cologne?" This is why.

As every other year, hundreds of young people gather in the shadow of Cologne's cathedral to celebrate New Year's Eve. But there won't be much to celebrate on this evening. Near the train station and around the cathedral, many women and young people are sexually assaulted. Young men, mostly from northern Africa or Arab countries, surround women, younger and older, clutching their breasts and grabbing them in the crotch, in some cases even getting beneath their underwear. Victims file over 700 charges. On top of being sexually assaulted, most of the victims also have their cellphones stolen. Other European cities report similar incidents that night. Cologne's police force is severely criticized, as there were too few officers in place to ensure law and order.

In the aftermath, Syrian and Afghani refugees who were not present during the assaults tell interviewers of being panic-stricken and returning to their quarters before midnight. The assaults receive widespread attention. The international press report—not without gloating—that Germany is struggling with the refugee situation. Cologne's police are accused of not having the situation under control and of airbrushing their report the next day. The chancellor is "appalled" and promises speedy explanations.

JANUARY 2016

Cologne provides ammunition for arguments that have always been strongly represented in the country—arguments against foreigners, against refugees, against things that are alien. The head of the AfD, Frauke Petry, in the wake of the shift in the German political climate, even suggests the last-resort use of weapons against refugees at the closed borders. The party's EU representative, Beatrix von Storch, adds on Facebook that it's "reasonable" to also shoot at women, but she draws the line at firing on children.[10] In the newer German states—the former East Germany—the AfD message finds support among members of PEGIDA, a grassroots protest movement whose members include neo-Nazis. Dangerous groupings of interests have formed.

AfD functionaries are now invited as guests on talk shows. And the journalist Heribert Prantl bluntly notes, "Those who begin the discussion [on internal security] with a link to refugee politics are being taken in by right-wing politicians." He adds, "The AfD should not be given the opportunity to brutalize society."[11]

The shift to the right even reaches parts of the country that have traditionally favored environmentalist, pacifist, cosmopolitan, and feminist views. For instance, after the incidents in Cologne, a tornado seems to sweep through Freiburg; even the locals agree. Night spots seek to refuse entry to refugees—because they steal, is the reasoning, but above all because they assault women.[12] The AfD is ecstatic: finally the refugee crisis has reached the left. But, as always, when you peer behind the headlines and captions, things are different. The Freiburg plan to exclude refugees never becomes reality. Only one live music club makes the attempt, intending to admit only people with membership cards issued after a briefing on the club's code of conduct. A dozen refugees appear at the first opportunity.

But other things do happen. The mayor of Freiburg has been requesting a larger police force for several years; suddenly, he gets it. If the incidents in Cologne have done any good whatsoever, then it is this: there has been some progress in tightening German laws on sexual crimes. Sexual assaults are not committed only by a few migrants but also by a great many German men. There is still a lot to do.

The German federal government also comes under pressure after Cologne, resulting in Asylpaket II, the new asylum laws. Family reunifications of refugees from secure countries of origin are suspended for two years. This mostly affects refugees with subsidiary protection. Of course, family reunifications do follow whenever there is an influx of refugees as men, mostly young men, arrive before their wives and children.

This new law includes provisions for the establishment of registration centers, and reception facilities are planned in which certain groups of asylum-seekers can be fast-tracked, to better cope with the influx, and stronger measures put in place for the quick deportation of those whose applications for asylum have been rejected. Simple illness can no longer protect against deportation; a more stringent set of criteria must be met for a medical certificate.

Even before Asylpaket II becomes law, the German government begins considering more amendments, including to grant officials the power to send refugees to specified places and to prevent them moving away while their applications are being processed. Additionally, there are plans to ensure that refugees contribute to the cost of their integration courses.

This month also, new statistics are published without attracting much attention. In 2015, twice as many asylum-seekers were deported as the year before: 20,888 foreigners had to leave the country; an additional 37,220 left voluntarily. Some 50,200 others should have been deported but for a variety of reasons weren't; among those reasons, without passports, their identity couldn't be ascertained. In early 2016, the government works with Morocco, Tunisia, and Algeria in the hope that these countries can help in the identification process. This they all promise to do. But the path to implementation is long.

"Angela against the rest of the world," writes *Stern*.[13] The chancellor is under ever-increasing pressure. Three state elections are coming up in March. The AfD, founded partly in opposition to the Greek debt crisis bailouts, is making headway on an anti-refugee ticket. The perpetrators in Cologne were demonstrably North African asylum-seekers who had entered Germany illegally. Some 2,000 refugees still land on the Greek islands every day. Most are heading for the Balkan route.

A cold wind blows for Angela Merkel. The last European allies closed their borders this month—first Sweden, then Austria. The rift between her federal party and its state-level equivalent is tangible. But the chancellor refuses to bend, saying at month's end, "It is perfectly normal to hold differing opinions within a party." She holds talks with the Turkish government and continues to negotiate with the Europeans in Brussels. Political scientists point to her "heroic serenity."[14] Her opponents continue to bray, "We have to close the borders." Former general secretary of the Christian Democrats Heiner Geissler quips, "Those suggesting bricking up the borders must be a few bricks short of a load."[15] That must have brought a smile to the chancellor's face.

RUMORS ON THE INTERNET

FEBRUARY 2016

In London on February 4, days after an ISIS suicide bomb killed seventy-one in Damascus and after King Abdullah II declared that Jordan can absorb no more refugees, a donor conference finally decides to provide funds for Jordan and Lebanon, the countries accommodating the most refugees—some U.S. $16.8 billion should help there. Germany contributes almost $3.4 billion. The UNHCR is pleased, as the previous summer the World Food Programme had to halve its monthly payments to refugees. This had been the impulse for the huge wave of asylum-seekers to move.

But fear of and prejudice against refugees and migrants spread. Cries that society is becoming "swamped by foreigners" can be heard, especially on social media, especially "after Cologne." Social inequality is increasing; the housing market is tightening; poorer Germans will soon have no chance at affordable housing... Rumors are rife, especially on the Internet.

The German economy counters these fears, supporting Chancellor Merkel's vision: *"Wir schaffen das"*—we can do it. From the beginning of the migration wave, the German economy and economists agree: immigration is good—for *everyone*. In 2015, 37,101 training positions went unfilled; high-ranking representatives of industry called for ways of making it easier for refugees to take on these apprenticeships. At that time, refugees weren't allowed to work while their applications were being considered. Many parts of the country sought to change this.

A Centre for European Economic Research study commissioned by the Bertelsmann Foundation dispels an oft-repeated myth.[16] Migrants, the study finds, are by no means a burden on social services. This is a prejudice often wheeled out in discussions about refugees. The opposite is closer to the truth: the 6.6 million citizens living in Germany without German passports pay more in taxes than they receive in services. Experts estimate the surplus paid by foreigners living in Germany at $154.7 billion, an average of $23,469 over the course of each foreigner's time in Germany—$3,500 a year. This number could rise as the educational level of foreigners rises. The study concludes that even added public spending on education for foreigners will eventually reap financial gains for the state, and thus for its citizens.

When Detlef Scheele of the Federal Ministry of Labor and Social Affairs reads in the news that asylum-seekers will take jobs away from Germans, he has to shake his head. "Germans can sleep soundly," he says. The refugees have too far to go to catch up, and the proportion of refugees is small compared with the 30-million-strong current workforce. He sees the future of the labor market as positive even if new asylum recipients don't find jobs quickly. Scheele reckons that in 2016, 335,000 refugees will rely on the social safety net. But studies show that after five years, half of job-seeking refugees have found work, and after fifteen years, 70 percent. This differs little from the data for German long-term unemployed individuals.[17]

At the beginning of 2016, a refugee costs the German government roughly €12,500 ($13,000) a year. With 1.1 million registered refugees, that adds up to about $14.3 billion. This figure, however, doesn't represent all costs: it leaves out German language courses, counseling, labor, and materials. To meet the costs, the Minister of Finance put aside €8 billion. In the first year of the refugee flood, 2,800 new staff were hired in the employment agency alone; €350 million was earmarked for them, a further €350 million for active labor market policies. Looking at the figures, you can only ask yourself, if Germany, with its population of 81 million and a famously efficient bureaucracy can't manage it, then who can?

In the winter of 2015–16 there were other incredible and surprising events. In a country where even twenty years ago refugees' homes were set alight, a touching solidarity began to emerge. From one end of the country to the other, people lent a hand, backed local governments' refugee policies. They stood in train stations in the cold with their welcoming banners, distributed clothing, served soup for days on end, helped refugees with the first bureaucratic steps. And all this was not just for a week or a month; it lasted throughout 2015 and into 2016. Finally, politicians understood what was happening in Germany. Certainly, from time to time discordant voices were raised, especially on the right-wing fringes, but most people realized that there were so many reasonable things that could be done: mentoring people from war zones and regions in crisis, preparing children for daycare and school, teaching German, offering counseling and other assistance before administrative appointments. Local authorities made empty buildings available as new living quarters for refugees. People offered jobs so that the refugees could earn a living and move into their own apartments. There is much to do still, and people are getting on with it.

THE EXAMPLE OF PASSAU

The eagerness of both citizens and the much-maligned bureaucracy has surpassed all expectations. Let's take the city of Passau as an example. Passau was under some of the greatest strain during the refugee wave—the Balkan route ends here. In just three months, 300,000 people arrived: six times the local population, a lot for a small municipality to learn to cope with. A few weeks into 2016, the local police announced, "We can cope with 500 to 1,000 people a day."[18] The mayor too was relaxed about the situation. On the day that Chancellor Merkel allowed thousands of refugees, crammed into trains in Budapest, to enter Germany, the mayor summoned a crisis team. They know all about crises in Passau: among others, they tackled the 2013 Danube River flood. Fifty Passau citizens were immediately ready for work, that very night, together with members of the police, the fire department, and the Red Cross.

Since then, the refugee routine has rolled along, day after day and night after night. One hundred of the roughly 2,000 volunteers are there every day for twelve-hour shifts, making sandwiches, serving tea, sweeping the asphalt. Thirty new positions have been created in the Refugee Office. Fifty soldiers help out. Officials claim that registration procedures are improving by the day—in Processing Line 2B, Hall 2, for example, where a police officer and an interpreter scrutinize passports, photos, and official stamps. Everything is translated into the language of the new arrivals. Officials ask if they want to come to Germany. Asylum? Some will have to join Processing Line Z . . . back to Austria. Once they've answered the questions and assuming they're not sent back, the migrants move on to the next table. Here officials are scanning the fingers of a woman and her children with a green laser; then each person is photographed. The police officer places a photo onto a grid on the monitor, storing the fingerprint in the Europol databanks. The refugee woman and her children are given a number and are registered. Name, photo, fingerprint. "The next one—next, please!" Everyone seems very friendly here. Since the sealing of the Balkan route and the EU treaty of March 20, 2016, things have become quieter in Passau. The question is, as the workers here also ask, for how long? The stream of refugees has only been slowed; it hasn't ended.

THE ENORMOUS GERMAN asylum operation is coordinated in Berlin, or, to be more precise, in the Department of the Interior. In the beginning things didn't run too smoothly. First, the extent of the situation was underestimated; then the welcoming celebrations were hyped up. Later, some localities were on the verge of collapse. Politicians seemed surprised, overwhelmed, overloaded. But in practice the crisis machinery at the general assessment center runs fairly smoothly from six in the morning on, day after day. Weekends, too—early shifts, late shifts.

All the information from around the country converges here. Here the current data, just an hour old, on refugees are analyzed. Who comes from where? How many are they? Who is still using the Balkan route? How rough is the Mediterranean right now? The army and police, supported by thousands of volunteers and experienced relief organizations, are in control. Not everywhere, unfortunately—for example, not in the capital, Berlin, of all places. There the regional authorities have demonstrated their incompetence for months. It is hard to believe that Berlin cannot accomplish what other parts of Germany manage to do quite successfully.

The refugee steering committee and the Chancellery meet once a week, so things seem to be progressing. In January and February 2016, accommodations and general provisioning of the great majority of new arrivals improve. The new objective is to reduce the numbers of new arrivals. Tasks for the coming years include faster asylum procedures and rigorous deportation of rejected applicants; language courses, practical training, and further education; housing construction; and labor-market integration. Logistics specialists in Germany will have plenty to do for quite a while yet.

FEBRUARY 2016

Criticism of the chancellor mounts: she has allowed a million refugees into the country, overturned democracy, didn't consult the people, let alone parliament; in doing all this she took Europe unawares and caused a rift, disgruntled her sister party, and broke the law. Mid-February, Merkel just says that she is "a little" disappointed with the Christian Social Union and Seehofer. Her popularity sinks. The AfD continues to gain ground in polls as the elections approach.

At the end of February, disputes in Germany about how to pay for refugees' needs heighten. The Treasury stresses that "every surplus Euro in the Federal Republic is, by law, reserved for the refugee crisis."[19] Record tax revenues are behind this announcement: in 2015, Germany saw the highest surpluses since reunification, some €19.4 billion. Financially, things are looking good—Merkel's "we can do it" seems to be justified on the financial side. As the *Süddeutsche Zeitung* reports, the government is planning for a total of 3.6 million refugees by 2020, half a million refugees a year.

At the end of the month, as a wave of Syrians flee the fighting in Aleppo, a new summit in Brussels is pending. Merkel intends to draw up an interim report on her refugee policies. Beforehand, she appears on TV. "When are you going to change course, Mrs. Merkel?" she is asked, and it becomes quickly obvious that she has no intention of deviating. It is, after all, her "damned duty and obligation" to do everything to enable Europe to find a common path. Unilateral border closings are not helpful. If one country closes its border, others have to suffer. That is not her Europe. She also objects to statements that she opened the borders in September—the borders were already open: she simply didn't close them.

MARCH 2016

On March 9, the Balkan route is closed. Macedonia won't let any more refugees through, not even Syrians or Iraqis with proper papers. In Passau, on the border, things are very quiet. Refugee workers sit in disbelief: they were prepared to be registering 500 to 1,000 refugees daily for the next few months. Now the refugees are all stranded at the tiny Greek border town of Idomeni. At least 14,000 camp out in the rain and cold in thin tents. The news hits hard in Canada, where refugee sponsors are protesting a slowdown in processing that will delay the next wave of refugees' arrival by months.

In Brussels, Merkel doesn't have a good hand for the EU negotiations with Turkey. Her pledge to reduce the number of asylum-seekers Germany accepts as refugees in 2016 rings true at the moment because of the closure of the Balkan route, but leading up to the state elections, a comprehensive solution to the refugee crisis is not in sight.

A week later, the news magazine *Stern* writes of a "divided Republic" and reports on the latest election polls in three German states: 57 percent of Germans think that none of the political parties have a good idea of how to solve the refugee crisis. Attacks on refugee hostels have increased nationwide; 83 percent of Germans are concerned about this, while 77 percent worry that large numbers of people are joining extreme right-wing groups. Thousands of followers of PEGIDA meet every Monday in Dresden, chanting right-wing slogans.

But it is also becoming clear that German attitudes to refugees themselves are in flux. In August 2015, 36 percent thought that the number of foreigners and refugees had reached an upper limit; by February 2016, that had reached 49 percent—very nearly half of all Germans.

Every day, images of refugees stranded at Idomeni flicker on German TV screens. The chancellor criticizes the closing of the Balkan route at every election rally. "Twenty-seven countries cannot just take it easy and leave one country, Greece, to solve the problem alone," she repeats time and again. But fewer refugees are arriving in Germany, and that might help her in the elections. Europe, with a population of half a billion, is presenting a pretty wretched image, both politically and morally—that, at least, is what can be read in the international press.

March 13, 2016: The Sunday of three state elections in Germany. The AfD makes significant gains, mainly because of their clear line against the government's refugee policies. But Malu Dreyer (Social Democratic Party) wins in Rhineland-Palatinate against Julia Klöckner (Christian Democratic Union) in part because she clearly backed the chancellor's refugee policies. The same applies to incumbent minister-president Winfried Kretschmann (Green Party), in Baden-Württemberg. His CDU rival had distanced himself from the chancellor, unlike Kretschmann, who records a comfortable victory. The AfD wins 27 percent of the vote in Saxony-Anhalt, but the CDU minister-president there, Reiner Haseloff, manages to form a coalition to exclude the AfD. Haseloff was the only CDU politician to campaign, against the wishes of Merkel, on a cap on refugees. Never since the building of the Berlin Wall has a crisis so affected the people in this country—whole families, people from all walks of life. This election is a barometer of the mood of the country at a time when many Germans feel that their own country has become alien to them.

THE WOMAN WHO DOESN'T CLOSE BORDERS

MARCH 2016

In the aftermath of the state elections, newspapers are claiming, vehemently, that Merkel is finally politically isolated. People are convinced that the end of Merkel's political career is imminent. *Der Spiegel* had already announced, the year before, the complete breakdown of her chancellorship (together with the failure of the euro) and continues to snipe at her, making her responsible for the apparent impending end of Europe. Besides political isolation and imminent downfall, other reasons for the supposed end of the Merkel era doing the rounds in the media are her frequent proclamations about concessions and tampering with her refugee policies—most recently shortly before the EU conference in Brussels.

In Brussels on March 17, Merkel wants, and desperately needs, an EU deal on refugee policies. She has worked for months on an agreement about Turkey. After the failure of plans for allocating refugees to all the EU member nations, settlement with the Turks is now what Merkel calls a "European solution."

March 18, Brussels: A day to remember. The Europeans reach an agreement with Turkey. All refugees arriving on the Greek islands after March 20 will be sent back to Turkey; repatriations will begin on April 4. For every Syrian deported in this way, a

Syrian refugee who tried to reach Europe through official channels will be accepted in return—the "one-to-one" agreement. In a further step, Turkey will be relieved of large contingents of refugees. The whole process will be executed "in full accord with EU and international law," as stated in the treaty signed by all the EU's heads of government and Turkish prime minister Ahmet Davutoğlu.

The day before, at a press conference, Merkel spoke of the death of her former Secretary of State Guido Westerwelle. "For me personally it is an extremely sad day," she said, then, after a short pause, she summarized the day in Brussels: "Europe will make it, Europe will survive even this major challenge." It is hardly surprising, given Westerwelle's death, that she was not radiant, but her satisfaction with the progress made was not completely concealed—after all, the plan that is now in motion was her idea. It just has to work.

ANGELA MERKEL IS anything but isolated in Europe. She succeeded in making the seemingly impossible possible, and on March 18, 2016, agreement with Turkey was reached. With this, one objective of a return to orderly conditions in Europe—that, above all, the Schengen Agreement works—became nearer. Her persistence, her tenacity, made it possible. True, the transit countries on the west Balkan route, following the example of Austria, closed their borders and brought pressure to bear on the EU—that is indisputable. Maybe they even made it easier to arrive at this settlement because of it. The most astonishing thing about the whole affair for everybody who saw the chancellor in front of the TV cameras was how calm, composed, and confident she was in weathering these times of crisis. Some people were saying that only now were we getting to know the real Angela Merkel. As one newspaper wrote, "Evidently the chancellor only begins to show her mettle in stormy times. This chancellor is seaworthy and steadfast."[20]

EPILOGUE

DO NOT FEAR

When this book is published, there will still be 60 million people in flight worldwide. Half of them will be women and children. In 2015, however, 75 percent of refugees arriving in Germany were men. Not until 2016 did more women and children than fathers, husbands, and brothers set out for Europe. Before these women started their trek with their children, I visited them in the refugee camps in Turkey and Lebanon and did some research in Jordan. Everywhere the women and children were stranded because the "stronger" men had been sent on the dangerous routes. At the end of my research, before the Balkan route was finally sealed off, I stood on the beaches on Lesbos and watched the women—mostly young mothers with children—arrive in their small, flimsy inflatable boats, all full of hope for a better future in Europe... hope for peace and a life fit for human beings. People witnessing these scenes without tears in their eyes must have no feelings at all.

So, after all these travels, all the interviews and other moving experiences, I hope that the welcoming culture of Germany will not change. I hope that the majority of people in my country will remain open to refugees from war zones, from countries that are politically unstable, from dictatorships where people's lives mean nothing. I hope that the hate campaigns of those to the right of the political spectrum, intimidating people to become entrenched behind their own four walls, bear no fruit. I expect from the Church, particularly my own Roman Catholic Church, clear statements about how we should deal with asylum-seekers and refugees: that is to say, considerately, caringly, and with help. Pope Francis's encyclical *Laudato si'* should give us strength and support in this crisis. The fact that this pope, on a visit to Lesbos in April 2016, spontaneously took twelve Syrian refugees back to the Vatican is itself a message. *Ecce homo*—behold the man. The Vatican has a population of 800, Germany around 80 million. Projecting these figures, those twelve Syrian refugees are equivalent to the 1.3 million refugees who came to Germany in 2015.

But we all need to be courageous. We who are often mockingly referred to as "do-gooders" should defend ourselves against such defamation. Former German chancellor Gerhard Schröder once demanded a revolt of the "decent." Such a movement is much needed now, in 2016, in the second year of the wave of refugees. We simply cannot allow refugee centers up and down the country to be burnt down, allow explosive devices to be thrown through windows of the places where people have found refuge. Only if we "revolt" will the necessary pressure reach the government. Only then will they stop courting the far-right fringes for fear of losing votes.

As a convinced TV journalist and publicist, I am certain that the majority of people aren't stupid and that they do have hearts.

Proof of this in Germany can be found in the election of Malu Dreyer and Winfried Kretschmann, who backed the Christian Democratic chancellor. Their party colleagues lost. This was encouraging: we have politicians with the strength of conviction to take a humane stance.

On the basis of my experiences and conversations with refugee women, I want to see urgent political action and a clear "yes" to more funding. It simply cannot be that Syria's small neighbors—Jordan and Lebanon—are kept at arm's length and allowed to starve. These countries desperately need financial support, and plenty of it. Lebanon, with a population of 5.8 million, has taken in 2 million refugees, more than a third of its population; Jordan, with a population of 6.7 million, has taken 1.6 million, 22 percent of its population. And Europe with its population of 500 million? Here there are ongoing discussions about the distribution of just 160,000 people. It's a disgrace.

At least Germany, in 2015, offered refuge to around 1.3 million people. Not all of them will be able to remain; not all of them *should* be allowed to remain—we have asylum laws with clear conditions that must be observed. But everyone covered by the asylum laws has to be treated humanely and, should they wish to remain, be integrated. Thus it is written in our constitution, and of that we should be proud.

But Turkey also needs help. That country, with 79.5 million citizens, is also temporary home to 2.8 million refugees, mostly Syrian, 80 percent of whom don't live in the twenty-five camps along the border with Syria. The EU decided in the spring of 2016 to transfer €3 billion to Turkey, assuming that the repatriation of refugees from Greece—of the ones who don't apply for asylum in Greece—runs smoothly. However, the Turkish government's handling of the Kurds and of freedom of the press should not be disregarded or forgotten.

What I fail to understand at all is why the Arab oil-producing countries don't do more to help their Muslim brothers and sisters in their hour of need. Countries on the Persian Gulf have the highest per capita income in the world but refuse to accept even a small number of Syrian refugees. They don't even send a decent-sized check, and though this was severely criticized by Human Rights Watch, it seems to have had very little effect on the governments of the Arab states.[1]

But back to the Germans. The surge of refugees shows that what we desperately need, in my opinion, is an Immigration Act along the lines once proposed by the late former president Richard von Weizsäcker, one similar to the Canadian system.[2] With this we could both offer protection to people who need it and take in the people we need. It is as simple as that. Why the Christian parties have difficulties with this is a mystery to me—after all, it works perfectly well in other countries.

If increasing numbers of women and children continue to follow their husbands, fathers, and brothers to Germany, then Germany is obliged to make allowances for their special needs. The hundreds of thousands of volunteers, the local authorities, and the states' institutions and politicians have to act. This is particularly the case regarding the needs and worries of women and children, so that, for example, reception centers have washroom facilities for women and girls that can be locked, and so that women learn that sexual violence is a crime in Germany and that it has to be reported. Enough interpreters need to be available so that the women can speak openly and don't have to be silent. It must be pointed out to the women that in Germany, at least in law, the sexes are equal and attacks on women and children are rapidly and rigorously punished. I am well aware that there is a lot to do, but with the right attitude, it is possible to see the glass as half full.

Just one more comment to the glass-half-empty faction: Fear eats the soul. It is above all to the worriers, the doubters, the pessimists that I would like to hold up the title of Fassbinder's great film: "Fear of fear" will get us nowhere, and certainly not now. What have we got to be frightened about? We are clearly Europe's number-one economic power. Nobody in recent times has profited from the economic and political shifts of power like we Germans. GDP per capita, despite drops in domestic wealth, is still 22 percent above the European average. The budget, for the first time in decades, is in surplus.

It surprises me that, even among the elite, the influx of refugees over the last two years has created the impression that Germany has become one huge refugee camp. And then people go on to suggest that we are at the "breaking point" and that people are "at the end of their tether." What on earth is that supposed to mean?

By the way—and I can no longer hold myself back—Germany has been a country of migrants for some time now: 16.5 million people with a migration background—first- and second-generation immigrants—live here, almost one-fifth of the population.[3] In Munich, Stuttgart, and Nuremberg the proportion is almost 40 percent. What's the point of all this scare-mongering for 1.3 million people in a year?

It will make the country more colorful, wake us all up from the lethargy of prosperity. We have a Herculean task in front of us. But it is just that—a task. Not to mention that we Christians may read to our loved ones beneath the Christmas tree the story about Mary, heavy with child, and Joseph, the story in which "there was no room for them in the inn." Do we want to be like them, the rich people of Bethlehem long ago, and turn women and children away?

ACKNOWLEDGMENTS

Such a book cannot be written without the help and support of a vast number of people. They have given advice and provided me with current information, given me insights into their countries and cultures, given me useful tips, and protected me from the embarrassment of hurting the feelings of the fleeing women and children. Above all I would like to thank the many women in the refugee camps who, despite their dire living conditions, still enjoyed talking to me, admitting me into their small tents or dwellings, willingly telling me stories from their lives. They all assured me that they were happy that someone was writing down their stories—stories of the helpless, the often vulnerable, the abandoned. Huge thanks in particular as well to the following:

IN TURKEY

Feray Olcer, a teacher, who cleverly and sensitively translated five different dialects of Kurdish and who enlightened me to the problems of her Kurd people, particularly in these dramatic times.

Mansur, who calmly and with great composure drove us through "wild Kurdistan." His experience was a great asset in handling the military and police checkpoints, and in the evenings he was perfectly at ease leaving us to our own devices without his protection.

Peter Müller, assigned to me again by former editor in chief of *Bild* Kai Diekmann. His unfaltering good mood, creativity, and understanding of the refugee women and children consistently impressed me.

Mechtild Buchholz of Medica Mondiale, who facilitated contact with women's organizations in eastern Turkey.

IN LEBANON

Berta Travieso, the UNICEF director in Zahlé in the Beqaa Valley. Since my research in eastern Congo, I have learned to treasure her straightforward manner, her talent for organization, and her warmth. Without her I would not have been able to have had so many conversations in the settlements. She provided me with priceless background information.

Cecilia Dirani, born in Lebanon, brought up in the United States, and extremely helpful with interpreting and in selecting the right settlements to visit.

Mohammed Mansour from the small town of Zahlé. He drove us knowledgeably and cheerfully through his country. We always felt safe with him, in part because he would always exchange a few friendly words with the police at checkpoints.

ON LESBOS

Angela Marda, who, as interpreter and English teacher, cordially took me by the hand and accompanied me everywhere on the small Greek island where a great refugee drama was unfolding.

Helpful Stella from the pretty Hotel Paradise Theofilos in Mytilene, who recommended our perceptive driver, Vangelis Vangelakis. Vangelis knows the island like the back of his hand and was always prepared to drive me to important places even in the wee hours.

IN GERMANY

Beate Jung at the UNICEF branch in Cologne, who, as always, was a great help in the initial stages of my research.

Condrobs, the aid organization for refugees in Munich, and in particular press officer Beate Zornig, who was always able to point me to more people to talk to.

Lila Grunow in Hamburg, with Fördern und Wohnen. She was always of assistance in organizing the often not so simple meetings with refugee women.

Kristina Rezkalla, who interpreted with understanding and enthusiasm the conversations with "my" Syrian refugee, Miryam, and her children.

My editor, Angela Stangl. She edited the text with a keen eye on the subject and also supplied a number of helpful comments.

Last but not least: My husband, Klaus Häusler, who again, from the initial idea until completion, actively supported me with love and care. He supplied me with endless cups of coffee and tea, did the shopping when I was tied to my desk, and encouraged and invigorated me when I was weighed down by the difficult and taxing subject matter.

NOTES

PREFACE TO THE ENGLISH EDITION

1. Bill Trott and Matt Spetalnick, "Critics Push U.S. to Help Europe by Taking More Refugees," Reuters, September 6, 2015, http://www.reuters.com/article/us-europe-migrants-usa-idUSKCN0R60SE20150906.
2. "PM House Statement on the Terrorist Attack in Quebec," January 30, 2017, http://pm.gc.ca/eng/news/2017/01/30/pm-house-statement-terrorist-attack-quebec.
3. Matthias Kolb, "Wo die Angst den Kürzeren zieht," *Süddeutche Zeitung,* February 7, 2017, http://www.sueddeutsche.de/politik/usa-wo-die-angst-den-kuerzeren-zieht-1.3366404.

INTRODUCTION

1. Thomas Gutschker, "Wie der Hunger die Syrer in die Flucht trieb," *Frankfurter Allgemeine Flüchtlingskrise,* August 11, 2015, http://www.faz.net/aktuell/politik/fluechtlingskrise/wie-der-fluechtlingsandrang-aussyrien- ausgeloest-wurde-13900101.html; World Food Programme, "WFP forced to suspend Syrian refugee food assistance, warns of terrible impact as winter nears," December 1, 2014, https://www.wfp.org/news/news-release/wfp-forced-suspend-syrian-refugee-food-assistance-warns-terrible-impact-winter-nea.
2. "Flüchtlinge sind nicht krimineller als Deutsche," *Zeit Online,* November 13, 2015, http://www.zeit.de/politik/deutschland/

2015-11/bundeskriminalamt- fluechtlinge-deutsche-straftaten-vergleich.

3. Jonas Ulrich, "Verschwundene Kinder," *Hinz & Kuntz,* March 2016, p. 17.
4. "5835 minderjährige Flüchtlinge in Deutschland verschwunden," *Welt,* April 11, 2016, http://www.welt.de/politik/deutschland/article154195736/5835-minderjaehrige-Fluechtlinge-in-Deutschland-verschwunden.html.
5. Hannah Arendt, *The Origins of Totalitarianism* (New York: Harcourt, Brace, 1951).

CHAPTER 1: SYRIA: MYRIAM'S STORY, PART 1

1. Christian Böhme, " 'Kinder müssen Gras essen,' " *Der Tagesspiegel,* November 23, 2015, http://www.tagesspiegel.de/politik/krieg-in-syrienkinder-muessen-gras essen/12627202.html.
2. Steffen Gassel, "Der Islamische Staat ist nicht das Hauptproblem, sondern Assad," *Stern,* September 25, 2015, http://www.stern.de/politik/ausland/syrien--assad-ist-das-hauptproblemnicht-der-islamische-staat-6465738.html.
3. Steffen Gassel, "Der Islamische Staat ist nicht das Hauptproblem"; see Nicolas Hénin, *Jihad Academy: The Rise of Islamic State,* translated by Martin Makinson (New Delhi: Bloomsbury, 2015).
4. Hamish de Bretton-Gordon, letter to the editor, *The Telegraph,* September 4, 2015, http://www.telegraph.co.uk/comment/letters/11842481/Letters-A-lack-of-EU-leadership-has-sharpened-the-migrant-crisis-and-left-its-causes-unsolved.html.
5. Mike Szymanski, "In Kilis zeigt sich das Versagen der Weltpolitik," *Süddeutsche Zeitung,* February 10, 2016. http://www.sueddeutsche.de/politik/tuerkei-wir-teilen-gerne-aber-es-reicht-nicht-1.2857660.
6. Benjamin Bidder, Katrin Kuntz, Juliane von Mittelstaedt, Christian Neef, Maximilian Popp, Christoph Reuter, Mathieu von Rohr,

Christoph Schult, and Holger Stark, "Aleppo—Von allen verlassen," *Der Spiegel*, July 2016.

7. "Syria: War's toll on women," Human Rights Watch, July 2, 2014, https://www.hrw.org/news/2014/07/02/syria-wars-toll-women.
8. UNHCR, "Zahl der Syrien-Flüchtlinge übersteigt 4 Millionen," July 9, 2015, http://www.unhcr.de/presse/nachrichten/artikel/ab59d3b3184f9e2b113b72bd0125c06d/zahl-der-syrien-fluechtlinge-uebersteigt-4-millionen-2.html. As of February 7, 2017, UNHCR lists 2,854,968 Syrian refugees in Turkey, 233,224 in Iraq, 655,895 in Jordan, 1,011,366 in Lebanon, 166,013 in Egypt, and 29,275 in North Africa (http://data.unhcr.org/syrianrefugees/regional.php).
9. "A million refugee children mark shameful milestone in Syria crisis," UNICEF, August 23, 2013, https://www.unicef.org/media/media_70225.html.

CHAPTER 2: TURKEY

1. A more recent World Bank GDP estimate shows a decline to $717.9 billion. Turkey's place in the World Press Freedom Index has fallen two places, to 151. Reporters Without Borders explains, "President Recep Tayyip Erdogan has embarked on an offensive against Turkey's media. Journalists are harassed, many have been accused of 'insulting the president' and the Internet is systematically censored. The regional context—the war in Syria and Turkey's offensive against the PKK Kurds—is exacerbating the pressure on the media, which are also accused of 'terrorism.' The media and civil society are nonetheless resisting Erdogan's growing authoritarianism" (RSF, "Erdogan against the media," accessed February 7, 2017, https://rsf.org/en/turkey).
2. Mac McClelland, "How to build a perfect refugee camp," *New York Times Magazine*, February 13, 2014, http://www.nytimes.com/2014/02/16/magazine/how-to-build-a-perfect-refugee-camp.html.

3. Ahmet Davutoğlu, "Turkey cannot deal with the refugee crisis alone. EU nations need to help," Opinion, *The Guardian*, September 9, 2015, https://www.theguardian.com/commentisfree/2015/sep/09/turkey-refugee-crisis-christian-fortress-europe.
4. Luisa Seeling, "Überfordert und enttaeuscht," *Süddeutsche Zeitung*, September 27, 2015, http://www.sueddeutsche.de/politik/tuerkei-ueberfordertund-enttaeuscht-1.2664713.
5. Ibid.
6. Dietrich Alexander, " 'Darf ich eine schwangere Sklavin verschenken?' " *Welt*, September 22, 2015, http://www.welt.de/politik/ausland/article146734207/Darf-ich-eine-schwangere-Sklavin-verschenken.html.
7. Karin Laub, "Rising number of Syrian refugees returning to war-torn homeland," AP, CTV News, October 5, 2015, http://www.ctvnews.ca/world/rising-number-of-syrian-refugees-returning-to-war-torn-homeland-1.2594959.
8. Amnesty International, *Europe's Gatekeeper: Unlawful Detention and Deportation of Refugees from Turkey*, December 16, 2015.
9. Luisa Seeling, "Amnesty: Türkei schickt Flüchtlinge zurück nach Syrien," *Süddeutsche Zeitung*, December 16, 2015, http://www.sueddeutsche.de/politik/buergerkrieg-amnesty-tuerkei-schicktfluechtlinge-zurueck-nach-syrien-1.2785413.
10. Seeling, "Überfordert und enttaeuscht."

CHAPTER 3: LEBANON

1. Garance Le Caisne wrote about the conditions there in his book *Codename Caesar: Im Herzen der syrischen Todesmaschinerie* (Munich: C.H. Beck, 2016).

CHAPTER 4: JORDAN

1. "Syria conflict: Jordanians 'at boiling point' over refugees," BBC News, February 2, 2016, http://www.bbc.com/news/world-middle-east-35462698.
2. Christa Minkin, "Vizebürgermeister von Amman: 'Zahlen sind jenseits von Moral,' " *Der Standard,* January 25, 2015, http://derstandard.at/2000029658758/Ammans-Vizebuergermeister-Jenseitsjeglicher-Moral-Zahlen-festzulegen.
3. "Aktuelle Eindrücke über die Situation von Frauen in Jordanien," *Terre des Femmes,* April 6, 2013, https://www.frauenrechte.de/online/index.php/themen-undaktionen/eine-welt/aktuelles/archiv-iz/1183-aktuelle-eindruecke-ueber-die-situation-von-frauenin-jordanien.
4. "Frauen im Exil in Jordanien," *Emma,* January/February 2015.
5. Daniela Schröder, "Tochter zu verkaufen," *Die Standard,* August 27, 2014, http://derstandard.at/2000004716939/Tochter-zu-verkaufen.
6. Ibid.
7. "Jordanien, Libanon, Türkei: Flüchtlinge kehren nach Syrien zurück," *Spiegel Online,* October 5, 2015, http://www.spiegel.de/politik/ausland/syrische-fluechtlingekehren-zurueck-nach-syrien-a-1056163.html.
8. Thomas Gutschker, "Geschäfte hinter Mauern," *Frankfurter Allgemeine,* December 8, 2015, http://www.faz.net/aktuell/politik/ausland/naher-osten/fluechtlingslager-zaatari-in-jordanien-mitgeschaeften-von-syrern-13950585.html.
9. Ibid.
10. Ibid.
11. Ibid.

CHAPTER 5: ERITREA

1. Tobias Zick, "Im Griff der Angst," *Süddeutsche Zeitung,* August 21, 2015, http://www.sueddeutsche.de/politik/eritrea-im-griff-der-angst-1.2615907.
2. Leonie Feuerbach, "Ein Bericht aus der Hölle," *Frankfurther Allgemeine,* October 13, 2015, http://www.faz.net/aktuell/politik/fluechtlingskrise/massenflucht-nach-europa-das-elend-in-eritrea-13850121.html.
3. Zick, "Im Griff der Angst."
4. Freedom House, "Eritrea," *Freedom in the World 2013,* https://freedomhouse.org/report/freedom-world/2013/eritrea.
5. Oliver Meiler, "Die Verlorenen," *Süddeutsche Zeitung,* April 21, 2015; Paul-Anton Krüger, "Auf den Wellen des Todes," *Süddeutsche Zeitung,* April 11, 2015.

CHAPTER 6: LESBOS

1. Filippo Grandi, "Women refugees and asylum seekers in the European Union," speech to the European Parliament marking International Women's Day, Strasbourg, March 8, 2016, http://www.unhcr.org/56dec2e99.html; Don Murray, "Grandi concerned at reports of Balkan border closures," UNHCR, February 23, 2016, http://www.unhcr.org/56cd6d166.html.

CHAPTER 7: EUROPE: MIRYAM'S STORY, PART II

1. Bernd Dörries, "Zwischengeparkte Menschen," *Süddeutsche Zeitung,* September 8, 2014.
2. Miguel Sanches, "De Maizière schliesst Obergrenze für Menge an Asylbewerbern aus," *Der Westen,* September 7, 2014, http://www.derwesten.de/politik/es-gibt-keine-obergrenze-fuer-asylbewerberid9790852.html.

3. Yvonne Weiss, "Darum helfen so viele Hamburger Flüchtlingen," *Hamburger Abendblatt,* October 7, 2015, http://www.abendblatt.de/hamburg/article206008395/Darum-helfen-so-viele-Hamburger-Fluechtlingen.html.

CHAPTER 8: GERMANY 2015

1. Andreas Hoidn-Borchers and Axel Vornbäumen, "Angela gegen den Rest der Welt," *Stern,* January 28, 2016; Melanie Amann, Peter Müller, Ralf Neukirch, René Pfister, Michael Sauga, and Christoph Schult, "Die Uhr tickt," *Der Spiegel,* March 2016, http://www.spiegel.de/spiegel/print/d-141495073.html.
2. Interview, *ARD-Sommerinterview,* July 19, 2015, http://www.daserste.de/information/nachrichten-wetter/tagesthemen/videosextern/tagesthemen-6124.html.
3. Jörg Thomann, "Das Ende der kleinen, heilen Welt, *Frankfurter Allgemeine,* September 22, 2015, http://www.faz.net/aktuell/politik/fluechtlingskrise/fluchtziel-deutschland-das-ende-der-kleinen-heilenwelt-13810727.html.
4. "Gaucks Rede im Wortlaut," *Spiegel Online,* October 3, 2015, http://www.spiegel.de/politik/deutschland/joachim-gauck-rede-zum-tag-derdeutschen-einheit-im-wortlaut-a-1056019.html.
5. Markus Becker, "EU-Türkei-Flüchtlingsdeal: Ein unmoralisches Geschäft," *Spiegel Online,* March 17, 2016, http://www.spiegel.de/politik/ausland/europaeische-union-und-tuerkei-einunmoralisches-geschaeft-a-1082743.html.
6. Heribert Prantl, "Angst vor Merkels Courage," *Süddeutsche Zeitung,* October 5, 2015, http://www.sueddeutsche.de/politik/fluechtlinge-angst-vor-merkels-courage-1.2676009.
7. Matthias Iken, " 'Wer eine Grenze schützen will, braucht einen Zaun,' " *Hamburger Abendblatt,* October 17, 2015,

http://www.abendblatt.de/hamburg/article206300617/Wer-eine-Grenze-schuetzen-will-brauchteinen-Zaun.html.

8. Jochen Gaugele, Jörg Quoos, Miguel Sanches, and Christian Unger, " 'Militanz in der bürgerlichen Mitte,' " *Der Westen*, November 14, 2015, http://www.derwesten.de/panorama/militanz-in-der-buergerlichen-mitte-id11284759.html.
9. Joachim Gauck, speech, Frankfurt/Main, October 3, 2015, https://www.bundespraesident.de/SharedDocs/Downloads/DE/Reden/2015/10/151003-Festakt-Deutsche-Einheit-englisch.pdf.
10. "Flüchtlingspolitik: AfD-Vize will doch nicht auf Kinder schiessen lassen," *Spiegel Online*, January 31, 2016, http://www.spiegel.de/politik/deutschland/afd-vize-beatrix-von-storchwill-doch-nicht-auf-kinder-schiessen-lassen-a-1074950.html.
11. Heribert Prantl, "AfD-Vorschläge: Auf einmal darf gesagt werden, was unsäglich ist," *Süddeutsche Zeitung*, January 31, 2016, http://www.sueddeutsche.de/politik/fluechtlinge-afd-vorschlaege-aufeinmal-darf-gesagt-werden-was-unsaeglich-ist-1.2842762.
12. Carolin Buchheim and Joachim Röderer, "Kein Zutritt mehr für Flüchtlinge in Freiburgs Clubs und Diskotheken," *Badische Zeitung*, January 22, 2016, http://www.badische-zeitung.de/kein-zutritt-mehr-fuer-fluechtlinge-in-freiburgs-clubsund-diskotheken--116454714.html.
13. Hoidn-Borchers and Vornbäumen, "Angela gegen den Rest der Welt."
14. "Das EU-Abkommen," *Frankfurter Allgemeine Sonntagszeitung*, March 20, 2016.
15. Laura Himmelreich, " 'Wer Grenzen dichtmachen will, ist selber nicht dicht,' " *Stern*, January 28, 2016, http://www.stern.de/politik/deutschland/heiner-geissler-haelt-grenzschliessungfuer-irre-6669382.html.

16. Holger Bonin, *Der Beitrag von Ausländern und künftiger Zuwanderung zum deutschen Staatshaushalt* (Bertelsmann Stiftung, n.d.), https://www.bertelsmann-stiftung.de/fileadmin/files/user_upload/Bonin_Beitrag_Zuwanderung_zum_dt_Staatshaushalt_141204_nm.pdf.
17. Thomas Öchsner, " 'Wir sind gut vorbereitet,' " *Süddeutsche Zeitung,* January 31, 2016, http://www.sueddeutsche.de/wirtschaft/montagsinterviewwir-sindgut-vorbereitet-1.2842348.
18. Christian Unger, "Wie die Stadt Passau den Ausnahmezustand organisiert," *Der Westen,* February 1, 2016, http://www.derwesten.de/politik/wie-die-stadt-passau-den-ausnahmezustand-organisiert-id11513667.html.
19. Cerstin Gammelin, "Regierung erwartet 3,6 Millionen Flüchtlinge bis 2020," *Süddeutsche Zeitung,* February 26, 2016, http://www.sueddeutsche.de/politik/haushaltsueberschuss-schaeuble-hat-schon-alles-ausgegeben-1.2878192.
20. Volker Zastrow, "Merkel muss noch immer nicht weg," *Frankfurter Allgemeine,* March 20, 2016, http://www.faz.net/aktuell/politik/fluechtlingskrise/merkel-erntet-erfolg-im-tuerkei-gipfel-14134852.html.

EPILOGUE

1. Ben Hubbard, "Wealthy Gulf nations are criticized for tepid response to Syrian refugee crisis," *New York Times,* September 5, 2015, http://www.nytimes.com/2015/09/06/world/gulf-monarchies-bristle-at-criticism-over-response-to-syrian-refugee-crisis.html.
2. The Canadian immigration system sets an annual immigration quota and judges applicants for permanent resident status from outside the country on a points system, as well as having economic and family classes. In Germany, non-EU citizens can apply for a

temporary residence permit for skilled work purposes, or an indefinite but nonpermanent residence permit if they already have a job, but can apply for permanent residency only after five years in Germany. "Ethnic German resettlers" from Eastern Europe can move to Germany at any time.

3. The comparable number for Canada is about 39 percent (22 percent foreign-born); for the United States, about 25 percent (13 percent foreign-born). In the UK, about 13 percent are foreign-born.

INDEX

H

I